Evidence-based practice in education

Conducting Educational Research

Series Editor: Harry Torrance, University of Sussex

This series is aimed at research students in education and those undertaking related professional, vocational and social research. It takes current methodological debates seriously and offers well-informed advice to students on how to respond to such debates. Books in the series review and engage with current methodological issues, while relating such issues to the sorts of decisions which research students have to make when designing, conducting and writing up research. Thus the series both contributes to methodological debate and has practical orientation by providing students with advice on how to engage with such debate and use particular methods in their work. Series authors are experienced researchers and supervisors. Each book provides students with insights into a different form of educational research while also providing them with the critical tools and knowledge necessary to make informed judgements about the strengths and weaknesses of different approaches.

Current titles:
Tony Brown and Liz Jones: *Action, Research and Postmodernism*
Gary Thomas and Richard Pring: *Evidence-based Practice in Education*
John Schostak: *Understanding, Designing and Conducting Qualitative Research in Education*
Lyn Yates: *What Does Good Education Research Look Like?*

Evidence-based practice in education

Edited by Gary Thomas and Richard Pring

Open University Press

Open University Press
McGraw-Hill Education
McGraw-Hill House
Shoppenhangers Road
Maidenhead
Berkshire
SL6 2QL

email: enquiries@openup.co.uk
world wide web: www.openup.co.uk

and Two Penn Plaza, New York, NY 10121-2289, USA

First Published 2004

A catalogue record of this book is available from the British Library

ISBN 0 335 21334 0 (pb)   0 335 21335 9 (hb)

Library of Congress Cataloging-in-Publication Data
CIP data has been applied for

Typeset by RefineCatch Ltd, Bungay, Suffolk
Printed in Great Britain by MPG Books Ltd, Bodmin, Cornwall

Contents

List of Contributors

Richard Andrews is Professor of Education at the University of York and Co-coordinator of the English Review Group for the EPPI-Centre. He is the author of *Narrative and Argument* and *The Problem with Poetry* (Open University Press), *Teaching and Learning Argument* (Cassell) and editor of *The Impact of ICT on Literacy Education* (Routledge Falmer). He is Associate Editor of *Education, Communication and Information* and sits on the editorial boards of *Informal Logic* and *English in Australia*.

Philippa Cordingley is the founder and the Chief Executive of the Centre for the Use of Research and Evidence in Education (CUREE). As adviser to the DfES, the National Union of Teachers, the National College for School Leadership, the GTC and as Chief Professional Adviser on research to the Teacher Training Agency from 1995 to 2001, she has instigated, designed and developed a range of strategies, policies and support programmes to increase teacher interest in, access to and use of research. She is a board member of The Education Network (TEN), a member of the National Steering Group for the Networked Learning Communities Initiative and a school governor.

Philip Davies is Director of Policy Evaluation in the Prime Minister's Strategy Unit, which is part of the Cabinet Office. Previously he was Director of Social Sciences in the Department for Continuing Education at Oxford University and a Fellow of Kellogg College, Oxford. Philip was responsible (with colleagues in the University of Oxford Medical School) for developing the University of Oxford Master's Programme in Evidence-based Health Care. Philip is a founder member of the Campbell Collaboration and is on its international steering committee. He is also a Visiting Honorary Fellow of the UK Cochrane Centre.

John Elliott is Professorial Fellow within the Centre for Applied

Research in Education, which he directed from 1996 to 1999 at the University of East Anglia. He is well known internationally for his work in developing action research and has directed a number of collaborative classroom research projects with teachers and schools. These include the Ford Teaching Project (1972–74) and, more recently, the TTA-funded Norwich Area Schools Consortium (NASC) on the 'curriculum and pedagogical dimensions of student disaffection' (1997–2001). He is currently an Advisory Professor to the Hong Kong Institute of Education and a consultant to the Hong Kong Government on the strategic development of its curriculum reform proposals.

Michael Eraut is a Professor of Education at the University of Sussex. His research over the last decade has focused on the nature of professional knowledge and competence, the role of tacit knowledge in professional practice, how professionals and managers learn in the workplace and factors affecting learning in professional apprenticeships. His recent research projects have addressed the training of junior doctors, the development of competence and judgement in postgraduate medical education, the vocational training of clinical and biomedical scientists, and how nurses learn to use scientific knowledge. He is Editor in Chief of a new Blackwells journal, *Learning in Health and Social Care.*

Deborah J. Gallagher is Professor of Education at the University of Northern Iowa. Her research interests centre on the philosophy of science as it pertains to research, pedagogy and policy in education and special education. This work focuses on how choices of methodological and conceptual frameworks affect the possibilities of achieving equitable and inclusive schooling for students labelled as having disabilities. Among other recent publications, she is the lead author of a book entitled *Challenging Orthodoxy in Special Education: Dissenting Voices* (Love Publishing Company 2003) with co-authors Lous Heshusius, Richard Iano and Thomas Skrtic.

David Gough is Reader in Social Science and Deputy Director of the Social Science Research Unit and its EPPI-Centre, Institute of Education, University of London. Previously he was Senior Research Fellow at the University of Glasgow and Professor of Social Welfare at Japan Women's University, near Tokyo. His main areas of research interest are the implicit social policy of social interventions for children and families and methods of systematic research synthesis to address all policy, practice and community questions. He is Editor of the journal *Child Abuse Review*.

Martyn Hammersley is Professor of Educational and Social Research at The Open University. Much of his work has been concerned with the methodological issues surrounding social and educational research. He has written several books: (with Paul Atkinson) *Ethnography: Principles* *in Practice* (2nd edition, Routledge 1995); *The Dilemma of Qualitative Method* (Routledge 1989); *Classroom Ethnography* (Open University Press 1990); *Reading Ethnographic Research* (Longman 1991); *What's Wrong with Ethnography?* (Routledge 1992); *The Politics of Social Research* (Sage 1995); (with Peter Foster and Roger Gomm) *Constructing Educational Inequality* (Falmer 1996); *Taking Sides in Research* (Routledge 1999); and *Educational Research, Policy-making and Practice* (Paul Chapman 2002).

Phil Hodkinson is Professor of Lifelong Learning at the University of Leeds. He was founder Director of the Lifelong Learning Institute, which works to interrelate research expertise with that of policy-makers and practitioners. He has considerable experience of qualitative case study research, and has written about hermeneutical and interpretivist methodologies. He has regularly engaged with policy-related research in vocational education and training, workplace learning and career progression. In one major project (on-going at the time of writing) he is co-leader of a mixed team of university and practitioner researchers, exploring ways in which research can improve teaching and learning in further education.

Ed Peile is a professor and Head of the Division of Medical Education at Warwick Medical School, University of Warwick. Previously a general practitioner, he started the Aston Clinton Surgery in 1983. He has been involved in postgraduate medical education for 16 years: as an Associate Advisor at Oxford Postgraduate Medical Deanery, he directed the Higher Professional Education programme as well as the New Teachers' Course in one-to-one teaching in Primary Care. In undergraduate education he was Associate Director of Clinical Studies at University of Oxford, where he is Hon. Senior Clinical Lecturer in Primary Health Care. His research interests are in interprofessional education and in process and outcome in GP Registrar training.

Richard Pring was Professor of Educational Studies at the University of Oxford from 1989 to 2003. He was previously Professor of Education at the University of Exeter, lecturer in Curriculum Studies at the University of London Institute of Education, a teacher in London comprehensive schools and Assistant Principal at the Department of Education and Science. His book *Philosophy of Educational Research* was published by Continuum in 2000. His main areas of academic and professional interest are in the philosophy of education, especially in relation to vocational education and training, religious education and comprehensive schooling. He retired from being Director of the Department of Educational Studies at Oxford in May 2003, and is now an Emeritus Fellow of Green College, Oxford.

Judy Sebba is a professor in education at the University of Sussex. Previously she was Senior Adviser (Research), Standards and Effectiveness

Unit, Department for Education and Skills (DfES) where she was responsible for developing the research strategy and quality of research relating to schools. She supports the National Educational Research Forum, which is developing a research strategy for education and manages the EPPI-Centre on behalf of the DfES which is developing systematic reviews in education. She was previously at the University of Cambridge, where she was involved in a number of projects on evaluating the use of school effectiveness grants, post-inspection action planning in special and primary schools, school improvement and inspection and special needs.

John K. Smith is Professor of Education at the University of Northern Iowa. Among his numerous publications are two books, *The Nature of Social and Educational Inquiry: Empiricism versus Interpretation* and *After the Demise of Empiricism: The Problem of Judging Social and Educational Inquiry*.

Gary Thomas is a Professor of Education at Oxford Brookes University, having previously worked as a teacher and an educational psychologist. His interests are in inclusive education and research methodology, and his books include *The Making of the Inclusive School* (Routledge 1998) and *Deconstructing Special Education and Constructing Inclusion* (Open University Press 2001).

Harry Torrance is Professor of Education and Head of Research in the Institute of Education, Manchester Metropolitan University. He was formerly Professor of Education at the University of Sussex, where the research on which his chapter is based was carried out in collaboration with Dr John Pryor.

Introduction: evidence and practice
Gary Thomas

What is evidence?

None of the contributors to this book denies the importance of evidence in shaping and enhancing practice. At issue is not the significance of evidence but its nature – and its value contingent on that nature. At issue are the potency and value ascribed to certain forms of evidence in supporting propositions that arise in educational practice. Many kinds of evidence are available to practitioners in support of ideas and propositions that arise as part of their work: from observation, from documents, from the word of others, from reason or reflection, from research of one kind or another. It is the respect and worth credited to these that I shall explore in the first section of this introduction, and I shall hinge that exploration around notions of evidence in various spheres of inquiry.

Evidence may take different forms, and be valued differently, in different places – in the legal system, in the natural sciences, in medicine, in the humanities. Those who promote evidence-based practice in education are not seeking evidence in the way that an historian might seek evidence of the existence of factionalism in England at the fall of Cromwell in 1640. Neither will they be looking for evidence in the way that a physicist might seek evidence for the existence of Higgs boson.[1] Likewise, they are unlikely to be satisfied with the kind of implicit and eclectic evidence-gathering involved in the accumulation of the tacit knowledge of which Polanyi (1969) speaks.

They will be following a path of reasoning that encourages the seeking, marshalling and dissemination of evidence of a particular kind, different from these others, and it is the character and distinctiveness of this particular kind of evidence that I shall principally examine in this comparative overview.

First, a story from one of those other spheres of inquiry . . .

Mary was scanning the slope when suddenly she saw a tooth pro-
jecting from it, just a speck of gray fossilized enamel. She looked once
more and then shouted for me to come.

Together we slowly cleared a little of the rock face with dental
picks, the ideal tools for such delicate work. As the rock came
away, we discovered that behind the tooth lay another tooth, and
something more behind that. Perhaps, we thought with growing
excitement, there might even be an entire jaw and skull.

(Leakey and van Lawick 1963)

Whether Mary Leakey's find yet constituted evidence, evidence for a
new kind of hominid, remained to be established. And the potential constitution of the find as evidence rested itself on other work. That anyone
should bother to look here, in this area, at all for our human forebears
rested on lucky accident and intuition rather than careful pre-planning
or strong *prima facie* evidence. The 1931 team of palaeoanthropologists
led by Louis and Mary Leakey was drawn to the area by the earlier work
of entomologists and geologists who had by chance, as part of their
insect and rock hunting, unearthed a human skeleton. This was thought
at first to be an ancient fossil, but only much later was discovered to be a
relatively modern intrusive burial in older deposits. Its constitution as
evidence of the presence of fossil *Hominoidea*, drawing palaeoanthropologists to the area like a magnet, was thus mistaken. And the Leakeys'
subsequent moves around the area were determined as much by what is
often called 'intuition' as 'evidence'. As Louis Leakey himself put it, 'For
some reason both of us [he and his wife] had been drawn again and again
to this particular site' (Leakey and van Lawick 1963: 134).

It is the 'For some reason' that is primarily of interest here, for it gives a
clue about what is meant by 'intuition', a meaning residing in personal,
tacit knowledge built out of information – data, evidence – accumulated
both deliberately and fortuitously about the world. Ideas often emerge out
of confluences of circumstantial evidence in the minds of those who are
steeped in a problem, a discourse or a technology. Often those individuals
have a feeling, a hunch that this way or that way is the right way to
proceed, without being able to articulate its evidential provenance. There
is a playing around with bits and pieces of everyday evidence that in some
way enables practitioners of one kind or another to discover – in the
words often heard nowadays in relation to evidence-based practice –
'what works'. The discovery by the Wright brothers that the aeroplane
worked (see Dyson 1997: 17) was made outside the theoretical frameworks within which evidence is supposedly used and from which it
supposedly emerges. The evidence behind the design of their aeroplane
came from observation, trial and error, and from noting the trials and

tribulations of others; the evidence of its success came from the fact that it flew – no more and no less. No randomized controlled trials were necessary.

The discovery of penicillin, the invention of nylon, the discovery of superconductivity (see De Bruyn Ouboter 1997) are all well-documented cases of the 'intelligent noticing' of evidence that emerged outside the intellectual infrastructure from which evidence is expected to materialize. Clearly, all were discovered by able people working with the tools of their trade and immersed in the ideas of their intellectual communities. But their significant breakthroughs – and this applies as much to the everyday insight in practical activity as to the important breakthrough – occurred out of evidence collected almost incidentally and worked on with personal knowledge and the knowledge of the intellectual communities of which they were a part.

All scientists – whether physicists, chemists, biologists, palaeo-anthropologists – use particular kinds of evidence and meld it in particular ways relevant to their fields of work and the methodological traditions that have developed there. As Michael Eraut puts it in Chapter 7 of this volume, 'The process of evidence generation is situated within the context, practices and thinking patterns of its creators.'

The interesting thing about scientists' discourse in reflecting on these methodological traditions is that there is generally accepted to be no particular, no correct or proper way of generating or marshalling evidence. As Einstein put it, the creative scientist must be an 'unscrupulous opportunist'. The essence of science, he said, is the seeking 'in whatever manner is suitable, a simplified and lucid image of the world . . . There is no logical path, but only intuition' (cited in Holton 1995: 168). In a similar vein, Feyerabend (1993: 14) asserted that thought actually moves forward by 'a maze of interactions . . . by accidents and conjunctures and curious juxtapositions of events'.

This use of the word 'intuition' by Einstein in the context of scientific endeavour is an interesting one. Clearly he is not denying the significance of evidence. Rather, he seems to be promoting a kind of spatchcock use of evidence – a playing with almost any piece of seemingly relevant information – by scientists in their everyday work. And here scientists are very much like teachers or doctors, operating on their own and as part of a community, and drawing eclectically from many and varied streams of information: a bricolage of potential evidence.

Leakey, for example, describes how what could have been mere infor-mational noise became evidence. First of all came the pieces of supporting evidence to complete a jigsaw:

> . . . after several days we had all the pieces out and began putting our fossil jigsaw puzzle together. At last we could see what we had: Mary

had discovered a nearly complete skull of *Proconsul africanus*, an early Miocene creature.

(Leakey and van Lawick 1963: 135)

Then came corroborative evidence of the fossil's age from potassium argon dating, and confirmation of its significance from other experts in the field. The presence of a canine fossa, for example, is accepted in the scientific community as evidence of presence on the branch to *Hominoidea* – the canine serving, as it does, as an anchor for a muscle which controls the movement of the upper lip, and therefore probably being important in some form of proto-speech.

The example of palaeoanthropology is given here to address some common themes in the search for evidence. In palaeoanthropology and elsewhere, in order for information to constitute evidence, that information has to pass a number of tests.

First, its relevance has to be determined, for the notion of evidence assumes that something less than established fact – an assertion, a proposition, an hypothesis – has been put forward and data of some kind is wanted in support of that position. The data inscribed on my Beatles *Revolver* CD is not in itself evidence for anything unless assertions are made about it (for example, that the Beatles were an outstanding pop group, in which case the data would constitute evidence about which judgements would have to be made). Evidence is thus information supporting (or refuting) an assertion, and must pass the test of relevance if it is to move from informational noise, to potential evidence through to *prima facie* evidence.

In helping to determine relevance will be other pieces of information, and this raises the second test – of sufficiency: the potential evidence has to be considered with other pieces of information to determine its place in support of the assertion. Is there, in other words, corroborating evidence? As Russell points out, the person who asserts that unsupported bodies in air fall, has merely generalized from insufficient evidence, '. . . and is liable to be refuted by balloons, butterflies and aeroplanes' (1956: 91). Quality and sufficiency of evidence here begin to be related to the epistemological ambitions of the proposition.

Third, and again linked to sufficiency, decisions have to be made about the veracity of the evidence: were these, in the Leakeys' example, more modern 'intrusions', and if so what was their status – were they perhaps fakes, as had been the case with Piltdown Man? Or, are commitments so intense that the strong possibility of selectivity and misinterpretation make the 'evidence base' untrustworthy?[2] There are cases in the education archive of commitment being so powerful that deliberate manipulation and distortion of evidence can be postulated.[3] Such questions arise principally because of the interests that exist in any research enterprise –

interests usually surrounding personal gain of one kind or another. Here, the existence of corroborative evidence is again essential in helping to determine veracity.

These various tests for evidence are summarized in Table 1.1.

Table 1.1   Criteria for judging evidence

Criterion	Enabled by
1. relevance $\updownarrow$	establishing that the information constitutes information for (or against) some proposition
2. sufficiency $\updownarrow$	corroboration with other instances of the same kind of evidence or other kinds of evidence
3. veracity	establishing that the process of gathering evidence has been free from distortion and as far as possible uncontaminated by vested interest

There is a second reason for using palaeoanthropology as an example, and that is to demonstrate how notions of evidence and of research practice can vary across different domains of inquiry and practice. One is struck by the fact that there appears to be little role for experimentation in this respected science: there is a reliance on idiographic evidence with a trust in the testimony of expert peers and commentators, and large doses of trust in those who made the find.[4] Replication of the work, in any meaningful sense, is not feasible.

Perhaps here, in examining the routes taken by different communities of inquiry in establishing evidence, one can borrow from the distinction that Lévi-Strauss draws between *bricoleurs* and *engineers* (see Norris 1987: 133–4). The *bricoleur* begins with a broad proposition and collects evidence *ad hoc*, within the broadest parameters and using the least delimiting rules, expecting to discover useful *prima facie* information. This *prima facie* evidence is examined for its veracity while additional corroborative evidence is sought. This seems to reflect the practice in the Leakeys' work, where clues led to finds which were then verified with corroborative evidence. The engineer, by contrast, is assumed to be bound initially within strict theoretical frameworks, beginning with a clear view of the object to be constructed, and ultimately developing a blueprint that will be closely followed.

In fact, as both Lévi-Strauss and Derrida (Derrida 1978: 285) note, processes are not nearly as cleanly distinct as the metaphors of bricoleur and engineer imply. In real life, engineers and physicists, as much as anthropologists, cast the net far and wide in their search for evidence. Wright Mills (1970) quotes a number of Nobel Prize-winning physicists on the process of gathering evidence and using it to establish reliable knowledge. Bridgman, for example, says that 'There is no scientific method as such, but the vital feature of the scientist's procedure has been merely to do his utmost with his mind, *no holds barred*' [original emphasis], and Beck says that 'The mechanics of discovery are not known . . . I think that the creative process is so closely tied in with the emotional structure of an individual . . . that . . . it is a poor subject for generalisation' (Wright Mills 1970: 69).

A problem for scientists in discussing evidence and its use is similar to that faced by teachers and educational researchers: of being seen in one's public face to be rigorous, methodical and meticulous; of creating and maintaining an impression of the kind of systematic study assumed by the general public to be the hallmark of science. The problem was well expressed by the renowned biologist Peter Medawar, who – in discussing scientific method – talked of 'the postures we choose to be seen in when the curtain goes up and the public sees us' (Medawar 1982: 88). Gough, in Chapter 4 of this volume, makes the same point about education: of public legitimacy coming from the perception that research evidence feeds into rational processes of decision making. The danger, of course, lies in a community believing its own rhetoric. As Medawar points out, mathematicians eschew – unwisely – the role of the fortuitous finding that emerges from intuition, from playing with bits and pieces of random evidence: 'Most [discoveries] entered the mind by processes of the kind vaguely called "intuitive" . . . this is seldom apparent from mathematical writings because mathematicians take pains to ensure that it should not be' (1982: 87–8).

This brief overview of domains of study has thus far explored some different kinds of evidence that are sought and employed in certain scholarly fields, and I have tried in particular to draw attention to the idiographic and implicit nature of evidence in many areas of inquiry. I have also stressed the importance of sufficiency – the significance of the *weight* of evidence. It is this consideration of weight – the accumulated quantity of reliable evidence – that motivates proponents of evidence-based practice (see especially Chapters 2 and 4 by Davies and Gough). In other words, they seek a synthesis made from a sufficient quantity of high-quality evidence.

It is worth pausing here to look at philosophers' 'take' on evidence, since they perhaps consider evidence *per se* more than scientists or educators. For them, evidence constitutes any information that bears on the truth or falsity of a proposition. One should note again that *sufficiency* is important also for the philosopher in determining the status of one's evidence in moving beyond information, and in particular for drawing distinctions between the status of the beliefs one holds. Many age-old philosophical debates, such as those about our knowledge of the external world, or the basis for moral judgements, are largely about whether the evidence we have in these areas is sufficient to yield knowledge – or merely rational belief. Is the evidence weak, strong . . . conclusive?

Rational belief is perhaps all that can be hoped for in practical circumstances, and it is unlikely that a practitioner will find conclusive evidence for a proposition, since conclusive evidence is so strong as to rule out any possibility of error. Conclusive evidence is always going to be lacking for beliefs about the external world, whether those beliefs concern the past, other minds, or the efficacy of Reading Recovery.

Aside from the significance of sufficiency, another strand has to be drawn out of this overview, and this is the *social and interpretative context of evidence*. In any community of inquiry – scientific, legal, artistic – both the collection of evidence and its assessment are part of a social process. In jurisprudence, for example, as in science, a premium is put on the process of corroboration for establishing both the relevance and valency of evidence. For lawyers, evidence constitutes the means by which disputed facts are proved to be true or untrue, and in English law the principal criterion determining the acceptability or admissibility of evidence is when it is relevant, that is to say when it has a tendency 'in reason' to prove or disprove disputed facts. And the employment of 'reason' to determine the relevance, value or effectiveness of evidence necessarily makes the process of the acceptance of potential evidence a social one, depending on how persuasive the evidence seems, for example to a jury. There is nothing inherently objective or acceptable in a particular piece of evidence: nothing to guarantee its verisimilitude. It may be an eye-witness testimony, a DNA fingerprint or a document, but its value depends not so much on its placing in the canon of good sources but rather on its position in the panoply of factors – kinds of evidence – that surround its discovery. And the process by which the assessment is made of that contextual, corroborative evidence is a social one. Who says, and who is prepared to accept, that this evidence is sound?

There is therefore a similarity in the ways in which the legal and the scientific communities approach the notion of evidence. In each, the ultimate determination of the value of the evidence will rest on the judgement of peers – those peers being twelve ordinary people in the case of the jury, and an expert scientific community (who will replicate, convene, confer, 'peer-review' and judge) in the case of science.[5] Both in the law and in science this social process will determine the quality and sufficiency of the corroborative evidence: has enough independent, admissible evidence confirmed, for example, that the accused has committed the crime? Or does one piece of very strong evidence outweigh several pieces of seemingly flimsier evidence? It is the 'seemingly' that is interesting here. The key matter is how the evidence *seems* to a community of assessors. The process of assessment is social.

And as soon as the process becomes social, questions arise about the interpenetration of notions that have travelled along different paths to the same question. Even for natural scientists, political is mixed with empirical for some of the evidential matters that they confront. As biologists Levins and Lewontin (1985: 4) point out, 'The denial of the interpenetration of the scientific and the social is itself a political act, giving support to social structures that hide behind scientific objectivity.' (Hodkinson and Smith, and Elliott make much the same point in Chapters 11 and 12 in this volume in relation to education.) Levins and Lewontin go on to note that 'Of course the speed of light is the same under socialism and capitalism' but that *social* questions – questions that arise about *the way people live* – cannot be answered without reference to an interrelated range of matters. Thus, the experimental evidence will suggest that the cause of tuberculosis is a bacterium, yet the evidence of epidemiologists tells us that the disease rarely takes hold where people's living and working conditions are adequate. In education, matters are no less complex: the denial of the interpenetration of the social and the scientific (or at least what is supposed to be scientific) in considerations of teaching and learning has sometimes led us to forms of school organization that discriminate against certain children and segregate them. The background to this debate is given in Gallagher's chapter (Chapter 9) in this volume.

This social context of evidence is crucial in determining its validity, and contributors in Part 2 of this book spend some time discussing this theme. I wish now, however, to return to the notion of sufficiency, for it is around the need for sufficiency – around the need for collection and collation of good-quality, reliable evidence – that arguments for the employment of evidence-based practice in education usually pivot. If a theme can be distilled from the discussion thus far in relation to sufficiency, it is that in strengthening a belief there must be a movement beyond the first piece of evidence to additional corroborative evidence (see Figure 1.1).

Questions arise, however, about the meaningfulness of such a typology when talking of evidence for practical activity and the beliefs inhering therein, for movement along the continuum in Figure 1.1 appears to be a deliberate, calculated process. Yet Polanyi (1969) reminds us that the scientist, for example, cannot specify the way in which facts become

Kinds of evidence	isolated observations	*prima facie* or inconclusive evidence	corroborative evidence	conclusive evidence
	←——————————————————————————————————————→			
Leading to	inspiration	hunch	rational belief	knowledge

Figure 1.1 A continuum of sufficiency

evidence. Neither, in dealing with the world more generally, is the process of gathering evidence and placing it in a theoretical or heuristic framework for practical purposes a conscious one. Polanyi (1969: 144) notes:

> We cannot learn to keep our balance on a bicycle by taking to heart that in order to compensate for a given angle of imbalance α, we must take a curve on the side of the imbalance, of which the radius (r) should be proportionate to the square of 5th the velocity (v) over the imbalance: $r \sim v^2/\alpha$. Such knowledge is ineffectual, unless known tacitly.

The same kind of thing could be said of much professional knowledge (sometimes called *craft knowledge*) in teaching. That knowledge in the classroom – whether to make eye contact, how to respond to an interruption, what sort of question to ask, what kind of language to employ in developing a theme – is often ineffectual unless known tacitly.

The issue, however, for some of the proponents of evidence-based practice is not in recognizing the significance of this kind of tacit knowledge, but rather in understanding practitioners' ability to reconcile it and meld it with knowledge from research: research evidence. Hargreaves (1996), for example, suggests that while medics achieve a good balance between craft knowledge and declarative research knowledge, teachers have been less successful in employing research evidence – in part because of the nature and presentation of that research evidence – alongside their craft knowledge: less successful in employing this additional corroborative evidence.

What Hargreaves seems to be suggesting is outlined in Figure 1.2: a more systematic incorporation of research evidence to the tacit knowledge/craft knowledge → practice cycle. This is essentially the position of many of those who promote evidence-based practice in education.

One must ask questions, though, about the status of the declarative knowledge and the kind of evidence needed to achieve it in different domains of practice, and Eraut, Peile and Hammersley examine this question in relation both to medicine and education in their chapters (Chapters 7, 8 and 10). How valid is it to make the assertion that this evidence, in the practical circumstance of the teacher – as distinct from the medic – is corroborative?

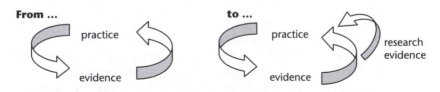

Figure 1.2   Evidence–practice cycles

In particular, one needs to examine the meaning of evidence-based practice among its proponents in education, for it is here especially that questions arise about what is likely to be gained in practical circumstances from particular kinds of evidence.[6]

If various stages in the employment of evidence are traversed in moving toward knowledge – a bricolage/hunch stage, an inspirational stage, a discovery stage and a corroborative/confirmatory stage – the notion of evidence-based practice focuses on evidence at the *confirmatory* stage, on the systematic collation of research studies for use by practitioners and policy-makers.

Oakley (2000) speaks specifically about this systematic collation. Drawing on a definition of evidence-based education that suggests that the establishment of sound research evidence must attend to the criteria of scientific validity, high quality and practical relevance, she suggests that systematicity is at the core of any gathering of such evidence:

> Systematic reviews are the primary method for managing knowledge in the evidence movement approach. This is because they synthesise the findings of many different research studies in a way which is explicit, transparent, replicable, accountable and (potentially) updateable.
>
> (Oakley 2000: 3)

Many proponents go further, to suggest that randomized controlled trials (RCTs) are at the core of the evidential armoury and that systematicity should centre around the collection of this kind of study. For them, the 'evidence' in evidence-based practice means a particular kind – a superior kind – of research evidence. Take what Robert E. Slavin had to say in the 'Distinguished Lecture' of the American Educational Research Association at its annual meeting in 2002:

> The most important reason for the extraordinary advances in medicine, agriculture, and other fields is the acceptance by practitioners of evidence as the basis for practice. In particular, it is the randomized clinical trial – more than any single medical breakthrough – that has transformed medicine.
>
> (Slavin 2002: 16)

Figure 1.3 summarizes the 'robust' position of proponents of evidence-based practice,[7] and the one that Slavin appears to take, drawing a central distinction between evidence from research, and evidence from personal or professional experience. Research evidence is itself delineated: nomothetic, idiographic; well designed, poorly designed. Certainly varied kinds of evidence can exist and they all have a degree of validity, it is conceded by Slavin, but *trustworthy* evidence, he seems to suggest, is obtained by following the heavy line that I have drawn in Figure 1.3.

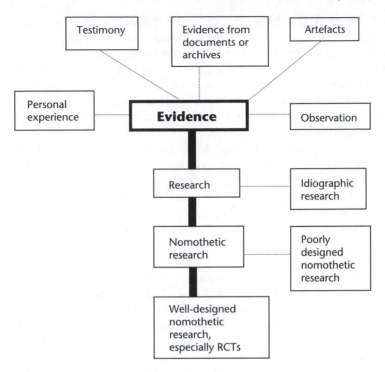

Figure 1.3   Evidence in evidence-based practice

Researchers and practitioners in other successful areas of professional inquiry, notably medicine, have followed it, and so should researchers and practitioners in education.

Slavin goes on to note that such experiments are in fact rare in education, concluding that '. . . the experiment is the design of choice for studies that seek to make causal connections, and particularly for evaluations of educational innovations' (2002: 18). Goldstein (2002) agrees that the randomized control trial (RCT) is generally accepted as a gold standard in applied statistical work, but in fact concludes that its use does not enable the establishment of causal connections. Nor is its use necessary for causal connections to be inferred.

It should also be said in relation to Slavin's assertion that although there have clearly been 'extraordinary advances' in medicine and agriculture in recent years, it is not clear (to me at least) how these can be attributed to the benefits of the RCT. The RCT plays an important but mundane, confirmatory role; it cannot provide the research work that leads to the advance. The recent remarkable discovery, for example, that the bacterium *Helicobacter pylori* causes more than 90 per cent of all peptic ulcers, came not from RCTs but from (as Medawar, above, would have predicted) a mix of inspirational thinking and serendipitous events (see

Blaser 1996). RCTs merely confirmed the efficacy of antibiotic therapy in the killing of the bacteria. Once the discovery had been made that bacteria were the culprits (by the 'Aha!' of an observant expert, not by a RCT) it required not a huge cognitive leap to get to the point that the bacteria needed killing in ulcer patients' stomachs. RCTs played a dull but important role in confirming the effectiveness of antibiotics in doing the killing. The point is that experiments and RCTs do not, as Slavin suggests, *lead to* 'extraordinary advances'.

Indeed, even in the RCT's workings as confirmatory agent, it may lead to falsely high or low expectations about the expected benefits of the change, and as Matthews (1998: 17) puts it '. . . can easily double the real efficacy of a useless drug' (see also Matthews 2001). This phenomenon, generated by the failure of frequentist methods to take into account *prior evidence* has of late led to calls for methods which contextualize *new evidence* in the context of *existing evidence* (see, for example, Spiegelhalter 1999; Howard *et al.* 2000).

Caveats notwithstanding, though, such experiments and their analysis are taken to be central to the building of an evidence base for practice. Some time ago, Parlett and Hamilton (1987) described this kind of work as emerging from an *agricultural-botany* paradigm[8] and pointed out some of the weaknesses of its adoption in education, and there have been many critiques both of this framework and the frequentist methods behind it in the social sciences (for example Cohen 1994; Howard *et al.* 2000). The particular criticisms of its use in education made by Parlett and Hamilton centred on assumptions made about the stability of 'before' and 'after' in before and after research designs, and about assumptions about the robustness of, for example, test scores and attitude ratings (often used to indicate 'effectiveness' of one kind or another) – which are assumed to be of the same order of robustness as the measures made, for example, of plant growth. In short, they argued, study undertaken in education in this tradition falls short of its own claims to be controlled, exact and unambiguous.

Dialogue, of course, continues about the need for and value of such research, with questions about both its technical capacity to deliver (questions that can be met with the answer that technical improvements in the instruments will be made[9]), and about the nature of the evidence provided: does this kind of evidence – can this kind of evidence – enhance practice? The nature of practice and practitioners' beliefs about that practice are central here, and are themes that several of this book's contributors take up. Teachers come to teaching with a set of beliefs and understandings, and these sometimes seem to be impermeable (or at least only semi-permeable) to the kinds of evidence emerging from certain kinds of educational research. One of the interesting aspects of teachers' practice, examined in this volume by both Gallagher and Hammersley, is its resistance to evidence of particular kinds and its solidarity in a certain commonality of purpose, which can perhaps be located in what Oakeshott (1967: 157) called 'an inheritance of feelings, emotions, images, visions, thoughts, beliefs, ideas, understandings'. It may be that certain kinds of research evidence – particularly if these are perceived in any way to be imposed by authority – do not mesh easily with this sort of inheritance, a problem noted by Peile to exist also amongst medics in Chapter 8 of this volume. As Onora O'Neill pointed out in her 2002 Reith Lectures (O'Neill 2002: 46), 'Central planning may have failed in the former Soviet Union but it is alive and well in Britain today', and if teachers and other public servants perceive 'what works' evidence as a clandestine way of imposing government's agenda and new checks on performance in meeting that agenda, they will reject it.

Practitioners accumulate evidence in practice and distil it in everyday heuristic, knack and rule of thumb. They engage in, and have confidence in, a kind of vernacular accumulation of evidence that enables what Schatzman (1991: 304) calls 'common interpretive acts'. As Schatzman suggests, we are all – as professionals and as laypersons – using these interpretive acts all the time and unselfconsciously employing them to help us order and comprehend the world. We all find pieces of evidence, make links between them, discover patterns, make generalizations, create explanatory propositions all the time, emerging out of our experience, and this is all 'empirical'. It can, moreover, be systematized in the kind of action research processes described by Elliott and Torrance in Chapters 12 and 13 of this volume.

All professionals will collect evidence deliberately and tacitly in ways described eloquently by Schön (1991), and others, who emphasize the interconnectedness of professional knowledge. The evidence will be reviewed, talked about with colleagues, new things will be tried out as a consequence and informally evaluated. Practitioners' trust in the knowledge that such processes work is perhaps at the root of their resistance to the imposition of other kinds of evidence. The key question is perhaps about issues that Sebba, Hammersley, Hodkinson and Smith raise in their chapters: whether research evidence is *made available* to add to the evidential storehouse of the teacher, or whether it is seen as a means of imposing the putatively 'effective'.

What is in this book?

A political and academic debate began in the late 1990s about evidence-based practice in education and it has led to the opening up of some of the questions that I have discussed in the first part of this chapter. The debate is further examined and reflected on in this book. Our contributors range over key themes and move the debate forward with informed commentary and analysis.

The book is divided into three parts. In the first part, our contributors explain in detail what is meant by evidence-based practice, drawing from their experience in a variety of contexts. In the second part, contributors contrast the development of evidence-based practice in education with its development in medicine and in allied fields and they provide a searching commentary on that development. In the third part some critical questions are posed about the notion of evidence-based practice in education.

Phil Davies opens the first part by looking at systematic reviews and in particular at the rationale for and the work of the Campbell Collaboration. Davies, who is Director of Policy Evaluation in the Prime Minister's Strategy Unit, highlights the importance for practitioners and policy-makers of being able efficiently to harness what is already known about a topic and to identify gaps in existing knowledge. The Campbell Collaboration plays a particular role in this process for social scientists, akin to that of the Cochrane Collaboration for health professionals. The Campbell Collaboration has been established to provide high-quality systematic reviews of the effectiveness of interventions in education, crime and justice, and social welfare.

Judy Sebba continues the first section by stressing the importance of understanding and dialogue between researchers and practitioners in education. Drawing from her experience as a Senior Adviser for Research at the Department for Education and Skills, she outlines some of the government initiatives designed to promote evidence-informed policy and practice, emphasizing the right of access to research for practitioners.

The first part of the book is concluded by David Gough, who asserts that there is a crucial challenge for educational researchers in increasing the relevance of research in education. The challenge can be met, Gough argues, by establishing methods for systematic research synthesis. Such a process, he says, must use explicit, accountable and updatable methods for critically appraising and synthesizing different studies with their different designs. Calling on his experience as Deputy Director of the Evidence for Policy and Practice Information and Co-ordinating Centre (EPPI-Centre), he outlines the rationale for such a synthesis and the ways in which the EPPI-Centre operates.

The second part of the book is about evidence-based practice in operation. It begins with Richard Andrews (coordinator of one of the EPPI review teams) describing his navigation between Scylla and Charybdis – the Scylla being EPPI methodology, informed as it is by social science and medical models of systematic review, and the Charybdis being educational research. In a self-critical and reflective overview of the process, he describes both conceptual and technical challenges for his team in undertaking this work. Though Andrews uses Scylla and Charybdis as an allegory for the journey taken in confronting the issues facing his own group, it is in fact a nice metaphor also for the broader difficulties of steering a rational course between different notions of evidence and different understandings about inquiry.

Like Sebba in Part 1, Philippa Cordingley in her chapter stresses the need for the practitioner to be intimately involved in the process of developing an evidence base. Looking at the different forms that evidence can take for teachers, she discusses what kinds of evidence teachers need in their work, and identifies a wide range of initiatives in which teachers are involved both to produce their own research-based evidence and better to employ the evidence produced by researchers in the academy.

Much discussion, both in this volume and elsewhere, rests on the similarities or discontinuities between medical research and practice on the one side, and educational research and practice on the other. This theme is taken forward here by Michael Eraut and Ed Peile. Eraut focuses on the nature of evidence in medicine and the decision-making processes in which it is used. He distinguishes especially between cultural knowledge that is socially situated (including 'scientific' knowledge) and personal knowledge derived from an individual's experience. He makes the point that evidence-based medicine is focused on comparisons using research-based probability estimates of the effectiveness of respective outcomes. Diagnostic decisions, however, are mainly based on a combination of personal knowledge aggregated from experience of a large number of cases. Much of this personal knowledge is tacit, acquired implicitly and very difficult to incorporate into an accessible-to-all pool of evidence.

Both Eraut and Peile draw the distinction between a) evidence-based practice, and b) practice-based evidence. Peile, as a general practitioner and medical educator, takes this distinction further. He asserts that the challenge for evidence-based practice in medicine now is to find ways of incorporating not the type of studies that emerge from large RCTs, but rather the everyday evidence accumulated by individual practitioners. Against some up-beat commentary about the achievements of evidence-based practice in medicine, Peile suggests that in fact efforts to compile and promote an evidence base for medics are failing to have the expected impact on practice.

Deborah Gallagher concludes this part of the book with a close examination of the use of research evidence in one field: special education. From an American perspective, and reviewing the American dialogue on this issue, she notes that many researchers lament the fact that supposedly effective 'what works' treatments are not being implemented by teachers. The problem is not the distribution of the research evidence to the practitioners (they seem, in a fairly sophisticated practitioner community, to know about it) but rather getting them to accept it and use it. The research – even if it supposedly shows 'what works' – is about methods that reflective teachers often eschew, perhaps because they don't believe the evidence, perhaps because a consequence of using those methods is a tendency to segregate and exclude, perhaps because the methods seem to emphasize technical expertise at the expense of comprehension (see also Thomas and Loxley 2001). Whatever the reason, teachers (and their mentors) will sometimes – because of their own personal understandings and beliefs about education – reject methods that seem to work.

In the final part of the book, some critical questions are posed about evidence-based practice. Martyn Hammersley in his chapter argues that while some aspects of the evidence-based practice movement warrant support, others do not – in fact, 'false and dangerous promises' are offered. A major issue he raises is that the evidence-based practice movement privileges a certain kind of evidence – evidence from research (and a *particular kind* of research) – against that from other sources, including the individual's personal experience, a theme already raised by Eraut and Peile. Another major problem for Hammersley concerns the idea that research can 'ensure' that the best is being done: the facts of research are presented, information is provided about 'what works' and practitioners can be inspected to see whether they are following 'best practice'. Such a model is dangerous, Hammersley argues, in the way it over-simplifies the relationship of research to practice.

Phil Hodkinson and John Smith proceed with some allied arguments in their chapter. They begin by reviewing the status of particular kinds of evidence, noting that the view of knowledge that lies at the heart of the evidence-based practice movement has been the subject of much critique over the last three or four decades. After outlining this critique, they examine some recent policy introductions and argue that research in the human sciences often comes up with contradictory messages. It is messy, and the job of the researcher is not to provide 'what works' simplifications but rather 'to provide independent external critique, as well as, where relevant, providing assistance to bring the policies into being and to improve their effectiveness'. Using work-based learning as their canvas, they propose an alternative model to evidence-based practice in which researchers, policy-makers and practitioners work together to construct better understandings of the problems they face.

A similar stance is taken by John Elliott, who takes as his starting point a critique of Hargreaves's (1996) promotion of evidence-based practice. In doing this, Elliott draws heavily from Alasdair MacIntyre's (1981) critical appraisal of the value of generalizations in the social sciences. Elliott suggests that Hargreaves's conception of actionable knowledge in education and his belief in the value of generalizations couched in the form of statistical probabilities are mistaken. Further, he suggests that such beliefs meld easily with the ideology of outcomes-based education and cause stagnation in curricular development. He calls for reinvigorated educational theory that takes as its foundation the centrality of reflection on educational aims and processes. As part of this, he sees a need to reinstate Stenhouse's view of educational research as research-based teaching.

Following this, Harry Torrance provides an example of just such research-based teaching in practice. Taking Elliott's baton, he argues for the application of research *methods* rather than research *findings* to educational endeavours and problems. Calling for more responsive forms of research and development conducted at local level, he reports on a research project using an action research approach to test and develop knowledge about formative assessment in primary classrooms. Torrance discusses arguments about the nature and purpose of evidence-based practice in the light of the project.

Finally, Richard Pring draws together themes that have emerged in this book. Outlining the many different kinds of evidence that exist in different forms of discourse – all valid in their own contexts – he proceeds to suggest that there should be no imperialism from one favoured kind of discourse and its associated evidence. He notes three philosophical issues that confront the approach embodied in the evidence-based practice movement. First, there are the problems – given the multifactorial nature of social life – of attempting to predict all of the many and varied consequences of a particular course of action. Second, there are the difficulties of reconciling the methods of a scientific discourse with one concerned with persons. And third, the approach can lead to a separation of ends from means in education. This ends-means divorce makes for '. . . a quite impoverished way of talking about and understanding education, for the "ends" are more often than not embedded within the "means" '.

Pring concludes with an appeal for reflection about notions of evidence outside experimental research – for example, in craft and personal knowledge – and consideration of how that evidence can be systematically marshalled and used. The hope must be, he argues, that the collation and synthesis of findings that the evidence-based practice approach promises can occur more broadly across different kinds of evidence.

Notes

1 Higgs boson is a particle – postulated but never observed – widely believed by physicists to give mass to other particles.
2 The role of the peer review journal is significant in determining the quality of

the evidence here (see Grayson 2002). It is interesting to note that Hargreaves (1996) highlights the differential success of the peer review process in education and medicine for explaining the differential success of these disciplines in filtering and enabling the production of good evidence. He suggests that 'In a research field that is successful and healthy, peer review works well' (p 5), asserting that educational research is not healthy and that peer review here perpetuates 'a very unsatisfactory *status quo*'. In fact, discussion of peer review in medicine (see, for example, Garfunkel *et al.* 1990; McNutt *et al.* 1990; Flanagin *et al.* 1998; Godlee *et al.* 1998; Misakian and Bero 1998; Rennie 1998), or indeed the sciences (for example, Wennerås and Wold 1997; Relyea 1999; Savage 1999), reveals little if any evidence or commentary from informed observers that 'peer review works well' in those other domains – in fact, far from it. Assertion is here standing in the place of evidence.

3   A case for lies being told in the construction of the 'evidence base' about how to teach children to read is made by Coles (2002) in relation to the National Institute of Child and Human Development's assessment of approaches to teaching reading. In another example, a highly respected educational psychologist has been shown to have fabricated evidence (see Kamin 1977; Hearnshaw 1979).

4   Coady (1992) and Shapin (1994) discuss testimony in the law and in scientific inquiry.

5   It was Kuhn (1970), of course, who drew attention to the social nature of the scientific process: ' "normal science" means research firmly based upon one or more past scientific achievements, achievements that *some particular scientific community acknowledges* for a time as supplying the foundation for its further practice' (Kuhn 1970: 10, my emphasis).

6   Buntić (2000) points out that exhortation to make teaching a research-based profession depends on particular definitions of *teaching, research* and *profession*. One can equally say that calls for more evidence-based practice usually depend on particular understandings of *evidence* and *practice*.

7   The less robust position prefers the term 'evidence informed practice' and allows for the inclusion of a wider range of evidence, including the incorporation of action research undertaken by teachers – see the chapters of Sebba and Cordingley in this volume.

8   They originated in agriculture in the early part of the twentieth century, and are not in essence complex. Typically, set A will be compared with set B (and possibly set C, and so on) – the sets being fields of grain or legumes or whatever. Variables (such as levels and kinds of fertilizer) will be modified differentially among the groups and the effects will be noted of these differential changes on another variable (such as growth). Inferential statistics of one kind or another will then be used to assess the significance of the changes that had been noted.

9   . . . such as the introduction of Bayesian methods.

Part 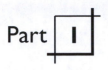 1

What is evidence-based practice?

2

Systematic reviews and the Campbell Collaboration
Philip Davies

Introduction

The idea that professional policy and practice can be based on evidence generated by sound research and scientific procedures is not new, and has little, if anything, to do with evidence-based medicine. It is at least as old as the Enlightenment, and its emphasis on replacing theology and metaphysics with *le concept positiv* as the grounding for knowledge and social action. Social and political science has spent the two centuries or so since the work of Comte and *les philosophes* arguing whether the positivist programme has any part to play in explaining the social world. These arguments will no doubt be played out once again elsewhere in the pages of this book. This chapter is less concerned about these well-rehearsed arguments, and more focused on how social and political science can harness what is already known about social and public affairs from the considerable volume of research that has been undertaken over the past years, decades and centuries.

The Campbell Collaboration is an international organization, inspired by the work of the Cochrane Collaboration, which seeks to help policy-makers, practitioners and the public make well-informed decisions about policy interventions by preparing, maintaining and disseminating systematic reviews of the effectiveness of social and behavioural interventions in education, crime and justice, and social welfare. This chapter will outline the contribution of systematic reviews to evidence-based policy and practice, and it will locate the work of the Campbell Collaboration within the writings of Donald T. Campbell. It will then discuss some tensions about the nature of evidence, and the role of social research in public policy and practice. The chapter will conclude by suggesting that the types of questions asked by policy-makers, and by people who teach, learn and manage in educational settings, requires a breadth and depth of evidence that goes beyond any particular methodology.

Systematic reviews and evidence-based policy and practice[1]

Systematic reviews are one form of research synthesis which contribute to evidence-based policy and practice by identifying the accumulated research evidence on a topic or question, critically appraising it for its methodological quality and findings, and determining the consistent and variable messages that are generated by this body of work. Systematic reviews of the existing research evidence also help identify what is not known about a topic or question and, thereby, to direct new primary research in areas where there is a gap in the evidence base.

Systematic reviews differ from other types of research synthesis, such as traditional narrative reviews and vote-counting reviews, by virtue of the way they formulate a research question, their comprehensive approach to searching, their critical appraisal strategy, and the transparency of criteria for including and excluding primary studies for review.

Formulating a question

The clarity of the questions asked of a systematic review is crucial. Questions should have a clear specification of the *interventions, factors* or *processes* in question; the *population* and/or *sub-groups* in question; the *outcomes* that are of interest to the user of the review; and the *contexts* in which the question is set. For instance, a systematic review on the effectiveness of peer group tutoring might pose the central question as follows: What is the effect of peer group tutoring (*intervention*) on students' participation in learning (*outcome 1*) and students' achievement of learning outcomes (*outcome 2*) among Key Stage 3 students (*population*) in UK state schools (*context*)? Such a question is far more helpful, and answerable, than the crude question 'does peer group tutoring work?', which begs the additional questions 'at doing what?', 'for whom?' and 'in which circumstances?'

A systematic review question posed in the above way, however, may turn out to be too specific for the purposes of identifying potentially relevant primary studies on a topic or question, and may yield no hits from electronic or print searching. In this case, it may be necessary to relax one or more of the constituent features of the question in order to establish how close the existing evidence comes to these exacting requirements. However, unless the question is posed in this precise way at the outset it will be difficult to know what the researcher is trying to achieve, and difficult to build an appropriate search strategy.

Systematic searching

One of the things that distinguishes a systematic review from a narrative review is the degree of comprehensiveness that goes into searching potentially relevant primary studies. Systematic reviews avoid the selectivity and opportunistic reading that one often finds with narrative reviews by searching for, and critically appraising, *all* of the available research literature on the question at hand, published and unpublished. This involves detailed hand-searching of journals, textbooks and conference proceedings, as well as exhaustive electronic searching of the existing research literature.

Systematic reviews also make explicit the search procedures for identifying the available literature, and the procedures by which this literature is critically appraised and interpreted. This affords a degree of transparency by which other researchers, readers and users of systematic reviews can determine what evidence has been reviewed, how it has been critically appraised, and how it has been interpreted and presented. This, in turn, allows for other interpretations of the evidence to be generated, and for additional studies of comparable quality to be added to the review, if and when they become available. In these ways, an interactive and cumulative body of sound evidence can be developed.

Critical appraisal

Systematic reviews recognize that not all published (or unpublished) studies are of equal quality in terms of the methodology used, the execution of the research design, the rigour of the analysis, and the reporting of the findings. This contrasts systematic reviews with vote-counting reviews,[2] which do not always take into account the fact that some studies are methodologically superior than others and, consequently, deserve special weighting. With systematic reviews explicit and transparent criteria are used to determine the quality and strength of studies that have been identified by systematic searching. Studies that are of sufficiently high quality are included in the review, whereas those that do not meet these quality criteria are not. There is always a danger that the criteria used for critical appraising and sifting existing studies may be too tight, and that potentially useful and relevant studies may be prematurely and unwarrantably excluded. This is why the researcher's criteria for including and excluding studies must be made explicit, so that any decisions can be revisited by the same researcher or by others.

The criteria used for critically appraising studies differs according to the methodologies of the primary studies. Some methodologies and research designs (for example, experimental and quasi-experimental methods) have more developed and explicit critical appraisal criteria than others (for example, qualitative research methods). This can be a source of tension about what constitutes acceptable and non-acceptable studies for inclusion in systematic reviews. This will be discussed in greater detail below.

Analytical framework

Systematic reviews vary in their analysis of primary studies, and different methodologies require different analytical approaches. However, an analytical framework for a systematic review should address the type, quality and validity of the data presented in the primary studies, the appropriateness of any comparisons, statistics or qualitative data that have been used, the quality of data presentation and reporting, and whether the findings and conclusions are warranted by the evidence presented.

Meta-analysis

Meta-analysis is a specific type of systematic review that seeks to *aggregate* the findings of comparable studies and 'combines the individual study treatment effects into a "pooled" treatment effect for all studies combined, and/or for specific subgroups of studies or patients, and makes statistical inferences' (Morton 1999). Gene Glass (1976) used the term to refer to 'the statistical analysis of a large collection of analysis results from individual studies for the purpose of integrating the findings'. In the two decades or more since Glass's original meta-analytic work on class size (Glass and Smith 1979; Smith and Glass 1980; Glass, Cahen, Smith and Filby 1982), and on psychotherapy (Smith, Glass and Miller 1980), meta-analysis has developed considerably in terms of the range and sophistication of data-pooling and statistical analysis of independent studies (see Kulik and Kulik 1989; Cook *et al.* 1992; Cooper and Hedges, 1994; and Egger, Davey Smith and Altman 2001 for more detailed accounts of these developments).

Meta-analysis is difficult, if not impossible, to undertake with certain types of data, the most obvious difficulty being the 'apples and pears' problem of not comparing like with like. There are tests for the heterogeneity and homogeneity of primary studies that use experimental, quasi-experimental and quantitative methods (Cooper and Hedges 1994; Deeks, Altman and Bradburn 2001). Attempts to develop meta-analysis of qualitative and ethnographic studies (Wax 1979; Noblit and Hare 1988) have not been successful, mainly because attempts to aggregate qualitative studies do not allow 'a full exploration of context', or the 'ethnographic uniqueness' of primary studies to be preserved (see Davies 2000 for a fuller discussion of the problems of meta-ethnography). More recently, methods have been developed to systematically review and synthesize qualitative studies without attempting to combine or aggregate primary studies into composite samples (Nutley, Davies and Walters 2002; Oakley, Gough and Harden 2002; Pawson 2002; Popay *et al.* 2002).

The work of Donald T. Campbell

Donald T. Campbell was a distinguished American social scientist who is perhaps best known for his interest in the 'experimenting society'. By this he meant a society that would use social science methods and evaluation techniques to 'vigorously try out possible solutions to recurrent problems and would make hard-headed, multidimensional evaluations of outcomes, and when the evaluation of one reform showed it to have been ineffective or harmful, would move on and try other alternatives' (Campbell 1999a: 9). Campbell was a strong advocate of randomized controlled trials on the grounds that 'detailed consideration of specific cases again and again reinforces my belief in the scientific superiority of randomised-assignment experiments' (1999: 24). In particular, randomized controlled trials (or randomized assignment experiments) were judged by Campbell to provide the best available means of dealing with threats to internal validity in quasi-experimental studies and other types of social science research (see Campbell 1999b: 80).

Despite this commitment to randomized controlled trials, and his acknowledgement that the experimenting society was somewhat Utopian, Campbell was also both eclectic and pragmatic about the contribution that social science research could make to public policy and practice. In recognition of some of the problems that can arise in doing randomized cotrolled trials in some social and political contexts, Campbell suggested that 'we must be elaborating high quality quasi-experimental approaches that, although more ambiguous in terms of clarity of scientific inference, are usually more acceptable as processes we will be willing to make a permanent part of our political system' (1999b: 26). Notwithstanding his lifelong concern about threats to internal validity, Campbell was also concerned about external validity and the use of research findings in different contexts. It was a repeated cause of concern for Campbell that 'we have no elegantly successful theories that predict precisely in widely different settings. . . . Our skills should be reserved for the evaluation of policies and programs that can be applied in more than one setting' (1999b: 20 and 22).

With this is mind, Campbell acknowledged the importance of qualitative research. He suggested that:

> There is the mistaken belief that quantitative measures replace qualitative knowledge. Instead, qualitative knowing is absolutely essential as a prerequisite for quantification in any science. Without competence at the qualitative level, one's computer printout is misleading or meaningless.
>
> (Campbell 1999c: 141)

Elsewhere, Campbell observed:

> Qualitative knowing is the test and building block of quantitative knowing. . . . This is not to say that such common-sense naturalistic observation is objective, dependable or unbiased. But it is all we have. It is the only route to knowledge – noisy, fallible and biased though it may be.
>
> (Campbell 1979: 186)

Campbell had a great interest in comparative ethnography, especially as a means of determining the *external* validity of programmes, projects and policies. He suggested that:

> To rule out plausible rival hypotheses we need situation-specific wisdom. The lack of this knowledge (whether it be called ethnography, programme history, or gossip) makes us incompetent estimators of programme impacts, turning out conclusions that are not only wrong, but are often wrong in socially destructive ways.
>
> (Campbell 1984: 142)

Qualitative research was also seen by Campbell as necessary for dealing with the problems that arise in the execution of randomized controlled trials and other forms of social experiment. He was fully aware of the problems of performance bias and that the measurement processes of trials often go awry. He proposed that one way of dealing with this was for 'all treatment-delivery and data collection staffs [to] keep laboratory notes' (Campbell 1999c: 230), and for 'well-placed observers' to be brought 'together in small groups when the major results were in, and ask them to speculate on what caused these outcomes'.

It is unclear whether Campbell appreciated the value of qualitative research in its own right, and not just as a hand-maiden of quantitative and experimental studies. However, his consistent reference to the importance of qualitative research is hard to deny. This raises a broader question of the sorts of evidence that should be included in systematic reviews, and what sorts of systematic review should be generated by the Campbell Collaboration.

The Campbell Collaboration

As has already been mentioned, the Campbell Collaboration is an international network of social scientists and policy analysts that prepares, maintains and disseminates systematic reviews of the effectiveness of social and behavioural interventions in education, crime and justice, and social welfare. The Collaboration was established in July 1999 following an exploratory meeting held at University College, London. Its membership is currently drawn from fifteen countries, and there are likely to be additional countries joining the Collaboration each year. There is a growing interest being shown in developing countries.

An organizational chart of the Campbell Collaboration is presented in Figure 2.1. It indicates that there are currently three substantive co-ordinating groups – in education, crime and justice, and social welfare – a methods co-ordinating group and a communications and dissemination group. Within each substantive co-ordinating group there are Review Groups undertaking systematic reviews on specific topics or areas (for example, school truancy, peer-assisted learning, second language training, problem-based teaching and learning). The Methods Co-ordinating Group is made up of a quasi-experimental group, a statistics group, a process and implementation group, and an information retrieval group. An economics methods group is currently being developed.

There are now two Campbell Regional Centres, one in Copenhagen, Denmark (the Nordic Campbell Centre), the other in Toronto, Canada. The role of these groups is to promote and disseminate systematic reviews according to Campbell Collaboration standards and principles, and to provide training in systematic review methodology. The Collaboration is led by an international steering committee of twelve members. An important feature of the Campbell Collaboration is the 'end-user' of systematic reviews and high-quality evidence. This includes policy-makers, practitioners (such as teachers, school principals, school governors), and the public (including students and parents). Ways of getting greater involvement of end-users in the work of the Collaboration (especially on the 'demand' side for good evidence and reviews) presents a constant challenge.

The funding of the Campbell Collaboration is for the most part decentralized in that each Review Group is expected to find the resources for the reviews that it undertakes. Some core funding has been provided by US research charities, and by the Danish and the Canadian provincial

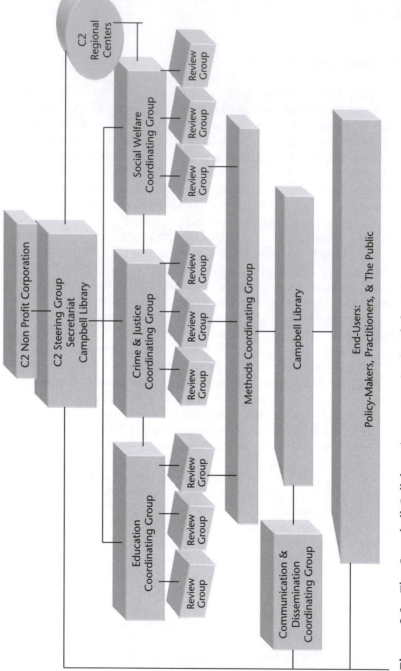

Figure 2.1 The Campbell Collaboration – organizational chart

governments (for the Nordic and Canadian Campbell Centres respectively). The British Home Office has also provided a modest amount of annual funding to the Crime and Justice Co-ordinating Group, which has allowed it to employ one person to undertake reviews and administrative tasks on behalf of the group. In August 2002 the US Department of Education awarded a five-year $18.5 million contract to a joint venture between the Campbell Collaboration and the American Institutes for Research in Washington, DC to develop a national *What Works Clearinghouse*. The clearinghouse will help provide education decision-makers with the information they need to make choice guided by the 'best available scientific research' (US Department of Education 2002).

A list of the nine key principles of the Campbell Collaboration is presented in Figure 2.2. These principles are matched by a low degree of formality and a high degree of voluntarism. There is no formal procedure for joining the Collaboration, such as application forms, acceptance or

---

The nine key principles on which the work of the Campbell and Cochrane Collaborations are based:

1. Collaboration, by internally and externally fostering good communications, open decision-making and teamwork.

2. Building on the enthusiasm of individuals, by involving and supporting people of different skills and backgrounds.

3. Avoiding unnecessary duplication, by good management and co-ordination to ensure economy of the effort.

4. Minimizing bias, through a variety of approaches such as abiding by high standards of scientific evidence, ensuring broad participation, and avoiding conflicts of interest.

5. Keeping up to date, by a commitment to ensure that Campbell Reviews are maintained through identification and incorporation of new evidence.

6. Striving for relevance, by promoting the assessment of policies and practices using outcomes that matter to people.

7. Promoting access, by wide dissemination of the outputs of the Collaboration, taking advantage of strategic alliances, and by promoting appropriate prices, content and media to meet the needs of users worldwide.

8. Ensuring quality, by being open and responsive to criticism, applying advances in methodology, and developing systems for quality improvement.

9. Continuity, by ensuring that responsibility for reviews, editorial processes and key functions is maintained and renewed.

Figure 2.2   Principles of the Campbell and Cochrane Collaborations

rejection procedures, or certificates of membership. People join the Collaboration at their will to work with existing Review Groups, or to establish new Review Groups where there is a gap in current provision. The only formality to the work of the Collaboration is that protocols for undertaking systematic reviews that wish to be published in the Campbell Library must meet the requirements of Campbell Collaboration's Protocol Guidelines (these can be found at www.campbellcollaboration.org).

At present the Campbell Collaboration's Protocol Guidelines reflect its strategic priorities for developing systematic reviews of i) randomized cotrolled trials, ii) quasi-experimental research designs, and iii) qualitative research designs that are part of controlled evaluations. In this way, the Collaboration seeks to establish both *summative* evidence of 'what works' in public policy and practice, and *formative* evidence of how, why, and under what conditions policies and practices work or fail to work. The latter is especially important for those responsible for effective delivery and implementation of policies, programmes and practices.

The Campbell Collaboration hosts the Social, Psychological and Educational Controlled Trials Register (*SPECTR*). This register was originally developed by the UK Cochrane Centre and was transferred to the Campbell Collaboration in December 2000 (and re-named *C2-SPECTR*). It contains over 10,000 randomized and 'possibly randomized' trials in education, crime and justice, and social welfare. *C2-SPECTR* is being updated and augmented regularly by the Campbell Collaboration and will serve as an important means for identifying experimental studies for inclusion in the Campbell Collaboration's systematic reviews. Each record in the registry contains citation and availability information, and usually an abstract. A primary purpose for maintaining *C2-SPECTR* is to provide support for individuals doing Campbell systematic reviews.

The inclusion of qualitative research designs only if they are *part of* controlled evaluations may be too restrictive for some social researchers and some policy-makers who commission and use systematic reviews. They need high-quality research synthesis of all types of social and political research, *regardless* of whether or not these are part of controlled evaluations. To date, the methodology for systematically synthesizing the full range of qualitative research studies has been under-developed. Currently, however, there is work underway to develop 'conceptual synthesis' (Nutley *et al.* 2002), 'realist synthesis' (Pawson 2002), and the systematic synthesis of qualitative research (Oakley *et al.* 2002) and evidence from diverse study designs (Popay *et al.* 2002). In addition, a Quality Framework for Qualitative Research is being developed (Cabinet Office 2003b) that will provide some consensus on what constitutes high-quality qualitative research and evaluation. These developments will put qualitative research on a similar footing to experimental and quasi-experimental methods in terms of having explicit quality frameworks, and will increase the pressure for a wider conception of qualitative research to be included in the Campbell Library of systematic reviews.

Other sources of systematic review evidence

The Campbell Collaboration does not have a monopoly on the provision of systematic review evidence in the areas of education, crime and justice, or social welfare. Other organizations synthesize studies using a wider range of research methods. The EPPI-Centre[3] at the Institute of Education, University of London (www.eppi.ioe.ac.uk) provides tools and procedures for helping groups undertake and disseminate quality-assured systematic reviews in education and health promotion. The EPPI-Centre's Research Evidence in Education Library (REEL) is the central means of disseminating the systematic reviews generated by its Review Groups. The Centre is also developing systematic review methodology, particularly in the area of non-intervention research. Similar work is being developed by the Centre for Research and Dissemination at the University of York (www.york.ac.uk/inst/crd), the ESRC Evidence Network (www.evidencenetwork.org), and the Social Care Institute of Excellence (www.scie.org.uk). All of this work is important for policy-makers and practitioners such as teachers, school management teams, and school governors, who often want sound evidence on *implementation* questions such as '*how* can second language teaching be implemented effectively in state primary schools?' and '*how* can peer-assisted learning be introduced in health education and health promotion curricula?' Systematic review evidence on the barriers to successful implementation, and how to overcome them, are also needed by policy-makers, practitioners and consumers of public services.

Synthesized evidence is also required by end-users on people's perceptions and experiences of policy and practice, and on the consequences of educational innovations for social interactions and behaviours. Work is also required on the *types* of context in which policies and practices are likely to work effectively. Much is claimed about the contextual variability of schools, classrooms, and sub-groups of learners. It is unclear, however, how infinite this variability is, and whether there may be patterns of contexts, or structures of variability that would help educators (and learners) be more effective in their everyday work and practice. Work is also required on the cost, cost-effectiveness, and cost-benefit of different educational policies and practices, particularly by teachers, school management teams and school governors who have to meet more and more targets with limited budgets and other resources.

As work in these areas of research synthesis develops and accumulates, it is likely that a range of institutions, centres and collaborations will emerge throughout the world. Arrangements are being developed within the Campbell Collaboration to recognize affiliated groups that provide sound review evidence in these areas. This, together with the close relationship between the Campbell Collaboration and the Cochrane Collaboration, should generate a breadth and depth of understanding of what constitutes sound review evidence that will enhance the systematic and rigorous work that is currently being undertaken by the Campbell Collaboration.

Conclusions

Systematic reviews make an important contribution to evidence-based policy and practice by providing a means of harnessing what is already known about a topic or question, and identifying gaps in the existing knowledge and evidence base. The Campbell Collaboration has been established to provide high-quality systematic reviews of the effectiveness of interventions in education, crime and justice, and social welfare. It also provides development, training and support in systematic review methodology. It is an international network of social scientists and policy analysts that is driven by the principles of collaboration, voluntarism and minimal formality. The Campbell Collaboration has taken a strategic decision to focus more on intervention studies than other types of research, and on experimental and quasi-experimental research designs. At the same time, there is a process and implementation methods group within the Collaboration, and increasing demands for the synthesis of qualitative research outside of the confines of controlled evaluations. These wider approaches to research synthesis are now being undertaken by organizations outside the Campbell Collaboration, and an opportunity exists via affiliated status for the Campbell Collaboration to be closely associated with these developments. This broader approach to research synthesis will be welcome to policy-makers, providers and consumers of public services whose demands for sound evidence go beyond any particular methodology or research design.

Notes

1 For a more detailed discussion of the issues covered in this section, see Davies (2000, 2003) and Cabinet Office (2003a).
2 Vote-counting reviews attempt to accumulate the results of a collection of relevant studies by counting those with positive findings, those with negative

findings, and those that have neutral findings. The category that has the most counts, or votes, is taken to represent the modal or typical finding, thereby indicating the most effective means of intervention.

3 The work of the EPPI-Centre is discussed in greater detail by David Gough in Chapter 4 of this book.

3

Developing evidence-informed policy and practice in education
Judy Sebba

> Sir Derek Raynor, a senior civil servant in the Heath and Thatcher governments, considered failure avoidance as the dominant trait of the Whitehall culture: '. . . the civil servant tends to be judged by failure. This . . . leads to the creation of an unnecessary number of large committees, all of which leads to delay in decision-making and the blurring of responsibility.' The inevitable result is that information is distorted at every level because no one wishes to communicate 'bad news' or to expose themselves to blame.
>
> (Chapman 2002: 59)

Introduction

The drive for evidence-informed policy-making is attempting to minimize distortion of information through greater transparency and better support for policy-makers and those who judge them, in regarding 'bad news' as formative and developmental. Following the publication of the Hillage *et al.* (1998) review of educational research which concluded that the impact of research on policy and practice was minimal, the Department for Education and Employment (now the Department for Education and Skills, DfES) set out its action plan (Budge 1998) to address the recommendations. These focused on two underlying aims: making better use of existing evidence and investing in a better evidence base for the future. Without re-rehearsing the debate about the conclusions reached in the Hillage *et al.* report, or the evidence from which it drew (see, for example, Goldstein 2000), this chapter attempts to review the progress made to date and the key questions still to be addressed.

Other chapters in this volume (by Davies, Gough and Andrews) discuss in greater detail systematic reviews in general and the work of the EPPI-Centre in particular, which is a key development for the DfES in investing in the future evidence base. Moreover, I have provided an overview of the elements of the strategy elsewhere (Sebba 2003), so instead will engage with the arguments raised by the authors in Part 1 of this volume about the nature of evidence-informed policy and practice. The emphasis in this chapter will be on policy, since the examples best known to me are from within the current policy process rather than within the education services, but comparisons are made where appropriate. Furthermore, the processes by which research informs policy and practice differ significantly and Philippa Cordingley addresses the relationship of research to practice in her chapter. For example, policy-makers do not generate new knowledge through their own activity in the way that it has been argued teachers theorize practice (Furlong 1998). Another main difference stems from the influence of the political context on the decision-making of the policy-maker, whereas the teacher is more likely to take into account the characteristics of the pupils and particular school context in mediating research evidence.

What do we mean by evidence?

There are many different types of evidence. Davies *et al.* (2000) argue that they include the means of proving an unknown fact, support for a belief, use of testimonies and witnesses. They note that however construed, evidence can be independently observed and verified and there is broad consensus as to its contents, even if the interpretation of it is contested. The view that they present of evidence as comprising the results of systematic investigation towards increasing the sum of knowledge, does not concur with the view of some others. For example, Martyn Hammersley in this volume argues that other kinds of evidence which do not necessarily emerge from systematic investigation may be more important. Hodkinson and Smith (Chapter 11) suggest that the contexts in which practitioners and politicians work are more influential than the evidence itself. Pawson (2001), adopting a realist synthesis approach, notes that it is the underlying reasons or resources offered rather than evidence of the policy itself which influence its impact. Hence, as Hodkinson suggests, the evidence and means of validating it are contested and problematic.

In the context of current policy-making, there are three types of evidence which policy-makers use predominantly and they are sometimes inappropriately treated as equivalent. Government departments employ statisticians and economists who conduct monitoring, evaluation and forecasting analyses using data collected through national surveys or other means. These data are mainly quantitative and subjected to different forms of statistical procedure rather than different possible interpretations of their meaning. Secondly, there are inspection data, which in the case of education are generated through Ofsted inspections. The validity and reliability of these data are discussed in detail elsewhere (see, for example, Earley 1998). While many policy-makers seek inspection data to illuminate policy options or evaluate their policies, those working in the education services in which these data are collected are more questioning of them.

Finally, there is research evidence, which is more usually collected through externally commissioned projects or programmes funded by the government department itself or external bodies including research councils and independent charitable foundations. A few departments such as the Home Office, in addition to externally commissioning research, employ their own researchers to undertake projects. The rest of this chapter focuses mainly on research evidence, while recognizing that confusion over types of evidence and their fitness for purpose is one of many factors that may be limiting its use.

Building a cumulative evidence base

The Hillage *et al.* review and other studies (for example, DETYA 2001) identified the need for a more cumulative evidence base. There are several aspects to this. First, it is essential for researchers, funders and users to be able to check not only what research has been published previously, but ongoing research that will be published in the future. Funders, in particular, also need information on the areas missing or under-represented in the present research activity. The Current Educational Research in the UK database (CERUK) was set up to provide information about ongoing projects, but to be comprehensive in coverage requires researchers to submit the details of current work and a few do not do so at present. Some funders have made it a requirement of their funding that researchers register on this database and want reassurance that they have consulted it prior to starting their research. Only with near complete information can this system enable cumulative evidence to be built up and unintentional overlap to be avoided.

Secondly, as the DETYA (2001) study concluded, single studies should have less impact than literature reviews and papers that synthesize research in a form accessible to practitioners. The contribution of reviews to the cumulative evidence base is therefore central and the EPPI user perspectives, which are summaries prepared by users for their constituent groups, are a major step forward in this respect. While systematic reviews may be desirable where possible, the contribution made by other types of reviews, in particular where the literature is very limited, should be acknowledged.

Thirdly, the building of a cumulative evidence base is hampered by the lack of replications and of reporting of negative results or research where the methodology did not meet the original expectations. Cooper *et al.* (1997) found that, of all the studies approved by a human subjects review committee, researchers submitted for publication 74 per cent of those with significant findings but only 4 per cent of those with non-significant results. The authors noted that editors are more likely to accept manuscripts reporting significant results. They also found that researchers were more likely to withhold results when they identify study design flaws. These publication biases are then exacerbated by any replications which are funded being based on previous published studies. These problems have emerged very clearly in the systematic review work where, as reported in other chapters of this volume, certain types of studies are much more likely to be published. The use of CERUK enables initiated research to be tracked through and these problems to be more readily identified.

Fourthly, the need to invest in the future evidence base provides the rationale for education foresight or what the National Educational Research Forum is now referring to as the Education Observatory. The Foresight process is justified by the Department of Trade and Industry (dti) as:

> ... *being ready for the future. No one can predict the future. What we can do is look ahead and think about what might happen so that we can begin to prepare for it.*
>
> *The future is shaped by the decisions we make today. If we wait for the future to happen to us the UK will miss out on opportunities for wealth creation and a better quality of life.*
>
> (Foresight, dti 2000, inside cover)

Thus, it is a means of moving from being reactive to being proactive. The present education research profile should be assessed against the future needs identified through foresight so that future planning can be better informed both substantively and theoretically.

Making research evidence more accessible

Elsewhere in this volume, David Gough describes the development and support for systematic reviewing through the work of the EPPI-Centre. In the US (Viadero 2002) and in the report of the review of educational research and development in England by the OECD (2002), these developments are held up as a world leader, the first to provide methods of integrating quantitative and qualitative studies in systematic reviews and meaningfully to involve users throughout the process. But in England, the critics are more evident. Hammersley (in Chapter 10 in this volume) describes systematic reviewing as linear, rational, based on a positivist view of practice and prioritizing randomly controlled trials. Yet the analysis of the first four reviews published in 2002 on the EPPI website (http://eppi.ioe.ac.uk) shows that 24 per cent of the studies included were process evaluations and 37 per cent descriptive studies. There are many theoretical issues highlighted by the reviewing, such as the nature of knowledge, nature of evidence used in the syntheses and how theory is presented in the reviews. But the reviews have provided transparency previously not evident; they have involved policy-makers and practitioners working alongside researchers in setting review questions, mapping the research and reporting the findings. As yet, they are insufficiently understood and assumed to be much closer to the medical model than they are in actuality. As Oakley (2000: 323) suggests: 'The paradigm war has set us against one another in ways that have been unproductive in answering some of the most urgent social questions facing us today.'

The Commission on the Social Sciences (2003) recommended that researchers should be supported in acquiring 'media-savvy skills'. This assumes that all researchers could write like successful journalists given appropriate training and that this would be desirable. Our approach has been to recognize the distinct skills of researchers and to use journalists to support them by mediating research rather than replacing them. Journalists work in teams with researchers or alongside them to do this. Examples include the General Teaching Council's *Research of the Month* initiative, which summarizes a piece of research that is of particular interest to the teaching profession (http://www.gtce.org.uk/research/romhome.asp), and the DfES *Research into Practice* initiative (http://www.standards.dfes.gov.uk/research/), which provides rewritten and summarized academic journal articles prepared by journalists for lay users but checked with the researchers for authenticity. More adventurous approaches to communicating research through the use of video or television are also being explored by the DfES and the ESRC's Teaching and Learning Research Programme (http://www.tlrp.org).

Building the capacity of research to address complex issues

Concerns have been expressed that the research 'system' lacks the human, intellectual and material resources to ensure that research of sufficient scale and quality can be produced that focuses on priority issues and can be used to inform policy and practice. The Commission on the Social Sciences (2003) provides strong support for the contribution of multidisciplinarity/cross-institutional research but notes that there is not much evidence of it at present. They also note that the need for some research to integrate quantitative and qualitative techniques to address key research questions is hampered by the lack of expertise in doing so.

Dyson and Desforges (2002) review the evidence of lack of capacity for both undertaking and using research. They note that it may be more helpful to think in terms of research capacities in the plural rather than of a single capacity. These, they suggest, include the capacity to produce scholarly research in order to build knowledge, the capacity for policy-makers to use such research, and the capacity for practitioners to produce or use research to inform their practice. This multi-dimensional view suggests that there is no one simple answer to increasing the capacity of the system.

Dyson and Desforges go on to note that capacity has to be seen not simply in terms of what the research system *can* do, but also in terms of what it *should* do. This implies a need for strategies which are more concerned with leveraging capacity in new ways as well as the maintenance and development of current capacity. They make a further distinction between strategies which *broaden* capacity (that is which enable the system to do 'more of the same') and those which *deepen* it (that is which enable the system to do new things or to do things better). Since strategies to increase capacity are rarely evaluated, there are no indications of which are the most effective approaches.

The paper by Dyson and Desforges identifies three themes around which research capacity may be built. The first is development opportunities for researchers to update, retrain or refresh their skills through courses, coaching, secondments and other means. The second is the development of the infrastructure for levering capacity through dedicated research centres, research networks, funding for information technology and other support. This includes further development of interdisciplinary research which provides the opportunity for complex research questions to be addressed from several different angles, with mutual benefit to each discipline involved.

The third area they identify is increasing the capacity for practitioner and policy-makers to produce and use research. Many of the initiatives in this area are discussed elsewhere in this chapter, such as the web developments described above which aim to make relevant research more accessible. The initiatives described below for developing better understanding between policy-makers and researchers are also relevant to increasing capacity to use research. Opportunities for practitioners to undertake research through scholarships or award-bearing study have increased but are still only reaching a tiny proportion of the profession. The establishment of practitioner secondments to research organizations and professional researcher secondments to schools, colleges and policy-making organizations are all making a contribution to capacity building. The networked learning communities established by the National College of School Leadership (2002) provide an innovatory process for building research capacity in schools.

Using research evidence in the policy process

In 2000, the National Educational Research Forum published the report of its sub-group on the impact of educational research on policy and practice. They made the distinction between dissemination and impact, arguing that whichever term is used, the process being described is usually dissemination, that is, the spreading of awareness about the research and its outcomes to people outside the research team. This, they note, is usually done after the research has concluded, will be publicly observable and might involve conferences and publications. Thus dissemination can be effective without having an impact. Walter *et al.* (2003) argue that explicit and active strategies are needed to ensure that research really does have an impact. They describe a taxonomy of interventions to enhance the impact of research on public sector policy and practice developed at the Unit for Research Utilisation at the University of St Andrews. It is cross-sectoral and includes ways of encouraging more conceptual uses of research to contribute to changing knowledge, beliefs and attitudes rather than being limited to behavioural interventions, which Hammersley (in this volume) and others (for example, Bates 2002) have criticized as overly rational.

Hodkinson (in this volume) similarly asserts that those promoting evidence-informed policy assume a linear relationship between research and its users, but the Forum's sub-group report made clear that linear models misrepresent the research process. They and others (for example, DETYA 2001) suggested that it is better described by an interactive approach to producing, disseminating and using new knowledge which requires a transformative process to overcome the hazards of transfer and application. Knowledge may not be transferred due to the way it is expressed or the receptivity of the recipient. Successful knowledge transfer does not guarantee effective application due to, for example, lack of opportunity or resources, adherence to deeply held beliefs or difficulties in translating theoretical knowledge into practical applications.

Hargreaves (2003) suggests that some research has had an impact by involving researchers and practitioners as co-creators of new knowledge that can be validated and transferred. He cites as an example the work on assessment for learning by Paul Black, Dylan Wiliam and others (see, for example, Wiliam and Lee 2001) which has involved a strong partnership between researchers and teachers providing a model of 'development and research' rather than 'research and development'. Hargreaves suggests that 'development and research' puts innovative practice in the lead and is thereby potentially transformative.

The professional development of teachers involved in this process draws on intellectual capital to generate new knowledge, social capital to support deep professional learning through experimentation within a context of trust, and organizational capital to ensure the dissemination of new knowledge. While the research on assessment for learning is only one of many areas of educational research to have influenced policy and practice, analysis of how this has occurred enables the process of impact to be better understood.

Use of research may be indirect, for example via teacher educators, rather than direct, and policy-makers can be informed by research without changing direction, that is, the research may suggest that they should not adopt a particular policy or action. They may be unaware of the source of the information they have used and there may be multiple sources being used simultaneously. Hence, policy that has not been explicitly informed by research may still have been influenced by it. Furthermore, political, economic and other pressures will come into play when policy-makers make decisions resulting in difficulties in identifying the precise contribution made by research. Researchers are not generally familiar with the policy-making process and may misinterpret the outcome as having ignored research. Since the methodology for evaluating impact is underdeveloped, it is difficult to establish precisely how these processes occur at present.

Encouraging policy-makers and practitioners to use research

Policy-makers and practitioners work in contexts and cultures which may not be conducive to using research. The quote at the start of this chapter was about the difficulties experienced by policy-makers in admitting to and using mistakes constructively. Developing an open dialogue between researchers and policy-makers may provide positive experiences for policy-makers in the potential of research use and help researchers to better understand the policy process. The Commission on the Social Sciences recognized the increasing involvement of academics on research steering groups, advisory groups and other work in government. Furthermore, it recommended increasing the programme of secondments in both directions between staff in academia and those in government as a means of creating greater mutual understanding and knowledge transfer.

Within the DfES, far greater investment has been made in larger and longer-term research projects and in longitudinal data sets and analyses of them. Since policy decisions in any given area need to be made frequently during the four- or five-year periods over which these analyses are completed, it is important that researchers are willing and able to give their 'best guesstimate' at a given time of what they think the evidence might mean. Trust is needed on both sides to do this. This does not assume, as the critics elsewhere in this book suggest, that the question being asked is always researchable, that the evidence is infallible or that highly reliable evidence of what works will be available. The fact that not all policy can be evidence-informed should not stop us from trying to encourage use of research when the alternative is decisions that are not informed by any evidence.

A similar analysis can be applied to educational practitioners. Teachers have traditionally worked in isolation. Like civil servants, an admission of a mistake is regarded as weakness. Hargreaves (1996, drawing on the work of William Taylor 1993) noted that teachers who cite research in a staffroom discussion would be assumed to be studying for a higher degree, rehearsing for an Ofsted inspection or more generally 'showing off'. The lack of an expectation to use research evidence in teaching or the civil service is deeply embedded in the culture, and despite the rhetoric of developing evidence-informed policy and practice and 'modernizing government', many will continue to be resistant to change. The work of the National Teacher Research Panel (www.standards.dfes.gov.uk/ntrp) and initiatives designed to encourage schools to be more engaged in using, and in some cases generating, research (for example, Essex County Council 2003) are contributing to addressing this. The experience of greater openness and more debate about what evidence exists and what it means should surely be welcomed.

Conclusion

What do we need in the policy-making process to enhance the use of research? A greater emphasis is needed on improvement driven by users rather than by the suppliers (researchers and funders) of research. This means identifying perceived needs to tackle a real problem and providing appropriate support to policy-makers to help them express their needs as researchable questions. In order to address many of the complex questions facing policy-makers and practitioners, quantitative and qualitative data may need to be integrated to provide information about what to do and how to do it. Existing evidence needs to be summarized clearly and presented accessibly, and flexible approaches adopted to address mismatches of timing between policy decisions being made and research results becoming available.

Chapman (2002) argues that we need interventions that introduce learning and support processes rather than specifying targets. The current initiative on networked learning communities (National College of School Leadership 2002) provides a means of engaging practitioners which is based on listening and co-researching rather than telling and directing. The dialogue between policy-makers, practitioners and researchers needs to be built into the research process from the outset to ensure that the research questions, design, data collection, interpretation and dissemination are all influenced by multiple perspectives. Initiatives such as the National Teacher Research Panel are helping to do this. Many research projects now have teachers part-time on their teams, but few are able to involve policy-makers similarly, so other means of establishing ongoing dialogue need to be found.

However much the procedures and processes are changed to increase the capacity of policy-makers and practitioners to use research, long-term sustainability of using it will only come about if embedded in their beliefs and values: 'The impact of research in schools and in policy formulation depends greatly on educators' valuing research, and on their ability to apply and critique it' (DETYA 2001, summary p. 8).

Like other areas of education, the value of research will be enhanced through positive experience. What are researchers, funders, politicians, policy-makers and practitioners doing to ensure that these positive experiences happen?

4

Systematic research synthesis
David Gough

Aims, users and quality of primary research

This chapter makes an argument for the use of systematic research synthesis. As such synthesis attempts to make productive use of primary research, attention needs first to be given to aims of that research; who it is produced for, how it can be accessed and how one can assess whether it should be trusted.

Educational research is undertaken for many diverse reasons, ranging from the furtherance of philosophical and theoretical understanding of the nature of learning to the no less fundamental issue of providing fruitful employment for university academic staff. In between these extremes of idealized and personal needs is the practical use of research evidence to inform policy and practice; the provision of conceptual understandings, predictive theories and empirical evidence articulated within different conceptual frameworks to influence decision-making. The nature of that influence can be complex. Research evidence may be used instrumentally to support decisions made according to other agendas rather than a more straightforward or naïve rational input into decision-making (Gough and Elbourne 2002). The research evidence will, of course, be dependent on particular world views which are part of wider ideological debates and contests being fought in many arenas, including both the supply of research and its use. Although research may be derived from many different conceptual and ideological bases, have differential legitimacy with different producers and users of research, and be used in many rational and non-rational ways, it loses much of its public legitimacy if it is not seen as being at least in part feeding into rational processes of decision-making.

Users of research

Research is undertaken for different purposes for different types of users of research, including policy-makers, practitioners, users of services and other members of society. These users have a variety of overlapping roles, responsibilities, interests and agendas and, most importantly, power and resources, so it is unsurprising that the role and importance of research evidence varies between and within such groups. Those who believe that research evidence should have an increasing and a rational role in influencing decision-making are in effect advocating a change in balance in current decision-making powers and processes and thus for political change. Currently we have little knowledge of the detail about how research evidence is so used, and so this is in itself an important research priority (Newman *et al.* 2001; Nutley *et al.* 2003).

The importance of research to policy-making has become increasingly overt recently, with knowledge being seen to be given a higher profile in government. In Britain, the 1999 White Paper on Modernizing Government (Cabinet Office 1999) gave a central role to the Cabinet Office for social science research, and the 2002 Treasury Spending Review required evidence of the effectiveness of funded programmes. Senior members of the government have publicly proclaimed the importance of social science research to policy (for example, Blunkett 2000), though politicians and other policy-makers may still be unwilling to accept research evidence when it conflicts with deep-seated views or policies. Policy-makers have many other issues to consider than research evidence and are relatively powerful in deciding the role research will play and in what research will be funded. An example is the £14 million research budget to evaluate the effectiveness of the Sure Start initiative, a programme of support to families of young children in socioeconomically deprived areas across England. Government officials made it clear that only non-experimental research designs would be funded. Experimental designs might be efficient at assessing the impact of new programmes, but such designs were politically unacceptable as it might seem as if provision to families in need was dependent on a toss of a coin. In health research there are similar concerns about withholding promising new interventions from those with health needs, but the scientific rationale and balance of power between research and policy is differently drawn. New drug therapies, for example, are required to be evaluated using random controlled trials.

Another issue for policy is the extent that research is able to deliver relevant and timely answers to a quickly changing policy environment. This is partly a problem of the time taken to commission and complete research, but may also be an issue of the framing of research questions by academics rather than policy-makers and the communication of the results of previous research activity and evidence to policy-makers. Both these latter problems could be reduced by greater involvement of policy-makers in the research process, greater effort to predict upcoming policy issues, and improved methods for synthesizing and communicating previous research activity and findings. The more that social research can be seen as relevant to policy, the more power that it will have compared to other influences on policy decision-making.

Another central group of potential users of research is professional practitioners. Hargreaves (1996) argues that teachers make insufficient use of declarative research knowledge such as research evidence compared to the craft knowledge of knowing how to be a teacher through learning from others and from individual experience. He argues that other professions such as medicine have a more even balance between declarative and craft knowledge. Professional practitioners can have subtle insights lost to research and are involved in an enormous amount of innovative activity that can develop professional thinking (Foray and Hargreaves 2002). Where codification of this tacit knowledge is possible, the knowledge may be more easily shared and its generalizability more easily assessed through research. However subtle and innovative human sensitivity and professional skills may be, they are also fallible (as is research itself, of course). Individual practitioners can be misled into believing that a particular form of educational provision is responsible for some educational successes whereas failures are perceived as due to failures in the recipients of the service. Such misperceptions have often been found in health where, for example, clinicians thought for years that albumin was the best treatment for children suffering from shock from extensive burns, although we now know that the treatment increases the risk of death compared to other treatments (Bunn *et al.* 2000). Similarly, many parents accepted the advice of Dr Benjamin Spock that infants should sleep on their fronts, but the change of advice that infants should sleep on their backs has over halved the incidence of sudden infant death syndrome in England and Wales within two years (Chalmers 2001). There are also examples of similar well-intentioned but problematic inter-ventions in people's lives in education and criminal justice, such as the fashion against teaching phonics in the 1970s and 1980s (Chalmers 2003, National Institute of Child Health and Human Development 2000) and the idea that frightening children by showing them prisons as a con-sequence of crime would reduce their rates of delinquency (Petrosino *et al.* 2003).

Users of research also include actual and potential users of services, such as school students and their parents. As our understanding of user perspectives in the choice and organization of services has increased, so has the relevance of research to inform service user decision-making and the consequent effects on practitioner and policy-maker decision-making. These issues are important in terms of democratic rights of choice and participation but also impact on the efficacy of services. Experimental research often examines services in ideal research-created settings, but implementation in the field depends upon user acceptability, and so user perspectives as well as user-framed research need to be examined in reviewing research evidence on efficacy (see, for example, Harden *et al.* 2003). Similarly, members of society in general need to have an understanding of research to properly participate in public discussions in a knowledge-based and an evidence-informed decision-making society. Research thus becomes an issue of public accountability of decisions made by policy-makers and practitioners on the behalf of citizens. Smith argues that:

> We are, through the media, as ordinary citizens, confronted daily with controversy and debate across a whole spectrum of public policy issues. But typically, we have no access to any form of a systematic 'evidence base' – and therefore no means of participating in the debate in a mature and informed manner.
>
> (Smith 1996: 369–70)

Finally, researchers are themselves users of research, using findings to address empirical and theoretical issues and plan further research. As those actively involved in formulating research plans, undertaking and disseminating research they often have a central role in the planning of research and in the use made of its findings.

Critiques of educational research

Notwithstanding the view about the role that research evidence may play, there may be variation in the efficiency in which such evidence is produced and implemented. Recently there have been a number of critiques of educational research in both the United States and Britain arguing that the field contains too much work that is inadequate in terms of research quality, practical relevance, or is inaccessible to those who might apply such research evidence (Gage 1972; Hargreaves 1996; Hillage *et al.* 1998; McIntyre 1997; Tooley and Darby 1998; McIntyre and McIntyre 1999; Lagemann 2000; Feuer *et al.* 2002; Shavelson and Towne 2002).

Some of these critiques come from government and have led to new educational research policies. In the United States, the National Research Council (NRC) of the National Academies (Shavelson and Towne 2002) argues that all educational research can or should be at least in part be scientific, where scientific endeavours require (Feuer *et al.* 2002):

* empirical investigation
* linking research to theory

- methods that permit direct investigation of the research questions
- findings that replicate and generalize across studies
- disclosure of data and methods to enable scrutiny and critique.

The NRC report states that the federal government does seek scientific research for policy and practice decisions and the new federal 'No Child Left Behind Act' of 2001 requires recipients of federal grants to use their grants on evidence-based strategies (Feuer *et al.* 2002), but current educational research is perceived to be lacking in quality.

In England, a government-commissioned report on the state of educational research evidence concluded that greater coordination was required in terms of setting research agendas and priorities and the synthesis and dissemination of the products of that research (Hillage *et al.* 1998). The recommendations led to the setting up the National Forum for Educational Research (www.nerf.org) and the centre for evidence-informed policy and practice at the EPPI-Centre (http://eppi.ioe.ac.uk). Similar conclusions were drawn by a review of educational research commissioned by the ESRC's Teaching and Learning Research Programme. The report argued that the complexity of research, policy and practice issues in education made it difficult to produce a finite agenda of research priorities, but there was a need for improved collation and dissemination of both quantitative and qualitative research (McIntyre and McIntyre 1999).

The critiques of educational research in America and Britain often argued for the importance of all forms of research as fit for answering different types of research question. Many of the critiques focused on the inadequacies of qualitative research (Tooley and Darby 1998), or argued for greater use of random experimental methods in education and the social sciences more generally (Gage 1972; Oakley 1998, 2001; Fitzgibbon 1999). The promotion of particular views about science, government involvement in these developments, and the nature of some of the strategies initiated to further research in education has led some to argue against the political assumptions and agendas that they believe to be implicit in such changes (Erikson and Gutierrez 2002; Hammersley, this volume).

Accessing evidence from educational research

Before undertaking any new policy, practice or new piece of research, it is sensible to first examine what other people have found out about the issue. Research, whatever its limitations, is one form of activity that might have found out such relevant evidence. The issue then becomes one of how one might find out about such previous research evidence.

A traditional method for ascertaining what is known in a research field is to consult a literature review. This is a common academic task undertaken by students in reports and dissertations and by fully trained academics in academic and public publications. Considering the large amount of research and publications produced each year, a literature review can be a difficult undertaking, but until recently little guidance was given in academic training as how to undertake such reviews. It was just assumed that people knew and maybe students were embarrassed to ask further. In practice, this probably meant that students gleaned what they could from reference lists and looking around the university library. Academic staff had experience and skills in a research area and could use this as a starting point for bringing together the literature on a topic.

Such informal and implicit approaches to reviewing have been criticized for not having an explicit methodology for undertaking and thus interpreting the review (Jackson 1980). As Glass, McGraw and Smith (1981) commented, it is curiously inconsistent that literature reviews of scientific research often have no explicit scientific procedures. Without such explicit procedures it is impossible to know what has been reviewed and in what way. Even slight changes in topic focus of a review can have major implications for the strategy used for searching for studies and criteria for including studies. For example, a comparison of six literature reviews on older people and accident prevention (which did have explicit review methodologies) found that 137 studies were reviewed in total, but only 33 of these were common to at least two of the six reviews and only two studies were included in all six reviews (Oliver *et al.* 1999). If reviews seemingly on the same topic actually have different foci and are thus examining different studies, then it would not be surprising if they came to different conclusions. What is essential is explicit explanations of the focus of the review and the associated inclusion criteria for studies.

Expert opinion is another common method for ascertaining what is known in a research field to inform policy-makers and practitioners and members of the public. It is also the main method used by courts of law in the form of expert witnesses. Expert assessments can have many useful qualities in terms of knowledge of the academic evidence, quality assessment of its relative worth, knowledge of professional tacit knowledge including contextual aspects of any evidence.

The problem with experts as with traditional literature reviews is that without explicit details about which, if any, of these many positive qualities applies, what evidence has been considered, and how it has been assessed and synthesized to come to a conclusion, then it is not possible to assess the quality of those conclusions. The main method of assessment is the reputation of the person providing the review or expert opinion. A consequence for policy-making is that experts may be chosen for the acceptability of their views. Also, policy-makers may become disenchanted with academic evidence when different experts proffer such different opinions. The effect may be to lower rather than increase the power of research evidence within a rational model of contributing to the policy-making process.

Another consequence of non-explicitly derived syntheses of research evidence is that the conclusions of such reviews may be wrong. In the previously mentioned example of albumin treatment for children with shock from extensive burns there were theoretical reasons why albumin might be an effective treatment plus some experimental studies showing positive outcomes of treatments. It was only when a more thorough search and synthesis of published and unpublished studies was undertaken that it was realized that it caused more deaths than previous treatments (Bunn *et al.* 2000). Similar problems can occur with expert testimony. In a recent case in England a woman solicitor was given a life sentence for murder of her child after expert evidence that the chances of two children in the same family dying from unexplained sudden death were only 1 in 70 million, though it is now thought that the chances are at most 1 in 8000 and probably less (Watkins 2000). The expert witness had high credibility in the court as a properly famous well-respected clinical professor, but the court was unable to assess the basis on which his incorrect conclusions has been reached. Such inaccurate synthesis has serious practical consequences; the woman spent three years in prison before being released on appeal. It can be argued that education has less dramatic impacts on people's lives, but what evidence do we have to say when we are doing more good than harm or more harm than good (Chalmers 2003)?

A final issue is that non-explicit synthesis of research evidence reduces the likelihood of being able to systematically build upon what we already know. This not only results in inefficiency of effort and sustainability but may also increase the chances of error.

Trustworthiness of research

Accessing what is known from research evidence is bound to include some assessment about the credibility and relevance of the evidence being considered. This includes the theoretical and ideological assumptions implicit in the research questions being addressed, the focus of each of the primary research studies, the research sample and context under study and the research design used to address the research questions. It also includes issues of quality in terms of how the aims and research design were operationalized in practice.

These issues of research assumptions, focus, method and quality of execution are highly contested areas. For example, some research designs are better able to address some research questions and so advocates of those designs may rightly or wrongly be seen as advocates of particular research questions and taking particular ideological and theoretical positions (Oakley 2000).

Even within particular research traditions there are differences in how researchers evaluate quality of execution of research. In random experimental research a number of quality criteria checking systems have been developed (for example, Valentine and Cooper 2003; see also the Campbell Collaboration's systems described by Davies in Chapter 2). Even if the research has been undertaken according to the highest standards there will always be limitations from the fact that a study is just one study. Research based on sampling assumes a hypothetical population from which the sample is drawn and so such studies are subject to sampling error; others replicating the study exactly are thus unlikely to obtain exactly the same results. Also, research is reported in aggregate form which often hides variability in the data (Ridgeway *et al.* 2000). Such data also typically hides contextual data which may be a crucial factor affecting the results and their interpretation (Hammersley, this volume).

In qualitative research fewer checklists have been developed and contain much fewer categories for checking, but these categories are remarkably similar to the basic components of the much longer quantitative lists including criteria such as (Oakley 2000; Harden 2002; Spencer *et al.* 2003):

- An explicit account of theoretical framework and/or inclusion of literature review
- Clearly stated aims and objectives
- A clear description of context
- A clear description of sample
- A clear description of fieldwork methods including systematic data collection
- An analysis of data by more than one researcher
- Sufficient original data to mediate between evidence and interpretation.

The trustworthiness of research is also affected by reporting issues. Not all research studies are reported and those finding positive or new interesting findings are more likely to be reported, which leads to reporting and awareness bias (Boston Medical and Surgical Journal 1909; Hedges 1984). Studies finding no statistical effect can be seen as less informative than those identifying such effects, but publication policies and research user interest in favour of the 'positive' studies has the unfortunate effect of biasing the whole field of study. An example is the previously mentioned study of albumin which found that clinical practice probably leading to greater mortality was being informed by a couple of non-representative studies (Bunn *et al.* 2000). There can also be commercial pressures where the suppliers of an intervention are more likely to want to advertise studies supporting their product than maybe a higher number of studies reporting no effect or a negative effect.

A further issue is that studies vary in the manner and extent that they report their methods and findings so that the studies may be mis-represented or wrongly judged as of relatively high or low quality on the basis of incomplete information. This can include lack of contextual data, which can make some sceptical of the validity of the findings of the research and thus of the whole research process.

Approaches to systematic synthesis

In the same way that the findings of primary research are dependent on the aims and the methods of a study, so are the conclusions of any secondary research dependent on the methods of review. In other words, any synthesis of research by others (secondary research) needs to be just as explicit in methods as primary research. Such an approach is described as a systematic research review or synthesis and has been applied most extensively to research questions of efficacy of interventions, though is applicable to virtually all research questions.

The concept of review and synthesis is in essence as old as the idea of science as it involves the development of previous ideas and theories with new empirical and conceptual work. Despite this, many have commented on the lack of consideration by scientists of previous research. An example is provided by this quote from a Cambridge professor of physics from 1885 from the James Lind Library:

> The work which deserves, but I am afraid does not always receive, the most credit is that in which discovery and explanation go hand in hand, in which not only are new facts presented but their old ones are pointed out.
>
> (Rayleigh 1885: 20, quoted by Chalmers *et al.* 2002)

The last 30 years have seen an increasing recognition of the need for a systematic approach to review and synthesis (Jackson 1980; Cooper 1982) and much of the work to date has been concerned with methods for the reduction in bias in synthesis and methods of statistical meta-analysis of experimental research studies to assess the effect of interventions (Chalmers *et al.* 2002). This work is well illustrated by the work of the Cochrane Collaboration undertaking systematic reviews of the efficacy of health interventions. The Cochrane Collaboration has international review groups using rigorous and explicit methods of review and statistical analysis to combine effect sizes of individual studies to create a combined effect size. The impact of this approach in promoting rational use of research evidence in health is illustrated by the setting up of the National Institute of Clinical Excellence by the British government to commission systematic reviews and to assess the economic, clinical and social effects of recommending different health interventions. This approach is beginning to have an influence in other areas as demonstrated by the publication of this volume of papers, government funding for a centre for evidence-informed education at the EPPI-Centre, ESRC funding of an evidence centre and network, and the setting up of the Campbell Collaboration to undertake similar work to the Cochrane Collaboration but systematically reviewing social interventions (see Chapter 2 by Davies).

The statistical meta-analysis work of the Cochrane and Campbell Collaborations is primarily addressing questions of the efficacy of interventions; in other words 'what works'. In many cases, there may not be research of sufficient quantity or quality on a topic to allow for systematic meta-analysis, so systematic methods for assessing narrative data have also been developed. As such systematic narrative approaches are not limited to statistical data this means that they are also not limited to research questions that use research designs with quantitative data that can be statistically meta-analysed. If there is a need to have explicit systematic methodologies for synthesizing research data for efficacy questions, then there is a similar need for explicit methods of synthesis for all research questions, though there may be differences in the detail of the methods of synthesis used (Gough and Elbourne 2002).

This logic also applies to research questions that use qualitative methodologies. In some cases the data from such qualitative research may be empirical and can be combined in narrative synthesis. For example, Harden and colleagues (2003) have compared syntheses of experimental data on the efficacy of interventions for young people with data on young peoples' views about interventions relevant to their needs.

In other cases the data are concepts that are synthesized into more macro concepts. Examples of this are found in meta-ethnography where different conceptual understandings derived by individual studies are brought together into a new macro conceptual understanding (Noblit and Hare 1988; Britten *et al.* 2002; Campbell *et al.* 2002). Conceptual synthesis can also be used to examine theoretical constructs within a topic of research (Paterson *et al.* 2001). Others mix conceptual and empirical approaches by using systematic methods to test out whether there is evidence in different domains to support particular theories using principles of realist evaluation (Pawson 2002b). Although most research can be subject to systematic synthesis, there may be some research questions or approaches to science and research that are so relative in approach that the concept of synthesis is intrinsically alien and their work cannot be easily subject to the same logic or processes of synthesis.

Stages of review

Apart from the highly relativist tradition and perhaps realist synthesis, all approaches to systematic research synthesis have some shared basic stages, though the data used in each stage and their treatment may differ.

1. Research question

As with primary research it is necessary to have a research question. If there is no question it is difficult to develop a focus of method for the review or to undertake a process to find some sort of answer to the question. Also, if different users of research evidence are involved in the framing of such questions then these constituencies are likely to have an increased impact on developing primary research agendas and increased participation and understanding of research.

2. Conceptual framework

The research question is bound to contain some sort of theoretical or ideological assumption that needs to be clarified. If not, then it will be difficult to operationalize the question into a meaningful systematic review study.

3. Review protocol

Again, just as with primary research, there is a need for an explicit methodology (or protocol) for the review to be developed. Within any approach to systematic research synthesis there are likely to be generally agreed processes, but there will always be further details that need to be specified. For some, this methodology needs to be fully stated before undertaking the systematic review in order to minimize biases from a data-driven review. This is typically the approach in statistical meta-analysis for efficacy questions, though sometimes a degree of iterative process can be observed. For others, a more iterative approach is considered necessary. For example, in meta-ethnography, as advanced by Noblit and Hare (1988), the quality of primary research studies becomes evident during the review process, whereas for Britten, Campbell and colleagues quality assessment is done at initial screening of studies into the review (Britten *et al.* 2002; Campbell *et al.* 2002).

4. Inclusion criteria

Part of the protocol for the review needs to specify what counts as data for the review – in other words, criteria to decide which studies should be included in the review. In traditional literature reviews, this information is often lacking, so it is difficult to identify the parameters for the review and why some studies are included and others are not.

5. *Search strategy*

The protocol also needs to specify the details of the strategy to search for research studies that meet the inclusion criteria. The strategy needs to be exhaustive within specific limits of the inclusion criteria. A danger is that the methods of searching may in themselves have hidden biases. For example, the inclusion criteria may not specify English language studies but these may make up the bulk of studies listed on many electronic databases.

6. *Data extraction*

Some method is necessary to pull out relevant data for synthesis such as the findings of the study. In addition, some form of process may be necessary to make judgements about quality or relevance in order to qualify the results of a study. In some reviews this is not necessary as such measures are included within the inclusion criteria, so only studies meeting such quality and relevance criteria are included at all.

7. *Synthesis*

The synthesis is the process by which the results are brought together in order to answer the question posed by the review. The method of synthesis will vary considerably between statistical meta-analysis, systematic narrative empirical and conceptual synthesis, but will always be dependent on the conceptual framework of the review. In some cases, there may not be any good-quality studies addressing the review question, so the review will have informed us of what is not known rather than what is known though this is still an important finding. It informs strategies for future research to inform policy and practice. In some areas of research, there may be many studies designed and executed by academics but few that address the issues relevant to specific users of research such as policy-makers or practitioners.

Broadening of questions and designs

An issue for statistical meta-analysis is how narrow should be the inclusion criteria for research design of primary research studies. For those undertaking such reviews, randomized controlled trials are often seen as the strongest design to establish efficacy, but some quasi-experimental designs or non-controlled studies might also contain useful evidence. This is partly an empirical question that continues to be a major issue of study and debate, but early statistical meta-analyses were criticized by Slavin for being strict about research design but not about the quality of the randomized controlled studies (Slavin 1984, 1995). Slavin argued that there might be more useful evidence available from a very well-undertaken quasi-experimental design than from a poorly executed random experimental design. The same thinking has been evident in review groups supported by the EPPI-Centre in London. The 13 review groups supported by the EPPI-Centre to date have undertaken reviews on efficacy questions but have been concerned to have broad inclusion criteria in terms of research design so as not to exclude studies that might contain useful information for the review question. This broad approach has led the EPPI-Centre to develop two aspects of the review process: mapping and weight of evidence.

Mapping

Mapping is a process that maps research activity. It involves coding each included study in a review on a number of mapping key words. Approximately ten of these sets of key words are generic to all educational reviews and describe basic aspects of research design and topic and study population focus. The rest are further key words developed specifically for an individual review and focus on areas of interest to that review; for example, contextual information, theoretical aspects or policy aspects of each study. These mapping key words allow the research studies that have been identified (by the inclusion criteria and search strategy) to be mapped out using the mapping key words. An example is shown in Figure 4.1 from the Personal Development Plan (PDP) review (Gough *et al.* 2003), illustrating that there have been many descriptive studies and few experimental studies in Britain while the opposite is true for the United States.

This mapping of research activity produces a useful product in its own right to describe what research has been undertaken in a field (as defined by the inclusion criteria) and so can inform policies for future research. For example, Figure 4.1 shows that there have been many descriptive studies of PDP in the United Kingdom providing a description of the nature of PDP and suggesting hypotheses of the process by which it may affect students' learning. However, there are few experimental studies to test any impact that is hypothesized. In the United States, by contrast, there are a number of experimental studies of impact but few studies describing the contexts and processes by which such impacts may have been achieved. Systematic maps can also be used in this way to describe

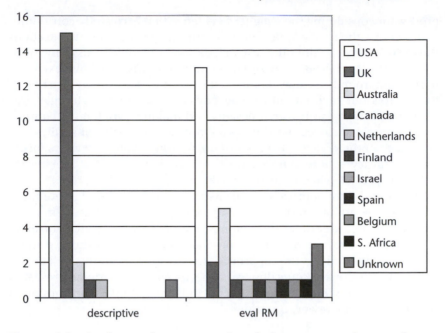

Figure 4.1 Study type by country of study from systematic map of research on personal development plans (Gough *et al.* 2003)

(N = 53 studies; mutually exclusive codings)

any other features of studies such as theoretical perspectives, samples, or contexts in which the studies were undertaken.

In addition to describing the research field as a product in its own right, a systematic map can also provide the basis for an informed decision about whether to undertake the in-depth review and synthesis on all of the studies or just a sub-set. The map can show whether the total population of studies are sufficiently homogeneous for a coherent synthesis, whether they will help answer the review question, as well as pragmatic consider-ations about the resources available to complete the review. If only a sub-set of studies is included in the in-depth review, then this requires a further set of inclusion criteria to be applied to define this sub-set of stud-ies. In the PDP review, for example, only the 25 studies using experimental designs with hard outcome data from the 157 studies in the map went through to synthesis, but further syntheses on different sub-questions can still be undertaken on different sub-groups of studies in the map.

Weight of evidence

The second development to take account of the use of broad review questions and thus heterogeneous studies in the review was to develop a process for considering the weight of evidence that each study contributes to answering the review question. In narrowly specified review questions the inclusion criteria limit the research designs and topic focus of included studies. As Slavin (1985, 1995) has pointed out, this may have excluded useful data from the review. Some inclusion criteria also apply strict quality controls but reviews with broad questions, allowing heterogeneous studies with different research designs and making only limited controls on quality, need to deal with the resultant heterogeneity of studies at a later stage of the review. These issues do not only apply to reviews focusing on efficacy of interventions but to all review questions looking for different types of evidence to address their review questions.

The EPPI-Centre approach to this issue is to clearly differentiate three aspects of the primary research studies that need to be addressed in order to consider the extent that the findings of an individual study contribute to answering a review question. These are the quality of the execution of the study design, the appropriateness of that study design for addressing the review question, and the focus of the primary research study. These can then inform the overall judgement of the contribution to the answering the review question:

A. *Quality of execution of study*   The quality of the study in terms of accepted standards for carrying out a research study of that design. This is not a judgement about the research design itself but how it is has been undertaken in practice, so a good-quality case study, pre/post outcome evaluation and a randomized control trial should all be scored the same.
B. *Appropriateness of that research design for answering the review question* In Slavin's view, a randomized controlled design was the strongest design for addressing efficacy issues, but if the best available evidence was from a quasi-experimental design then that should be used. Similarly, qualitative studies are often best for addressing process issues, but some relevant data may be identified from an experimental quantitative design. In this way, dimension A on quality of execution is distinguished from strength of design for addressing different questions.
C. *Appropriateness of study focus*   The authors of the primary studies may not have had the aims of the systematic review in mind when they undertook their study and it should not be assumed that the focus of the primary and secondary studies are the same. If a broad review question is used with wide inclusion criteria then heterogeneous studies may be included in the review, with the result that studies are likely to vary in the extent that the particular focus of the primary study fits the focus of the review question. The dimension C allows studies to be judged as relatively central or not to the review question. This may

be on the basis of topic focus, theoretical perspective, sample, context, or other features of the study. What is important is that the basis of the judgement is made explicit.

D. *Overall weight of evidence*   All three dimensions, A, B and C can then be combined to make an overall judgement D of the weight of evidence that the results of a study have in answering the review question.

The weight of evidence system is simply a process. The EPPI-Centre does not stipulate how each judgement A to C should be made but helps identify issues that might be considered for each judgement. The Centre also does not stipulate the relative emphasis that is put on each dimension A to C to make judgement D. Some review groups give equal emphasis to each, others emphasize topic focus C, while others emphasize research rigour A on the basis that if the quality of the study is poor then all other issues should not be considered. Over time a consensus may develop in the research and research user communities about how these judgements should be made; a flexible process that requires the basis of the judgements to be made explicit may enable this to occur. Empirical work is then required to assess how these judgements are being made in practice and the impact that these have on conclusions of reviews.

Challenges to systematic synthesis

Critiques of systematic synthesis

A number of the critiques of systematic research synthesis are due to different views about the nature of science, evidence and scientific development. Some of the critiques, however, may be due to simple misunderstandings. Five such issues are listed here (Gough and Elbourne 2002).

First is the view that methods of research synthesis involve a naïve conception about the development of research knowledge and its use (Hammersley 2001). This criticism creates a straw man by over-stating the case claimed for systematic synthesis. It is not proposed that such synthesis replaces all forms of scientific debate and progress, but that policy, practice and research decisions should be made with knowledge of what research has been undertaken and an understanding of their results. This approach may be considered naïve in believing that the rational role for research evidence in decision-making can be increased. It may also be naïve in believing that research effort can result in researchers becoming better informed of the work of others and thus making more efficient use of the collaborative effort. This is not an argument for all research to be the same or that synthesis should dictate all research agendas.

An additional area of potential naïvety is the argument proposed in this chapter that users of research can become more involved in agenda setting of systematic review questions and thus also in the evaluation of the relevance of research to addressing their needs. This should enable greater democratic participation in research and also increase general understanding of research to allow further participation. Involvement in systematic research synthesis is a powerful method for developing understanding about how different types of research help address different research questions and thus of understanding research methodology.

A second criticism is that research synthesis is positivistic in the types of research that it synthesizes and also in its own processes. This criticism depends upon seeing positivism as a negative attribute and upon the breadth of definition of the term. Systematic synthesis can include qualitative primary research and use qualitative methods in the review process. Of course, the use of quality criteria and views of bias may be different from synthesis of quantitative synthesis but many of the main principles are the same. The only research not open to this form of synthesis is research that is so relativist that the whole concept of synthesis is untenable.

A third charge is that the research synthesis agenda is promoted and controlled by government which has a technocratic managerial agenda that will control critical and creative research. It is quite possible that government does have such an agenda, but increasing the overt methodology of synthesis and moving away from traditional reviews and expert opinions with no explicit account of the source of conclusions should make it more difficult for any one interest group including government to hijack or misuse the research agenda for non rational purposes. Furthermore, there is the democratizing effect of a review process that involves users of research to help define the synthesis agenda.

A fourth and similar criticism is that research synthesis will control professional practice (Elliott 2001, and Chapter 12 in this volume). My belief is that the involvement of users of research such as teachers in the review process will ensure that questions relevant to those users will be addressed as has happened in nursing where professional staff have been enabled to become more active in their own learning and practice (Evans and Benefield 2001).

Fifthly, and maybe most damning, is the suggestion that systematic research synthesis is boring and can not compete with the excitement of interpretive synthesis (Schwandt 1998) or new primary research. This might help explain the situation identified by Professor Rayleigh in 1885 (Rayleigh 1885, p. 20, quoted by Chalmers *et al.* 2002). Maybe it is simply too much effort and not sufficiently rewarding systematically to review what research has already been done.

Other problems and dangers

A more fundamental problem for systematic research synthesis is the synthesis of syntheses. Each individual synthesis exists within a particular conceptual framework and because of the limits of that framework and the narrowness of individual in-depth reviews there is the danger of many little bits of non-connected knowledge. For such bits to be joined up and for systematic synthesis to deal with synthesis of different types of research evidence, different contexts of research, short- and long-term influences, and with complex research questions, a much greater emphasis on theory-building is required. This is not so much a criticism of systematic synthesis but acknowledgement of the danger that an emphasis on process may lead to a neglect of theory development. The lack of explicit process in secondary research can account for the recent energy directed at developing such systems, but the underlying problem of focus on method not theory is also a problem for primary research. Empty empiricism is not a danger solely for research synthesis.

A related issue is the inherently conservative nature of synthesis (Ridgeway *et al.* 2000). Professor Rayleigh urged us to look back as well as forwards in time (1885, p. 20, quoted by Chalmers *et al.* 2002) but this is not an argument for not continuing to look forward. New research should be partly driven by what has gone before, but theory building and creative new insights are also an essential part of this programme.

All primary and secondary research needs to be fit for purpose and we need to guard against bad research and misinformed gatekeepers of the research process. This is as true for research synthesis as any other form of research. Research synthesis is not the road to salvation or to all forms of knowledge development. It is but one important and previously under-utilized tool for making research more relevant and useful to the many users of research. As a relatively new method it is in its early stages of development and must not be seen as a fixed method for which all problems have been resolved.

A relatively new methodology research synthesis does face a number of challenges. There are conceptual challenges raised in this chapter and by other authors in this volume related to the synthesis of weights of evidence from quantitative and interpretative qualitative data as well as operationalizing research-user involvement in the research process.

There are also technical, structural and financial challenges arising from a lack of infrastructure to support this work, a lack of understanding of the resources required for these types of reviews, a lack of research capacity and wider understanding of the principles of systematic reviews and a lack of funding for pure methodological work rather than for the production of reviews.

Last, but not least, there are ideological and political challenges. There is the fear of central political control of research rather than the potential of the democratization of the research process. There is confusion between experimental methodologies and systematic research synthesis related to a polarization of 'quantitative' and 'qualitative' paradigms, which is a misunderstanding of the methodology and purpose of systematic reviews. There is scepticism about 'negative' results of reviews. Few of the infinite and ever-changing aspects of human life have been studied so it is not surprising that research synthesis cannot answer all these unknowns, but if decision-makers decide that the rational use of research knowledge is not worth the price then we will revert back to the non-rational use of research in the policy and practice decision-making process. Users of services and other members of society will have no alternatives to such political processes and agendas. Systematic research synthesis which gives users a direct role in framing the research agenda may lead to less control by politicians, practitioners and researchers and may have a greater impact on democratic accountability of research and other forms of decision-making.

Note: Thanks to Ann Oakley for her helpful comments on an earlier draft of this chapter.

Part 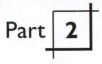 2

Evidence-based practice in practice

Section A: in education

5

Between Scylla and Charybdis: the experience of undertaking a systematic review in education

Richard Andrews

Introduction

As coordinator of the English Review Group for the EPPI project, much of my role is to navigate the review team's work (steered by the advisory group) between the Scylla of EPPI methodology, informed as it is by social science and medical models of systematic review, and the Charybdis of educational research (see Nicoll 2000). Our first topic for review, undertaken during the period February 2001 to January 2003, was the impact of information and communication technologies on 5–16-year-olds' literacy learning in English. The report of the first year's work, resulting in a mapping exercise of the entire topic and an in-depth review of the impact of *networked* ICT on literacy learning, is published by the Research Evidence in Education Library (www.eppi.ioe.ac.uk/reel) as Andrews *et al.* (2002). Various other articles and papers arising from the project have also been published, some relating to content and some to process (Andrews 2002a; Andrews 2002b; Andrews forthcoming; Elbourne *et al.* 2002; Oakley *et al.* 2002).

The English Review Group has an advisory function, and consists of members from primary and secondary schools, from a Local Education Authority advisory service and from the Open University, the Institute of Education and the universities of York and Durham. It also includes a parent governor from both a primary and secondary school and representatives from the EPPI-Centre. The function of this group is to steer the review team, to read and comment on its reports and to help disseminate its findings. To give two specific examples of how the advisory group has contributed: it was instrumental in the choice of the topic to review systematically in the first two years of operation; and it provided user summaries of the first report, written by and for policy-makers, parent governors, teachers and 5–16-year-olds. The latter, written by a 15-year-old and taken from the REEL site, will give a succinct picture of what the review group achieved in the first year:

Summary from a Year 10 pupil

Do Computers Help Us To Read and Write?

In 2001 and early 2002, a group of researchers has been investigating the impact of ICT on literacy learning.

What exactly are they trying to investigate?

This research study is aiming to investigate how ICT (Information and Communication Technologies – the use of computers) can help us learn ... especially in literacy (that is, in reading and writing in English). The study is focusing on how ICT can help students who are still in compulsory schooling (age 5–16).

The researchers are asking this question:

'What is the impact of networked ICT on literacy learning in English, 5–16?'

Or, in other words:

'How does using ICT (especially the internet and e-mail) in our English and language lessons affect us?'

Why do they need to investigate this?

Many pupils use computers to help them with their work, and knowing about how ICT can help us will be useful for all sorts of people.

- ☑ *Teachers* will be encouraged to involve more ICT in their teaching, which will make the lessons more fun and interesting. From this study, the teachers can also learn about other ways of using ICT in their English and language lessons, and can assess their current use of ICT.
- ☑ The *Government* (especially the people who decide on what we learn) will find it useful so that they can assess our current use of ICT, and so that they can encourage more people to use ICT to assist education.
- ☑ *Parents* need to know the facts about ICT so that they can help with home/school communication electronically, in terms of homework for ICT education.
- ☑ Most importantly, we as *students* will find out about more ways to make our work more interesting by using ICT in our English lessons.

How did they go about researching this topic?

In order to research the use of ICT in literacy learning and answer the research question, the researchers ...

- ☑ Wrote a plan to map out what they were going to do.
- ☑ Searched, using the internet, books, journals and reports, for studies that were relevant to the topic. There were nearly 200 of them.

☑ Looked more closely at those studies to find the ones that were specifically about *networked ICT in literacy learning* (16 were found).
☑ Made a list of the different topic areas within ICT and literacy (e.g. word-processing, the internet, using multimedia).
☑ Took out the data (or information) needed from the 16 studies identified.

Results

Many studies on various sub-topics were found, mostly from the USA but also some from the UK, Canada, Australia and New Zealand. Some were focused on primary/elementary schools, and some on secondary/high schools. Some referred to literacy as reading and writing in English, and some referred to it as a matter of social communication in learning (that is, communicating with other people while learning). Some focused on writing, and some on reading.

Overall, the results are inconclusive (that is, the research did not provide a definite answer to the question). Information was found about ICT in out-of-school activities; word-processing; ICT used in speaking and listening in education; and also ICT used to help special needs education.

The results suggest that using ICT helps to 'widen the concepts of literacy', extending literacy education to more than just reading and writing. They also suggest that using ICT helps to increase confidence in pupils, makes learning in English and language more enjoyable, and helps education to keep up with modern technology in the world. In conclusion, the use of networked ICT in literacy learning affects students aged 5–16 in many positive ways, but more and better research is needed to answer the research question fully.

Over the next year, the English Review Group is going to look at the effects of other aspects of ICT (like CD-ROM use and reading onscreen) on 5–16-year-olds.

The review team is a smaller group, consisting of six researchers from the advisory group who undertake the actual reviewing.

Challenges

What have been the difficulties, problems and challenges of the first phase of systematic reviewing in education? First, let's take the navigational problems. Scylla 'was sometimes described as originally human but turned into a monster by a rival in love' and 'is represented as having six heads, each with a triple row of teeth, and twelve feet'. It has been acknowledged by the EPPI-Centre that the original methodology was too closely allied to research in a scientific paradigm. Within trials-based research or 'outcome evaluations', for example, there is a hierarchy of evidence provided by randomized controlled trials, pre- and post-test designs, post-test designs, in descending order. Such a hierarchy does not, however, apply to all evidence gathered in education research and certainly not to evidence gathered within the humanist (largely qualitative outcome-based) research paradigm. It was thus an important navigational decision to steer a course that allowed for both paradigms to be in play and that allowed for evidence of different kinds to be taken into account. The early EPPI methodology tended to see trials-based research as providing tangible results and other research as providing an insight into the processes of research ('process evaluations'). The relegation of such studies to the 'process' category put them in a secondary position, shedding light on the tangible results of the primary studies but not contributing much to meta-analysis – the statistical synthesis of quantitative results – nor indeed to overall synthesis (quantitative and qualitative data) in the research review.

One could say the original methodology defeated its own object in that it led researchers to favour research reports with tangible outcomes, thus biasing the systematic review against a comprehensive view of the research literature on a particular topic. There was ample categorization and coding of outcome evaluations, and insufficient recognition of and apparatus for categorization and coding of other study types.

Such an approach might have been justified if the main research question driving the review had been asking about the *effect* of ICT on literacy learning instead of focusing on the *impact* of *x* on *y*. Consideration of these terms is critical to the continuation of the discussion. If a research study is aiming to gauge effect, it will most probably adopt a randomized control trial design. It is hard, with the scientific paradigm implied by the term 'effect', to consider how else it could be measured. The scientific paradigm also assumes that an 'intervention' will be made into a state of affairs to measure what effect that intervention has. From the start, the English Review Group wanted to broaden the field and not focus merely on the effect of ICT on literacy learning. 'Impact', on the other hand, is a far more slippery term. The government is currently interested in gauging the impact of its interventions after a period in the 1980s and 1990s in which evaluation has been short-term, fitful and often compliant. It tends to use 'impact' (cf. the BECTa-informed ImpaCT2 study) rather than 'effect'. The English Review Group also chose 'impact' as the engine of the boat navigating the Straits of Messina. The term 'impact' would allow us to embrace 'effect' but also take into account studies that attempted to evaluate less tangible aspects of the ICT/literacy interface: strategic realignment, terminological shifts, changes in pedagogical as well as learning orientations. These might be termed intermediate outcomes, though our aim is to gauge the impact of ICT on the individual learner. The terms are discussed in more detail in Andrews *et al.* (2002).

Using 'impact' as a key term raises further issues. It is not synonymous with 'effect', although some have wished to see it as synonymous. Part of the challenge has been to keep the eye fixed firmly on the research question and not to be diverted into channels that would suggest a too narrow approach to the problem, or into the wider seas of trying to gauge 'influence'. Adopting 'impact' has forced us to consider how best to synthesize quantitative and qualitative data (a narrative synthesis is the best we have managed to date, though Bayesian theory is a possibility for future exploration); it has also allowed us to access a wider range of study types and to embrace most of education research within the purview of the research question.

Interestingly, one of the books revealed through electronic searching for relevant research reports has been Haas's *Writing Technology: Studies on the Materiality of Literacy* (Haas 1996). Haas suggests that rather than the relationship between ICT and literacy being one of the effect or impact of one on the other, the relationship can be better characterized as *symbiotic*. Such a perspective has implications for research designs, as most of the studies we have unearthed to date assume a one-way causal connection (ICT influences or has an impact on or affects literacy). The implications include choosing an appropriate research paradigm for further investigation of the relationship; working out methods for investigating symbiotic relationships; and understanding how causal one-way relationships can contribute to a symbiotic picture. To put the problem another way: schools are buying hardware, software and linking in various ways to the internet. They are not waiting for the results of evaluations or research to do this. The leap into a technologically supported classroom is a mixture of faith, economic realities and *force majeure* rather than a considered curriculum development programme. Literacy is changing as a result; it is not so much a question of how new technologies impact on pre-ICT notions of monolithic print literacy, but how new social and technological literacies develop in relation to advances in ICT.

One last point about navigation through the straits: we were faced, in pursuit of answer to our research question, with a Charybdis of existing research on ICT and literacy education in the education research literature. (I don't want to press the analogy too much – the whirlpool Charybdis sucked in seawater and spewed it out three times a day.) Our initial electronic and hand searches of journals, chapters, books and theses that might be relevant suggested 1871 titles published between 1990 and the autumn of 2001. Of these, 178 were judged to be relevant to the mapping study; and when we came to the in-depth review of the impact of *networked* ICT on 5–16-year-olds' literacy education, 16 of these were distilled from the seawater. The exclusion and inclusion criteria were strictly applied, the results at each stage moderated, and a high incidence of agreement noted throughout the distilling process. But what of the 16 studies?

Few of the 16 studies in the in-depth review provide a firm basis for accepting their findings and therefore can have little bearing on the answering of the main research question for the in-depth review. Of the remainder, two provide theoretical and practical insights into widening conceptions of literacy; five suggest increased motivation and/or confidence in pupils as a result of ICT use with regard to literacy development; and one sees empowerment and ownership as an important factor to bear in mind in an increasingly diverse digital world. The RCTs in the distillation of 16 studies were, on the whole, poorly conducted. The 'process evaluations' were suggestive of relationships rather than authoritative in their outcomes, leading to 'findings' rather than 'results'.

Our interim conclusions are not that there is a problem with education research in general, but that in the particular area of the sea we were exploring, there was not much research that we could depend on to give us valid or reliable grounds on which to answer our question substantially. This does not mean to say that in the wider review – the impact of ICT on literacy education – we will not find satisfactory answers. At the time of writing (October 2002) they do not exist as far as we know, but by September 2003 we will have completed an updated review of a number of further sub-questions, and will be better placed to provide an answer. The sub-questions we are exploring include the following aspects of ICT's impact on literacy education: English as a Additional Language, literature, pedagogies of English teachers, randomized controlled trials on the effect of ICT on literacy learning, dyslexia and moving image. Combined with our existing in-depth review on networked ICT (e-mail, the internet), and with the ImpaCT2 report on the impact of ICT on the core subjects at Key Stages 2 and 3 in the English National Curriculum, we should be in a better position to say something substantial as well as methodological.

To summarize thus far: the challenges have not been in identifying and screening the plethora of studies in the area of ICT and literacy. There are plenty of fish out there, though it has to be said that some abstracts (the principal means of identifying such studies) are better than others. Nor have they been consistent in finding agreement between reviewers, nor in gaining consensus on the advisory body about the direction of our research. Rather, the challenges have been in adapting key wording approaches to make them both usable and sensitive to the field; in 'extracting the data'; and in attempting to synthesize the results.

How the challenges are being overcome

It has been accepted all along by the EPPI-Centre and by the first wave of review groups that the first reviews are pilot-like in nature. Much has been learnt about the processes of systematic reviewing. The two 'sides' of the polemical argument are moving closer to each other (and here I leave my Scylla and Charybdis analogy for the time being, moving into calmer waters).

First, the key wording document has been revised generically at the EPPI-Centre to take account of the study types in the education research. Whereas in the first version, there was an implied hierarchy with outcome evaluations seemingly given precedence over process evaluations; and within the category of outcome evaluations, RCTs given pride of place as the gold standard in providing a hierarchy of evidence . . . in the second version here is a very different set of categories within which to identify study type. In the new version (EPPI-Centre Core Keywording Strategy version 0.9.5), the categories are:

Description
Exploration of relationships
Evaluation: naturally occurring or researcher-manipulated
Development of methodology
Review: systematic or other.

This is a significant shift, because it suggests that 'evidence' may not necessarily be the result of scientific data-gathering within a causal paradigm. It could be the result of a qualitative case study which suggests and/ or critiques relationships between variables.

At a specific review level, the English review group has reduced its key words from a brainstormed eclectic set to a refined set that is more workable and useful (see Figures 5.1 and 5.2). Key terms are glossed to improve clarity and reviewer agreement.

Similarly, the data extraction tool has been radically revised and simplified to give due weight to qualitative data. Readers are referred to the latest version of the data extraction tool (see www.eppi.ioe.ac.uk) and to Oakley (2000), Mays and Pope (2000), Nastasi and Schensul (2001) and Harden (2002) for recent discussions about the assessment and use of qualitative data in systematic reviewing of research.

In terms of synthesis, it was understood in the first in-depth review that synthesis would be of a narrative nature rather than statistical (a meta-analysis was not possible, given the unreliable nature of the data sets). Consequently, a narrative summary of the findings was written and checked by all members of the review team, the advisory group and the EPPI-Centre to make sure that it fairly reflected the individual studies on which it was based. It was not possible to integrate quantitative and qualitative data, though during the process a proposal was written to explore the value that Bayesian analysis might have on the relationship between the two data sets and approaches. Bernardo and Smith (1994) and Roberts (2002) suggest that the Bayesian approach, which accords 'an explicit place to the role of prior knowledge or prior information, belief and subjectivity within a quantitative approach to decision-making' (2002: 5) in research might be one way of reconciling the differences. It

11. *Focus of the report (tick all that apply)*

literacy	learning	ICT
genre	assessment	CAI/CAL
literacies	dyslexia hypertext	
literature	learning difficulties	moving image
multimodality	learning disabilities	multimedia
reading	motivation	word-processing
spelling	teaching	
writing	ESL/EAL	
	audience	
	comprehension	

12. *Type(s) of intervention or non-intervention (tick all that apply)*

computer – stand alone (software)
computer – networked (e-mail)
computer – networked (internet)
mobile phone
other technology _____ (please specify)

13. *What principal aspect(s) of literacy is the study focused on increasing? (tick all that apply)*

13a. psychological aspects or representations
social representations and/or cultural/critical representations

13b. writing, print and graphical or pictorial representation
reading print and graphical or pictorial representations

14. *Which outcomes are reported? (tick all that apply)*

test results - reading
       - writing
       - spelling
examination results
motivation/engagement
self-esteem/attitude
quality of writing
increased awareness of process
quality of reading
quality of response to multimedia

15. *If study type in question 10 is C.b. (researcher-manipulated) is it*

A. RCT
B. Trial
C. Other

The generic EPPI key wording document is numbered 1 to 10 (see Figure 5.2)

Figure 5.1 EPPI English Review Group: ICT and Literacy key wording document

EPPI-CENTRE EDUCATIONAL KEYWORDING SHEET V0.9.5 *Bibliographic details and/or unique identifier*.................

NB: Please refer to the EPPI-Centre Core Keywording Strategy Version 0.9.5 for guidance on how to apply keywording

1: Identification of report
Citation
Contact
Handsearch
Unknown
Electronic database
(please specify) ....

2. Status
Published
In press
Unpublished

3. Linked reports
Is this report linked to one or more other reports in such a way that they also report the same study?

Not Linked
Linked *(please provide bibliographical details and/or unique identifier)*
....
....
....

4. Language *(please specify)*
....
....

5. In which country/countries was the study carried out? *(please specify)*
....
....

6. What is/are the topic focus/foci of the study?
Assessment
Classroom management
Curriculum*
Equal opportunities
Methodology
Organisation and management
Policy
Teacher careers
Teaching and learning
Other *(please specify)* ....

*6a Curriculum
Art
Business Studies
Citizenship
Cross-curricular
Design & Technology
Environment
General
Geography
Hidden
History
ICT
Literacy – first language
Literacy further languages
Literature
Maths
Music
PSE
Phys. Ed.
Religious Ed.
Science
Vocational
Other *(please specify)*

7. Programme name *(please specify)*
....
....
....

8. What is/are the population focus/foci of the study?
Learners*
Senior management
Teaching staff
Non-teaching staff
Other education practitioners
Government
Local education authority officers
Parents
Governors
Other *(please specify)* ....

*8a Age of learners (years)
0-4
5-10
11-16
17-20
21 and over

*8b. Sex of learners
Female only
Male only
Mixed sex

9. What is/are the educational setting(s) of the study?
Community centre
Correctional institution
Government department
Higher education institution
Home
Independent school
Local education authority
Nursery school
Post-compulsory education institution
Primary school
Pupil referral unit
Residential school
Secondary school
Special needs school
Workplace
Other educational setting *(please specify)*.................

10. Which type(s) of study does this report describe?
A. Description
B. Exploration of relationships
C. Evaluation
    a. Naturally occurring
    b. Researcher-manipulated
D. Development of methodology
E. Review
    a. Systematic review
    b. Other review

Please state here if keywords have not been applied from any particular category (1-10) and the reason why (e.g. no information provided in the text)
....
....
....
....

PTO to apply review-specific keywords (if applicable)

Keyworded by.................   Date.................

Figure 5.2   EPPI-Centre educational key wording sheet

has to be acknowledged, however, that Bayesian theory still works within an overall scientific paradigm of hypothesis generation and testing.

It has been an important principle throughout the various stages of distillation that more than one voice has been present at each stage (protocol writing/screening/keywording/mapping/data extraction/analysis/synthesis) to minimize any possible bias. At three points in the process (protocol/mapping/synthesis) the whole advisory group has been consulted, and changes made accordingly. At two points in the process (protocol/first draft of report) the work has been sent out for independent peer review. Further blind refereeing has taken place when an article based on the research has been submitted to a national or international journal. It is probably fair to say that the process is one of the most tightly reviewed, systematic, transparent and replicable that you are likely to find in the academy.

Problems that remain

Results of our first in-depth review were disappointing in terms of substance, but intellectually challenging in terms of methodology. We expect that the results of the two-year study will be more satisfying, substantially because of an improved methodology, an updating of the database, a more comprehensive review and deeper understanding of the conceptual problems and issues in the field.

The most pressing problems are now conceptual rather than technical. They are as follows:

- The term 'impact', so current in educational evaluation and research, is unsatisfactory unless it is further defined; further work needs to be done before this term can be used with confidence.
- At the interface of ICT and literacy, Haas's insight (discussed in the first section above) that the relationship is symbiotic rather than one-way and causal will require new kinds of research to answer key questions about the interface/relationship. Far from being secondary, more qualitative case studies which investigate the complexity of the relationship in particular contexts will be required before any clear paradigm emerges for further investigation. These case studies and other small-scale studies will need, however, to be informed by theoretical frameworks within and against which new empirical data can be analysed.
- We need to get away form the positive and positivist assumption that the intervention of ICT is a 'good thing' irrespective of the evidence or of the kind of relationship suggested in the previous point. Too many studies within the positivist paradigm show 'a small benefit to literacy

because of the use of ICT' – an entirely predictable outcome, given the way the experiments have been set up to date.

- We also need larger and longitudinal studies of the use of computers and other forms of ICT in the development of literacy.
- In the literacy camp, there is still limited understanding of the changing nature of literacy itself, and still a preponderance of narrow conceptions of literacy as being a universal ability to read and write. The socially constructed nature of literacy, resulting in different literacies – either from the perspective of social groups and communication practices on the one hand, or from the use and combination of different media on the other – is well established theoretically and in a number of studies, but not well understood in the majority of research we have looked at so far.

The way forward

Navigating between Scylla and Charybdis has been difficult, but the holding to a course between opposites or the maintenance of a balanced position in the turbulent straits of dialectic has been salutary. It seems to me that the most interesting waters are those beyond the straits: interesting conceptually, in that there are gaps in our knowledge about the impact of ICT on literacy learning (and no doubt, other kinds and areas of learning) and there are difficult problems to solve in terms of the relationship between ICT and literacy. But interesting, too, methodologically, in that existing methods and methodologies seem to fall short of answering the initial questions that have been asked by the review group.

It may not be wise to return through the straits to the more well-known seas and rocks of the scientific research paradigm, nor to the whirlpools of conventional humanistic education research, as characterized in the early part of this chapter. To that extent, it may be that questions of 'impact' or more narrowly 'effect' are redundant, difficult to answer and unsatisfactory. It may also be the case that the most telling studies at this particular stage of pre-paradigm research are those that are modest, contextualized and suggestive of relationships between emerging factors.

The way forward seems to give systematic review methodology a chance to see if it can answer existing questions about learning, or pose new ones. To change the metaphor, if it does little more than clear the ground for the next generation of researchers, it will have performed a useful task. But the probability is that it will do more than that. It is likely that it will provide much firmer foundations for primary empirical research, contribute to the accumulation of reliable evidence, challenge existing theories and methodologies in education research, and provide a tool for sharpening conceptual categories in particular fields.

Acknowledgements

The work in producing the first reviews in English has been undertaken jointly with Sue Beverton (Durham), Andrew Burn (Institute of Education), Jenny Leach (OU), Terry Locke (Waikato), Graham Low and Carole Torgerson with assistance from Alison Robinson (all York). The review team has been supported and guided by James Durran (Parkside Community College, Cambridge), Katy Evans, Diana Elbourne (both EPPI-Centre), Peter Hatcher, Nick McGuinn (both York), Rebecca Rees (EPPI-Centre), Gloria Reid (City of Kingston-upon-Hull Education Services), Nancy Rowland (NHS Centre for Reviews and Dissemination), Maggie Snowling (York); and at distance by Wendy Morgan (Queensland University of Technology) and Eileen Shakespeare (Harvard). I am grateful for permission to quote the 15-year-old's summary of the first year of research. The views expressed in and shortcomings of this chapter, however, are my own.

6

Teachers using evidence: using what we know about teaching and learning to reconceptualize evidence-based practice
Philippa Cordingley

Evidence-based practice is not some sort of universal process that can be transferred from profession to profession: it has to be understood in terms of the specific demands that it makes upon practitioners' own learning processes. These have as yet not featured largely in debate about evidence-based practice.

Except in exceptional circumstances, learning builds upon and has to be related to previous knowledge, understanding and beliefs. For individuals who are adult professional learners the process is complex – and as differentiated as the adults involved. But evidence-based practice is often promoted as a single, undifferentiated process. So I shall start by exploring a little of the history of national efforts to promote evidence-based practice – in order to illustrate the foundations on which we can build.

The historical context

The Teacher Training Agency (TTA) for England started to promote teaching as a research and evidence-informed profession from its inception. By 1996 it had already started to tackle three specific aspects of this work:

- it launched a pilot programme to provide research grants of £3000 to teachers for carrying out small-scale studies and preparing materials from those studies designed to attract teachers' attention to the usefulness of research findings and processes;
- it had started to experiment with commissioning large-scale research whose focus from the outset was utility to teachers. Three projects were later published as the Effective Teachers of Numeracy (Askew *et al.*, 1997), Effective Teachers of Literacy (Medwell *et al.*, 1998) and Ways Forward with ICT (Higgins and Moseley 1999));

- finally, it had published a leaflet setting out:
  - its views about the need to support the development of a teacher voice within the research discourse and stating its intention to develop a National Teacher Research Panel to this end;
  - the need for much more research about pedagogy;
  - problems relating to the accessibility of academic research findings and the relative lack of educational research focused upon teaching and learning.

(TTA 1996)

In subsequent years, the TTA refined and enhanced its research grant scheme, increasing the emphasis upon the importance of collaborative work and partnership with mentors. It launched the School Based Research Consortia initiative (four, three-year partnerships between schools, LEAs and HEIs aimed at exploring the ways in which teacher engagement in and with research could improve teaching and enhance learning). It also supported a range of regional conferences, in partnership with HEIs and LEAs, to raise teachers' expectations about what research can do for practice, and commissioned a range of studies about teachers' views of and priorities for research. Finally, in order to increase teachers' sense that research and evidence is a natural part of professional practice it took steps to celebrate the work of those who chose to publish their work and expose it to a challenging question and answer process. It did this by publishing over 100 summaries of teacher case studies and initiating and supporting a national research conference for teachers.

This steady stream of activity found an increasingly receptive audience. In 1999 the DfES launched a much larger-scale programme of awarding grants for teachers – the Best Practice Research Scholarship scheme (BPRS). The government made research and evidence-based practice a priority, and the DfES supported the development of the National Teacher Research Panel. At the time of writing, the Panel itself has been in existence for over three years, and has presented papers to British Education Research Association (BERA) explaining teachers' perceptions on research outputs, drawing messages from its experience of reviewing large-scale research proposals and developing some of the questions that schools need to explore in considering hosting large-scale research.

In addition, the General Teacher Council for England (GTCe) has made teachers' use of research processes and findings a core priority. The National Union of Teachers (NUT) has developed a research and evidence-based continuing professional development strategy involving scholarships for teachers and peer coaching programmes developed in partnership with academic researchers. The NUT has also sponsored a Research Review Group (registered by the Evidence Policy Practice Centre) focused on the impact of Continued Professional Development (CPD).

The challenge: embedding evidence-informed practice in the profession as a whole

So far, so good. Even a conservative estimate suggests that these activities have directly involved well over 10,000 teachers. But this touches only a small proportion of the profession as a whole. This chapter explores what else might be needed if evidence-based practice or 'research and evidence-informed practice', which is the National Teacher Research Panel's preferred rubric, is to become truly embedded in professional practice. The emphasis is upon the practice of teaching both for individuals and the profession as a whole and the role that research and evidence can play in this.

Evidence-based or evidence-informed – a practitioner perspective

For teachers, the distinction between *evidence-based* and *evidence-informed* is not trivial. Decisions about how to respond to the hugely varying needs that emerge second by second in dynamic classrooms have to be made quickly. They are grounded in what is feasible. They are framed by the teachers' tacit knowledge and skills. Explicit knowledge derived from reflective scrutiny of evidence from research or from teachers' own pupils, must be insinuated into existing frameworks – rather as a car must insinuate itself into the flow of fast-moving traffic on a motorway. Teaching always involves sophisticated professional judgements about what evidence means for this group of learners, with these learning objectives at this particular point in time. This is just as true of the many hundreds of teachers now attempting to work with the findings about formative assessment from the large-scale and systematic review of evidence reported in *Inside the Black Box* (Black and Wiliam 1998), as it is for teachers seeking to explore the implications of a colleague's case study of pupils' approaches to, say, questioning skills, or to understand the significance of detailed and comparative performance data of specific sub-groups of their pupils.

Trying out new strategies based on evidence from elsewhere always involves the risk that those strategies may not work in this or that particular context. So teachers need to believe strongly in the relative gains before taking a risk with untried methods.

One thing that influences and encourages teachers to change their practice to take account of new knowledge, is credible evidence that new approaches will enhance their pupils' learning, an issue to which I will return later in this chapter. Another is belief in the importance of modelling in learning of any kind. Perhaps these don't really follow on – does belief in modelling encourage teachers to change their practice? Many teachers understand the positive impact of modelling and making learning explicit. Effective literacy teachers, for example, model their own writing for their students and demonstrate how editing and revision of writing is a powerful tool for everyone (Medwell, Poulson and Wray 1998). Research or evidence-informed practice has the potential to support teaching and learning precisely because it involves teachers in becoming learners again, and so developing their understanding of how their students feel, and in modelling learning for their students. Hence evidence-informed practice does not merely mean bringing new information about what works to bear on professional practice, it becomes part of an ongoing learning process on the part of the practitioner. This does not mean, however, that research and/or evidence-informed practice is an end in itself. Its worth to practitioners still depends upon its capacity to enhance teaching and learning.

The challenges of evidence-informed practice

The challenges involved in enabling evidence-informed practice are formidable. In the conference debate that led to the commissioning of this volume (BERA 2001), the analysis of the task focused mainly upon the quality of the evidence chosen to inform practice. Desforges (2000b) reminds us repeatedly of the length of time it took the medical world to embrace the relatively simple (and dramatic in its outcome) change of washing their hands thoroughly between patients, in order to reduce cross infection. Making changes to the complex, internalized skills, beliefs and knowledge of classroom teachers is recognized as difficult and time-consuming in those few studies that have explored the multiple variables and their influence in classrooms over time. For example, Joyce and Showers (1988) found that it was only when:

- theory and strategies were demonstrated at work in a relevant context;
- there were opportunities to experiment with and practise new strategies;
- practice efforts were observed and the observer offered feedback based on evidence;

that it was possible to find evidence of teachers using new strategies introduced through in-service education in regular use in classrooms.

The problems involved in factoring evidence into this dynamic, especially research evidence (which often takes a highly abstract form) are self-evident. They have been explored in some detail in the review of research about teacher acquisition and use of knowledge completed for the TTA (Cordingley and Bell 2001). This, and an earlier review, lay behind the TTA's programme of promoting teaching as a research and evidence-informed profession, taking as a starting point the challenges faced by classroom teachers. The report of the study of the Impact of Educational Research, a review by the Australian Higher Education Division of the Department of Education Training and Youth Affairs, approached the issues on a broader canvas. It contains three separate studies of the impact of education research. One of these attempted to explore the problem by 'Backtracking Practice and Policies to Research' (Figgis *et al.* 2000) through exploring four separate case studies of areas where research seemed to have had an impact on practice. This study summarizes the picture in 2000 thus:

> . . . it is now recognised that complex networks bridge the divide between researcher/practitioner and policy-maker and that neither policy-making nor school practice is so straightforward and logical an enterprise, that research findings can simply be slipped into the mix and automatically find themselves absorbed into the ongoing activity.
>
> (Figgis *et al.* 2000: 366)

The study goes on to pose what it describes as a user-centric model of the connections between research knowledge and practice derived from the four case studies explored in the study (see Figure 6.1).

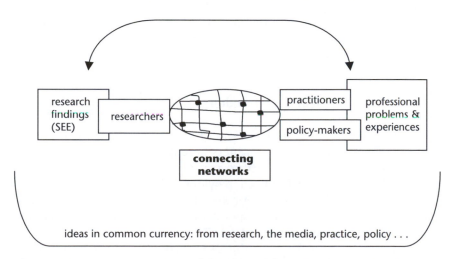

Figure 6.1 A user-centric model (adapted from Figgis *et al.* 2000)

This model emphasizes the importance of considering research and evidence-informed practice through the lens of the professional problems experienced by practitioners and policy-makers. Most of all, the study emphasizes that the connecting processes must be conceived as a network of activities and people and that practitioner and policy-maker networks are more rational and purposeful than might be supposed. It suggests too that such networks often do not involve researchers directly but introduce them in specific partnerships for specific purposes. There are quite a number of initiatives in the UK that expressly attempt to create and occupy a networked space between research and practice or policy-making. These include initiatives such as:

- the *Improving the Quality of Education for All* (IQEA) school improvement networks supported by the University of Nottingham;
- the TTA/CfBT funded School Based Research Consortia in 2002;
- the ESRC Teaching and Learning Research Programme networks and projects;
- some of the more co-ordinated bids for BPRS funding;
- the National College for School Leadership Networked Learning Communities programme in which groups of between six and twenty schools work together to create practical (and also, perhaps empirical and theoretical) knowledge and gains in pupil and adult learning. (Forty such networks were launched in September 2002. Forty more will start in January 2003 and a further forty still will start in September 2003.)

The rest of this chapter explores how this networked activity mirrors the teaching and learning processes in classrooms. Using the experiences of the networks, it focuses on the central proposition that evidence-informed practice can and should be understood and operationalized as a teaching and learning issue.

Triggering use of research and evidence

Effective teaching viewed from a learner perspective starts by considering how to motivate learners. The learners here are teachers, and given the pressures upon teachers we need to pay close attention to what might motivate them to become involved in evidence-based practice.

Why might practitioners look for and use evidence? In responding to a questionnaire a number of respondents – members of the National Teacher Research Panel, participants at TTA-funded research networking conferences and the teachers in the TTA's School Based Research Consortia – all reported a shared starting point. These teachers were willing to engage with evidence if they thought it would help them enhance pupils' learning. They cared passionately that learning was shown to be enhanced and they were curious about potential links between what they do and its effect upon learners. The Australian study underlines this point by emphasizing that characteristic of effective users of research in their study was a sense of hope that engaging with evidence would help them to make a difference. Certainly the school-based research consortia experience showed how teachers were spurred on to try out and test new strategies and to make use of others' research by evidence about improvements in learning. It also acted as a trigger for engaging with evidence and for drawing in more sceptical colleagues. Ensuring that evidence can be readily related to the professional problems pressing upon practitioners and policy-makers would, according to the TTA literature review and the Australian study, also be important triggers.

Supporting use of research and evidence

Now that practitioners have been encouraged to look to evidence as a means of improving practice and enhancing learning, what do we know about practice that affects how such engagement needs to take place? We know a good deal about student learning. The social construction of knowledge, particularly for school students was an important strand of research in the twentieth century. The importance of social exchange in learning, with roots in the work of authors such as Vygotsky and Dewey, is becoming increasingly understood and explored by teachers. For example, teachers involved in the School Based Research Consortia used systematic and sustained observation of practice to support their efforts to enhance thinking skills or speaking and listening. These activities, which have all been described in the reports of the Consortia for the TTA, brought significant benefits, not least from the dialogue that has occurred among teachers. The teachers also reflected on the importance of pupil-to-pupil exchanges in the process of improving teaching and enhancing learning. I want to argue that research and/or evidence-informed practice is, at its heart, a learning process for practitioners which is underpinned by the same pedagogical principles that operate in classroom practice. If practitioners are to use evidence, they need to work *together* to interpret it and to reflect upon its significance for their own particular context.

It has to be remembered that practitioner use of research or evidence is highly context-specific. The number of variables at work in every lesson and every school have significant implications for evidence-informed practice. Such practice means making decisions and taking action to take learning forward – effectively a process of sustained problem solving. Problems in education are context specific, because they depend upon chance and dynamic combinations of learner starting points, teacher skills and understanding, school and socially driven constraints and learning objectives. So there will always be a skilled professional job to do in interpreting the relevance of and implications of evidence for a practitioner's own setting, and students' end needs.

Supporting such interpretation of the implications of research for a specific lesson, practitioner or school calls for all of the stages and activities identified by Joyce and Showers (1998 – see above) as necessary for the transfer of an idea or approach into a teacher's embedded repertoire of skills and strategies. In particular, as the National Teacher Research Panel suggests in its comparative analysis of research outputs for BERA (2000), it requires vivid exemplification of qualitative and quantitative research findings in classroom contexts. This helps teachers to review their customary approach to a given situation and to compare this with other approaches and contexts. It also helps them to experiment with different ways of testing evidence in a classroom context.

The importance of experimenting with different ways of acting upon evidence is emphasized by Hargreaves (1999), who described the process as 'tinkering': a matter of moving forward incrementally on sustained and incremental steps. Such tinkering depends upon access to direct evidence about specific experiences that enables teachers to see the impact of potential changes in the round. Mechanisms for providing such evidence include coaching, enquiry, peer observation or video capture and review (see Cibulka *et al.* 2000). They also include collecting evidence of pupils' learning and outcomes, through observation, questioning or assessment. Evidence-informed practice therefore involves practitioners in wrestling with evidence from their own classrooms as well as from larger-scale research.

Does using research and evidence therefore mean doing research?

Perhaps it is the complexity of the processes required to put research or evidence to work in classrooms – and their close relationship with the cycles of research – that lead so many to argue, as did Stenhouse (1979b), that in order to use research teachers have to undertake research; to suggest that in order to be an evidence-based practitioner teachers must also become researchers. This seems to me to be an unhelpful and misleading proposition and one which will seem to teachers to show that evidence-informed practice is mostly about 'working harder not smarter'.

The systematic use of evidence needs to be recognized for what it is: a highly complex, sustained professional skill and one that involves a series of activities closely related to research. One of its most common manifestations will be practitioner enquiry. But this is not the only form of effective use. Some teachers in the School Based Research Consortia were keen to try out classroom strategies brought to their attention from research. So are hundreds of teachers involved in using Cognitive

Acceleration through Science Education (CASE), or Cognitive Acceleration through Maths Education (CAME). They engage with theory
and change their practice through a period of sustained collaborative
curriculum development or coaching. But only a fraction of the teachers
involved see this as research. Their entry-point is improving teaching
and enhancing learning and that is where their priority stays. They see
themselves engaging with research but not in it.

Nor is it sensible to look at all practitioner enquiry as research. Much
of this important work is undertaken as professional development by
individuals purely to meet their own learning goals. Some such practitioners will engage solely with evidence from their own classrooms and
students. Many will see the process of developing their own practice as
their goal. Such teachers rarely choose to publish their work and their
engagement constitutes reflection and challenge – but not research.

Some teachers, including some TTA research grant holders or consortium participants, engage systematically with evidence from others'
research and from their own classrooms and go on to publish their aims,
methods and interpretation of the literature, alongside their analysis and
findings, in order to enable colleagues to test and interpret their work.
Such practitioners are engaging in both evidence-informed practice *and* in
research. Teachers who have undertaken one rigorous research project
will not necessarily want to continue it forever – although experience to
date shows that they often remain passionate about retaining a problem-
atizing approach to their practice. This means that if we can improve the
accessibility and relevance of the research resources they can draw on,
teachers who have been involved in doing research will remain engaged
in evidence-informed practice on a continuing basis. They would enter
a virtuous circle where the benefits of engaging with evidence from a
range of sources becomes self-sustaining. There is now plenty of evidence
from collaborative projects such as IQEA and the School Based Research
Consortia that such teachers have genuinely moved towards evidence-
informed practice – which is of use both for themselves and for their
colleagues. User-friendly summaries of their work and the full research
reports are accessible and meaningful to other teachers, in a way that
academic reports are not. Web-based work where teacher case studies are
used to illustrate larger-scale studies (as can be seen in the GTC *Research
of the Month* website), seems also to offer a powerful combination of the
two approaches.

Given the fine distinction between engaging *in* and engaging *with*
research, comparisons between practitioner enquiry and academic
research need careful handling. We need to identify, support and value
the elegance, creativity, discipline and thoroughness of teacher research
that is developed for the purpose of adding to the current stock of public,
published knowledge. We need also to foster the professional skills

needed to engage with the research of others through personally oriented enquiry. This will, of course, involve critique of practitioner research – on a case-by-case basis. Practitioners will accept and welcome this – if it is appropriately calibrated. Having criteria which are capable of being applied to the assessment of both kinds of work is a cornerstone of the National Teacher Research Panel's efforts to ensure that practitioner research is not consigned to a ghetto.

Support

However they are interpreted, all forms of teacher enquiry, research or evidence-informed practice require significant support. The creation of the evidence capable of informing practice, hard as it is, is only a small part of the picture. There are many tasks being tackled incrementally and there is much more to be done.

The development of research reviews is underway. These work systematically, transparently and comprehensively through specific questions and weigh the evidence from different studies, and David Gough's chapter in this book makes it clear how this is being done. This is a slow and labour-intensive process, the benefits of which will begin to be realized as the methodology and support becomes better understood and streamlined and the review groups build a critical mass of reviews.

The Centre for the Use of Research and Evidence in Education (CUREE) is also developing techniques for creating web-based, user-oriented, non-linear summaries of research articles. Through the GTC Research of the Month website, large-scale evidence is being linked by CUREE with small-scale practitioner enquiry. Through the DfES Research Informed Practice website, larger numbers of recent research journal articles are being made accessible to practitioners.

There is need, nonetheless, for much more funding and thought to be given to making original research usable by teachers. Not many academics seem to realize how few of the extensive electronic resources, to which they have access through HEIs, are available to teachers. For example, the lay version of ERIC is built of shorter and much wider abstracts than those which academics use (see Cordingley *et al.* 2002).

Once funds and plans are in place there is also a need to sustain support for practitioner enquiry, and the nature and quality of this support is crucial. A study by Galton for TTA (Galton 2002) makes plain the unevenness of support and haphazard nature of the incentives and quality assurance mechanisms in this area.

Above all, there is a need to recognize that teachers themselves must be in the driving seat in identifying what they need if evidence-informed practice is to become genuinely part of 'working smarter' – rather than just harder. Desforges, long a champion of looking at research use through practitioners' eyes offers this baleful warning: 'The development of evidence-informed practice . . . is more likely to be achieved through manipulation of the inspection regime and key statutory measures than through the process of persuasion, or professional development based on professional responsibilities' (Desforges 2003: 10). I do not accept this assertion. I feel that evidence-informed practice could be developed and actualized through better listening to teachers, ensuring that they have a strong voice in figuring out the processes needed to make it work. Building on teachers' own successes and contributions is likely to be more powerful than compulsion.

Part 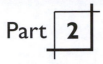 2

Evidence-based practice in practice

Section B: in medicine and allied fields

7

Practice-based evidence
Michael Eraut

This chapter focuses on the nature of the evidence used by practitioners in medicine and other professions and the decision-making processes in which it is used. Professional practice both generates and uses evidence. Sometimes these processes are linked by agency; the generator and user may be the same person, immediate colleagues or members of the same organization. Sometimes they are mutually interactive, with early evidence influencing the search for later evidence. Sometimes they are separated by time, space and lack of interaction between those who generate evidence and those who use it. Such separation may be bridged by the use of mediated, usually published, materials; but the distinction between the context of evidence generation and the context of evidence use remains important. The process of evidence generation is situated within the context, practices and thinking patterns of its creators; while the process of evidence use is situated within the context, practices and thinking patterns of its users. Even when the agent is the same, their pattern of thinking may differ according to their role at the time.

From a scientific viewpoint the key factors are the quality of the evidence and the population for whom it is deemed to be relevant. This ranges from a single client, or groups of clients deemed to be very similar on a range of variables, to large populations from which representative samples have been investigated. The scale of user application can also vary from a single client or small group of clients being 'treated' by a single or small group of practitioners to a local or national population for whom policy decisions are being made. While evidence from large populations may yield better outcomes than might be achieved by throwing a dice or the universal adoption of practices unsupported by research-based evidence, there always remains the problem of the variations in outcome within the population being researched. The question then arises as to whether there is any evidence or plausible theory about the variables that might be responsible for some of this variation and whether any alternative decision options might be advantageous for any sub-groups. Equally problematic is the implication for clients whose characteristics place them outside the populations selected for the research.

Social scientists, familiar with the literature on the transfer of innovations and on professional learning in the workplace, will add further factors. What is the awareness of the research evidence among potential users, and how do they interpret it? Does using the evidence involve significant changes in the practices of individual practitioners, teams or departments? Who would need to learn what if new practice(s) were to be introduced? Could support for such learning be acquired and resourced? Might there be an interim period of higher risk during the changeover period; and how could this be minimized?

Information generated by oneself or others is treated as evidence when it is cited either as evidence *of* the validity of an analysis or diagnosis or as evidence *for* or *against* an argument, conclusion or decision option. Labelling such information as evidence immediately triggers concerns about its validity or credibility, because it will only be publicly accepted as evidence if it is believed to be true, or to have a reasonable probability of being true. Hence attention is given to its provenance and reliability and its consistency with other evidence. Three kinds of credibility are in common use:

1. **Research-based evidence** from published research that satisfies the critical reviews of that area of research;
2. **Other scientific evidence** generated by a process involving scientific procedures with a proven record of producing valid and reliable results; and
3. **Practice-based evidence** from professional practices recognized by the relevant profession, and performed in accordance with the criteria expected by the relevant experts within that profession.

Practice-based evidence is always used in making decisions about a client; and in health care this may be provided by several members of a multi-professional team. Recognized professional practices whose evidence is accepted unless contravened include a doctor's clinical examination and history-taking procedures and a teacher's report on the progress of a pupil. Other scientific evidence may be gathered by either the practitioner(s) or specialists such as biomedical scientists, radiographers or educational psychologists. An interesting aspect of the evidence is the point on the inference chain at which evidence is normally reported, and the extent to which estimates of possible error are reported with it. Different cultural traditions can be found in the reporting of the results of biochemical tests to doctors and of achievement tests to parents with neither estimates of error nor information about relevant norms. In the former case information about estimated error and norms for different types of patient is in the public domain and assumed to be part of the medical knowledge base, and specialist scientists are available for consultation. In the latter case estimates of error are unavailable, the relevance of any publicly available norms is dubious and understanding of the issues of validity involved is not part of the knowledge base of most teachers, still less to 99 per cent of parents. Given the many sources of evidence and reporting practices, it is hardly surprising that complications occur wherever one seeks to combine evidence grounded in different types of knowledge, each of which is judged by a different set of criteria, or even evidence relating to different aspects of the situation under analysis.

The roots of the evidence-based practice movement lie in research on decision-making, aimed at improving rather than understanding human capability by amassing greater amounts of information, expanding the coverage of research and making increasing use of computers to organize, process and access relevant information. The two areas in which this has been most developed have been business and medicine. The term originally adopted was decision analysis or, in medicine, clinical decision analysis (Weinstein and Fineberg 1980). Its first main area of application was in drug testing where the use of randomized controlled trials (RCTs) moved from rarity in 1960 to mandatory by 1990. Since then this method has been increasingly applied to surgical therapies and diagnostic tests. At the same time principles of epidemiology, whose concern is with estimating the probable occurrence and distribution of illnesses and diseases, have been increasingly applied to mainstream clinical practice.

Two key publications in the early 1990s provide markers of its progress. Clinical decision analysis was introduced to the doctor in the street by the Royal College of Physicians publication 'Analysing how we reach clinical decisions' (Llewelyn and Hopkins 1993). This showed how decision trees could be used to represent a decision-making process, and how writing research evidence to assign probabilities to each successive branch, enabled us to calculate the probabilities of each of the possible outcomes. Assigning values to these outcomes then provided strong research guidance to decision-makers. One year earlier a paper entitled Evidence-Based Medicine was published in the *Journal of the American Medical Association* (1992) by the Evidence-Based Medicine Working Group at McMaster University in Ontario, whose radical new medical school had introduced problem-based learning some 20 years previously. Its opening sentence was more forthright than the RCP book, declaring that 'A new paradigm for medical practice is emerging' and describing how medical students were being initiated into EBM at the onset of their careers.

A fuller presentation of this paradigm is provided by a pocket-sized handbook *Evidence-Based Medicine: How to Practise and Teach EBM* (Sackett *et al.* 1997), authored by two leading members of the McMaster Group – David Sackett, now Director of the NHS R&D Centre for Evidence-Based Medicine in Oxford, and Brian Haynes, Head of the Health Information Research Unit at McMaster – and two professors of medicine. The intended readership of this handbook is practitioners rather than researchers, and it provides guidance on precisely when and how practitioners should be seeking to use evidence available from research. It also explains how the use of research evidence is integrated with much patient-specific evidence and informed by doctors' previous experience.

The McMaster paper, in particular, emphasizes that while the new paradigm is of critical importance, its implementation still relies on the old knowledge:

> Clinical experience and the development of clinical instincts (particularly with respect to diagnosis) are a crucial and necessary part of becoming a competent physician. Many aspects of clinical practice cannot, or will not, ever be adequately tested. Clinical experience and its lessons are particularly important in these situations. At the same time, systematic attempts to record observations in a reproducible and unbiased fashion markedly increase the confidence one can have in knowledge about patient prognosis, the value of diagnostic tests, and the efficacy of treatment. In the absence of systematic observation one must be cautious in the interpretation of information derived from clinical experience and intuition, for it may at times be misleading.

They also warn that theory also can mislead.

> The study and understanding of basic mechanisms of disease are necessary but insufficient guides for clinical practice. The rationales for diagnosis and treatment, which follow from basic pathophysiologic principles, may in fact be incorrect, leading to inaccurate predictions about the performance of diagnostic tests and efficacy of treatments.
>
> (McMaster 1992: 2421)

The key conclusion to be drawn from these authoritative sources is that evidence-based medicine is founded not only on research-based evidence and other scientific evidence but also on practice-based evidence. For practitioners and those who train them one of the most critical issues appears to be the balance between the two. Much of the current advocacy of evidence-based practice proceeds on the assumption that there is enough research evidence available to largely determine, not just inform, a large proportion of practitioner decisions. Medicine is of prime importance for two reasons. First, it involves a large number of high-risk, high-stakes decisions. Second, its research effort is much greater than that in other areas of professional work. It is difficult to imagine even the largest multi-national companies having as large an investment in knowledge production as that of worldwide medical research. It has also invested more than any other sector in knowledge management systems designed to make the results of that research available not only to policy-makers but also to individual physicians. This has been accompanied by increasing pressure to use this growing body of codified knowledge to maximum effect.

The 'gold standard' of medical research is the randomized control trial of a health care intervention, and its Fort Knox is the Cochrane Database of Systematic Reviews, an electronic resource with quarterly updates which are prepared, maintained and disseminated by the Cochrane Collaboration, an international organization. According to Sackett *et al.* (1997) the Cochrane database sets 'a newer higher standard for finding, rating, summarising and reporting evidence from trials'. But they also note that it will take many years to reach the stage where the 'Cochrane Collaboration succeeds in summarising all randomised control trials of health care interventions in any field'. Some knowledge retrieval pathways may be paved with gold, but others will remain less easy to find and less firm underfoot. During the course of a recent review of research in postgraduate medical education, I consulted a number of medical consultants about the proportion of medical decisions for which relevant 'gold standard' evidence was available, whether summarized by Cochrane or not. Nobody suggested a figure above 20 per cent, but all agreed that the figure was rising. However, opinions about the speed of that rise and when it would begin to plateau varied widely.

The key criteria for acceptance as 'gold standard' research relates to the description and sampling of the population, the consistent administration of the intervention and the avoidance of unintended influence by researchers or participating workers by the use of double-blind randomized controlled trials. Rigorous assessment of outcomes is necessary but not sufficient, because these additional precautions are needed to enable the more robust attribution of outcomes to the specified intervention rather than to other factors.

The practice of meta-analysis associated with Cochrane reviews involves first the exclusion of all research other than RCTs, then the careful differentiation of the included research studies according to their population (especially the nature and severity of the patient's condition), the effect size and other contingent conditions such as contextual variables and side effects. When other types of research are included, more research becomes available, but its value is usually lower because alternative interpretations of the data are more plausible. The process moves closer to that of a traditional research review, which at its best gives considerable attention to alternative interpretations to those offered by the authors of published studies. Hence their output is more likely to take the form of carefully considered judgements based on evidence and argument and/or warnings against giving too much credence to advice that is not sufficiently backed by research. However, it is still important to remember that much of the less robust research, which fails to meet the Cochrane criteria, is still very useful because it may still contribute to the probability of making a better decision even if the evidence is less reliable. But the use of such research demands greater expertise and critical assessment from the user, even when recent reviews are available.

We must note, however, that this 'gold standard' research applies almost exclusively to treatment and even that requires fine tuning to the characteristics of individual patients. It assumes the diagnosis is correct and will normally not apply to patients with multiple conditions, an increasingly likely problem as patients get older. Diagnostic decisions usually rely on a wide range of practice-based evidence; and the diagnostic process is best described in terms of a doctor recognizing the pattern created by piecing together several disparate types of information, derived from patient history (obtained by questioning), physical examination, routine tests and, if appropriate, X-ray or other forms of image, microbiological or other more sophisticated tests – all of which need interpretation by doctors and often by other health professionals as well. Some of this practice-based evidence is collected at the beginning and some, if needed, at later stages in the diagnostic process. When patients are acutely ill, stabilization and treatment of life-endangering symptoms may precede the collection of diagnostic evidence that cannot be quickly obtained; and the patient's response to such emergency measures may provide some of the most important evidence. Some diagnostic tests are mainly used for differential diagnosis after possible diagnoses compatible with the early evidence have been short-listed.

Research-based evidence may contribute to this diagnosis process in a number of ways. First, these are the results of epidemiological research that measures the probability of various medical conditions in particular populations. Populations in the medical context can be defined by a large number of variables, including: gender, ethnicity, age, family, occupation, locality of home and work, lifestyle (for example, smoking, diet, exercise, travel) height, weight and medical history of self and family. Such data allows early assignment of probabilities to possible diagnoses. Second, research has provided statistical evidence of how test results may vary with many of these population variables, thus enabling estimates of the abnormality of a test result by comparing it with data from 'similar' patients. Together with research or local audit evidence on the accuracy of such evidence, these provide an essential framework for judging its significance. Then, thirdly, research may provide evidence on the discriminating power of various diagnostic tests and procedures. What is the probability that a particular test will confirm a particular diagnosis? Will it significantly improve the choice of diagnosis; and what are the most likely errors to arise from its use?

Most of the research on diagnosis, however, is focused not on the use of research evidence but on the expertise of individual clinicians. Key features of this research, and also of research into expertise in many other domains, are

> the importance of case-based experience, the rapid retrieval of information from memory attributable to its superior organisation, the development of standard patterns of reasoning and problem-solving, quick recognition of which approach to use and when, awareness of bias and fallibility; and the ability to track down, evaluate and use evidence from research and case-specific data. Understanding the nature of expertise is important for self-monitoring one's use of heuristics and possible bias, sharing knowledge with others and supporting other people's learning. It is also critical for understanding the respective roles of clinical experience and research-based guidelines.
>
> (Eraut and Du Boulay 2000: 99)

Thus, according to the nature of the decision, whether it concerns diagnosis or treatment, and the amount of relevant research evidence available, the balance between system-based knowledge and expert-based knowledge will vary considerably. The chances of the expert being already familiar with the system-based knowledge will be high, the chances of the system capturing most of the expert-based knowledge near to zero. 'Those responsible for developing, disseminating, evaluating and modifying guidelines, decision aids, information systems and communications aids within teams and across teams need to match their procedures and modes of representation to the way doctors' minds work' (Eraut and Du Boulay 2000: 99). Our conclusion is that even in areas where the most sophisticated knowledge bases can be found, access to the individual human expertise developed through knowledge and experience is the most important part of a knowledge management policy.

When we move outside the hospital to community or even outpatient settings, other kinds of expertise become more prominent. Consultations, in particular, may involve treatment, even therapy, as well as diagnosis. Most of the conditions will be less severe or not yet sufficiently clear to diagnose, and the psychological element may be given greater attention. Some authors (such as Balint 1957) have argued that there is a psychological element in most consultations, and that it is the most significant aspect of at least a quarter of consultations in community settings. This gives a very different perspective on the kind of knowledge needed by family doctors.

A rather different psychological issue is associated with what the user-unfriendly literature describes as the problem of compliance. Whatever the merits of a doctor's diagnosis and advice, research indicates that a large proportion of patients do not follow it. This does not apply only to 'hard to change' unhealthy lifestyles but also to taking medication. Tuckett et al. (1985: 167–8), examining doctor–patient communication in general practice, found that in 'as many as one in every two consultations patients could not recall all the key points . . ., could not make correct sense of them, or were not committed to them'.

> Because doctors did not know the details of what patients were think-ing, the information they did give could not relate, in any precise or considered way, to the ideas patients themselves possessed. In short, doctors could have no way of knowing whether the information they offered was being understood 'correctly' or not. Equally, patients could have no way of knowing whether their understanding of what doctors said was 'correct'.
>
> (Tuckett et al. 1985: 205)

At a more general level, and particularly in community settings and clinics, it is important for the doctor to find out what is worrying the patient and why they have come for a consultation in order to frame the health problem in an appropriate way for progressing the situation. The doctor's problem may not be the same as that of the patient. I doubt if knowledge of how to conduct more effective consultations often appears in teaching sessions on prescribing medication. This analysis of professional–client interaction could apply to many other professions.

Let us now turn to a parallel debate outside medicine. The genesis of classical decision-making can be traced to Von Neumann and Morgen-stern's (1947) *Theory of Games and Economic Behaviour*. It comprises 'an abstract system of propositions that is designed to describe the choices of an ideal hypothetical decision maker – omniscient, computationally omnipotent Economic Man' (Beach and Lipshitz 1993). However, follow-ing Edwards (1954), this theory has assumed the role of a prescriptive standard against which the quality of decision-making by mere mortals has been measured. Unfortunately for its proponents, research has shown that 'real life' decision-makers very rarely behave in this way. Beach and Lipshitz (1993) discern four possible responses to this conundrum:

1. To damn the behaviour by branding the actors as irrational or incompetent
2. To narrow the gap between theory and practice by training people in decision analysis and/or providing them with decision aids
3. To adapt the theory by making minor modifications, a strategy that has now reached Ptolemaic proportions

4. To develop a rival approach based on research into how decision-makers behave in naturalistic settings.

The range of theories developed by this fourth approach is reviewed by Klein *et al.* (1993) book *Decision Making in Action: Models and Methods*.

Classical decision theory is more abstract and idealized than the practice of evidence-based medicine; but its decline provides an important warning about overemphasizing the importance of research-based practice and failing to develop decision-making practices in areas beyond its current scope, or where evidence indicates that research provides inadequate guidance. The proponents of naturalization decision-making (NDM) argue that contexts are rarely as simple as those envisioned by either classical decision theory or the stronger versions of evidence-based practice, because real settings have many of the following characteristics:

- Problems are ill-structured.
- Information is incomplete, ambiguous, or changing.
- Goals are shifting, ill-defined or competing.
- Decisions occur in multiple event-feedback loops.
- Time constraints exist.
- Stakes are high.
- Many participants contribute to the decisions.
- The decision-maker must balance personal choice with organizational norms and goals.

(Orasanu and Connolly 1993: 19–20)

The findings of NDM research correspond quite closely with those on medical diagnosis briefly mentioned earlier:

- Experts frequently generate and evaluate a single option rather than analyse multiple options concurrently.
- Experts are distinguished from novices mainly by their situation assessment abilities, not their general reasoning skills.
- Because most naturalistic decision problems are ill-structured, decision-makers choose an option that is good enough, though not necessarily the best (ibid: 20).
- Reasoning and acting are interleaved, rather than segregated (Weick 1983).
- Instead of analysing all facets of a situation, making a decision, and then acting, it appears that in complex realistic situations people think a little, act a little, and then evaluate the outcomes and think and act some more (Connolly and Wagner 1988: 19).

The research also demonstrates that reasoning is 'schema-driven' rather than algorithmic, as assumed by computer-supported decision analysis in the classical mode.

Even for problems with many novel elements (typical of NDM situations), decision makers use their knowledge to organise the problem, to interpret the situation, and to define what information is valuable for solution. Some information may be selected or distorted to fit the existing schema, a potential source of error. But it also enables speedy assessment, search, selection, and interpretation of relevant information, a definite advantage when faced with information overload and time pressure. A critical feature of the schema-driven approach is that people create causal models of the situation. They try to understand the significance of events and information by inferring causal relations.

(Connolly and Wagner 1988: 18)

The implications of this research are that:

1. the relationship between knowledge and decision-making is rarely simple,
2. good decision-making is critically dependent on how the decision is framed by the decision-makers in the light of their situational understanding, and therefore
3. the balance is tilted more towards the personal knowledge of the decision-maker and less towards a codified knowledge management system than might be implied by classical decision-making theory.

If there is very little time or several competing decisions, any consultation of the knowledge management system would be brief and only under-taken if there was a high expectation of getting a valuable pay-off almost immediately. Most of the research evidence has to be embedded in normal practice, if it is to be used on a regular basis.

This brings us back to the nature of practice itself. The term has several meanings in common use. The practice of medicine embraces every-thing a doctor does in his role as a doctor. To this must be added a set of activity-based meanings, for example the practice of physical exami-nation, history-taking or the interpretation of X-rays; and a set of con-dition-based meanings, such as the practice of diagnosing and treating asthma. The practice in EBP is normally condition-based, and its use depends on the condition being appropriately diagnosed. Also it implicitly defines practice as an explicitly desirable set or sequence of actions that can be replicated by any practitioner with the requisite competence. Aspects of that competence will include situational understanding, skilful action, ongoing monitoring and contingent responses to changes in a patient's condition. Not all of these aspects are, or even could be, explicitly described. Thus I would argue that in most situations there are two types of practice in evidence: the observable, socially constructed and approved, practice (possibly evidence-based); and the only partly observable, only partly describable experience-based practice of the performer (Eraut 2000, 2003). Thus practitioners need both the capability to obtain and interpret research-based evidence in general and the competence to perform the particular practices judged appropriate for each particular case. Under conditions of extreme urgency or pressure of work, the latter will always take priority. Hence relevant research evidence has to be embedded in normal practice; and this will only happen if there are periods of less pressured work that allow time for reflection, review and learning of new practices.

Organizational practices are important for both this and other reasons. The organization provides the environment, technology, administration and skill mix that characterize the working context of practitioners. Research in areas like health promotion or mentoring patients at risk has shown that interventions which address administrative practices as well as practitioner learning give more sustainable results; and the consequences of organizational deficiencies that had not been foreseen are reported in the research literature on technology transfer. Whereas the more general literature on transfer of practice reveal how the micro-political context can be an extremely important factor. The acceptability of a new practice many depend more on who introduces it, or champions it, than on its benefits for users.

Finally, let me stress the importance of attending to the many user practices which affect their health and the appropriate practitioner response. One set of practices, those which are deemed as damaging or risking one's health, need to be understood in the user's life context before they can be appropriately addressed. Helping users with chronic conditions or disabilities requires understanding both their physical and their social environment; and discussing how it might best support those practices of daily living which are most valued by the user. Priorities differ greatly and knowledge of how best to support certain practices may be difficult to find. User practices can also be subdivided, like professional practices, into observable activities and the experience-based practice which users may need help to acquire.

8

Reflections from medical practice: balancing evidence-based practice with practice-based evidence
Ed Peile

Why has evidence-based medicine become almost a shibboleth of medical and health care inquiry and practice, whereas the world of education is much more cautious about defining and promulgating its evidence base? Are the disciplines fundamentally different or is it culture and context that has led the one to embrace a concept which is still regarded with much suspicion in the other?

The history of evidence-based medicine

The core activities at the root of evidence-based medicine can be identified as:

- a questioning approach to practice leading to scientific experimentation;
- meticulous observation, enumeration and analysis replacing anecdotal case description;
- recording and cataloguing the evidence for systematic retrieval.

Each of these activities was recorded in the eighteenth century. The founder of modern experimentation is regarded as James Lind (1716–94). A Surgeon-Admiral in the Royal Navy, Lind was determined to establish a scientific foundation for practice. In 1747 he carried out what was probably the first controlled experiment. Lind took twelve men from a Royal Naval ship (all suffering from scurvy) and divided them (non-randomly) into six pairs. They were given cider, sea water, garlic, mustard, horseradish; or oranges and lemons. Only those given citrus fruit recovered enough to look after the others.

If Lind was the founder of modern experimentation, then the founder of medical statistics was probably the French physician Pierre-Charles-

Alexandre Louis (1787–1872). In sharp contrast to the prevailing climate in Paris, where physicians relied on their memory of striking cases in the discussion of diagnosis and treatment, Louis championed exact observation and the use of empirical deduction in medical studies. Devoting his time to observing and recording the work of other physicians, and conducting large numbers of interviews with patients and their families, Louis insisted that patients who died at the Charité Hospital, where he worked, had detailed post-mortem examinations. In this way he built up an unprecedented database of illness and treatment. He believed passionately in the scientific approach he propounded, and unlike his contemporaries, he was not afraid to publish negative findings. It was Louis who showed conclusively that many of the claims for blood-letting were unfounded (Louis 1836). He detailed his philosophy thus:

> Let us bestow upon observation the care and time which it demands; let the facts be rigorously analyzed in order to a just appreciation of them; and it is impossible to attain this without classifying and counting them; and then therapeutics will advance not less than other branches of science.
>
> (Louis 1836: 64–5)

Two hundred years after these elements were in place, the prevailing culture in medicine was still one of experiential learning. Much of the credit for today's techniques of critical appraisal belongs to Archie Cochrane, who is best known for his influential book, *Effectiveness and Efficiency: Random Reflections on Health Services* (Cochrane 1972). Cochrane's principles were straightforward: he suggested that because resources

Figure 8.1   Professor Archie Cochrane, CBE, FRCP, FFCM (1909–88)

would always be limited, they should be used to provide equitably those forms of health care which had been shown in properly designed evaluations to be effective (Cochrane Collaboration 2003). Cochrane was steeped in the science of epidemiology and maintained adamantly that the most reliable evidence was that which emanated from randomized controlled trials (RCTs). Cochrane's simple propositions were timely and were taken up rapidly throughout the world of medicine (see Dickersin and Manheimer 1998).

Cochrane's challenge to medical specialities was to develop a summary of all relevant randomized controlled trials, and this was taken up in the 1980s by an international collaboration to develop the Oxford Database of Perinatal Trials. In 1987, the year before he died, Cochrane referred to a systematic review of randomized controlled trials (RCTs) of care during pregnancy and childbirth as 'a real milestone in the history of randomized trials and in the evaluation of care' (Cochrane 1989).

The bandwagon rolling

The Cochrane Centre opened in Oxford in 1992 and was followed by the founding of the Cochrane Collaboration in 1993. The Collaboration consists of international collaborative review groups who prepare and maintain systematic reviews of evidence in many clinical fields. These reviews are published electronically in successive issues of *The Cochrane Database of Systematic Reviews*. According to the Collaboration's website:

> By the beginning of 2001, the existing review groups covered all of the important areas of health care. The members of these groups – researchers, health care professionals, consumers, and others – share an interest in generating reliable, up-to-date evidence relevant to the prevention, treatment and rehabilitation of particular health problems or groups of problems. How can stroke and its effects be prevented and treated? What drugs should be used to prevent and treat malaria, tuberculosis and other important infectious diseases? What strategies are effective in preventing brain and spinal cord injury and its consequences, and what rehabilitative measures can help those with residual disabilities?
>
> (Cochrane Collaboration website 2003)

The term 'evidence based medicine' (no hyphen) was coined at McMaster Medical School in Canada in the 1980s for a clinical learning strategy comprising four steps:

- formulate a clear clinical question from the patient's problem
- search the literature for relevant clinical articles

- evaluate (critically appraise) the literature for its validity and usefulness
- implement useful findings in clinical practice.

(Rosenberg 1995)

The strategy remains similar today (Sackett *et al.* 2000).

The present position of evidence-based medicine in Britain

Today there are innumerable paper and on-line journals on the topic of evidence-based medicine, some of the best known of which in the UK are *Evidence-Based Medicine; Bandolier; The British Journal of Clinical Governance; Effectiveness Matters; Effective Health Care; Quality and Safety in Healthcare*. All the main medical journals devote sections to the evidence base, and most medical specialities publish evidence-based topic reviews for specialists. Books abound in a field where no one can afford to be ignorant, and most niches of the subject have been explored, namely:

- Evidence-based medicine (Sackett *et al.* 2000)
- Evidence-based decision-making (Downie and Macnaughton 2000)
- Evidence-based health care (Gray 1997)
- Evidence-based patient choice (Edwards and Elwyn 2001)

Small wonder that *Bandolier* talks about 'Evidence based Everything' (Anon 1995a), and that websites on the topic abound.

On many, if not most, doctors' desks there is a computer with links to evidence-based resources, and in 1999 the use of the 'evidence-based cart' was pioneered on acute medical wards at Oxford, offering physicians access to electronic sources of clinical evidence in 15 seconds on the ward-round (Sackett and Straus 1998). There is even a section of the National Electronic Library for Health, called 'Evidence-Based On-Call', which is a database to help young doctors to find the evidence they need, particularly when it is needed most – namely, in the middle of the night when libraries are closed or remote, and when senior staff are not on the premises.

The practice of evidence-based medicine is the underlying paradigm for the new institutions of the NHS, such as NICE (National Institute for Clinical Evidence) and CHAI (Commission for Healthcare Audit and Inspection).

It is worth pausing to reflect how a movement based on ideas published in 1972, and given impetus by Canadian teaching in the early 1980s, could by the turn of the century become the prevailing paradigm in medicine in the developed world. 'As in political revolutions, so in paradigm choice – there is no standard higher than the assent of the relevant community' (Kuhn 1962). For a paradigm to become preeminent there has to be a collusion between stakeholders. In this case doctors, patients and government all stood to gain something from evidence-based medicine. (To understand *what* they gained, try applying the *'not*-test'. Would most doctors want to say, 'I do *not* want practice medicine based on best available evidence'? Are there many patients seeking treatment that is *not* supported by scientific evidence? Can governments afford to been seen funding health-care systems that are *not* supported by best available evidence of efficacy?) Indeed, the promotion of ways of identifying the best methods of health care and thus helping patients and doctors to make better informed choices has been described as constituting universally appealing ethical and clinical ideals (Kerridge *et al.* 1998).

Characterizing the knowledge-base

Conventionally, the practice of evidence-based medicine includes five steps (Sackett *et al.* 2000):

1. Converting the need for information about prevention, diagnosis, prognosis, therapy causation and so on into an answerable question
2. Tracking down the best evidence with which to answer that question
3. Critically appraising that evidence for its validity, impact and applicability
4. Integrating the critical appraisal with our clinical expertise and with our patients' unique biology, values and circumstances
5. Evaluating our effectiveness and efficiency in executing steps (1–4) and seeking ways to improve them for the next time.

Integral to these steps there are a number of skills underpinning the practice of evidence-based medicine. For example, in framing questions a common technique is to use the PICO model (Patient, Intervention, Comparison and Outcome) (Armstrong 1999). However, even experienced researchers encounter difficulties searching the literature for evidence – such difficulties may have more to do with the quality of the evidence than the skills of the researcher (Ely *et al.* 2002).

Several people have tried to simplify the steps to generate evidence-based answers quickly to pressing clinical problems (see Sackett and Straus 1998). Look also at Table 8.1 for an attempt at this kind of simplification.

Others have addressed the need to focus on a small number of questions. Strauss (1998) calculated that a typical inpatient generates five questions for clinicians who are willing to admit that they don't have

Table 8.1   Type and strength of evidence (from Anon 1995a)

1. Strong evidence from at least 1 systematic review of multiple well-designed randomised controlled trials
2. Strong evidence from at least 1 properly designed randomised controlled trial of appropriate size
3. Evidence from well-designed trials without randomisation, single group pre-post, cohort, time series or matched case-controlled studies
4. Evidence from well-designed non-experimental studies from more than 1 centre or research group
5. Opinions of respected authorities, based on clinical evidence, descriptive studies or reports of expert committees

all the answers. They therefore tried to introduce a process which reduced these to one answerable question by balancing various factors. These factors might be: which question is most important to the patient's well-being; which is it most feasible to answer in the time available; which is most interesting to the clinician; and which answer is most likely to be applicable in subsequent patients? (Straus and Sackett 1998).

Perhaps a more controversial aspect of academic evidence-based medicine is the 'hierarchy of evidence' (Barton 2000), whereby RCTs remain the gold standard. This view reflects the positivist approach to scientific method, based on setting up falsifiable hypotheses and testing them, which underpins medical science. However, even Barton, the editor of *Clinical Evidence*, admits a place for more than one methodology in constructing evidence:

> The typical problem with observational studies is not their ability to detect significant changes, it is their difficulty in excluding systematic biases that could also explain those changes. Randomised controlled trials rarely provide all the evidence needed to answer clinical questions. Few randomised controlled trials are designed to provide good evidence about harms, and good quality observational studies are likely to remain essential in any thorough review of the adverse effects of treatments.
>
> (Barton 2001: 165)

There are some doctors, particularly those working in primary care, who are uncomfortable with the positivist emphasis (Sweeney 1996). Some would place a higher premium on well-designed qualitative research designed to look at questions such as, 'in what circumstances and for which patients will this treatment work?' These doctors might be seen as working in the 'swamplands of practice' (Schön 1991) as distinct from the 'high, hard ground' of research.

Evidence of the relevance of this is to be found in a fascinating study by Freeman and Sweeney, using Balintian methodology. They summarize their conclusions tellingly:

> This study suggests that the general practitioner acts as a conduit in consultations in which clinical evidence is one commodity. For some doctors the evidence had clarified practice, focused clinical effort, and sometimes radically altered practice. But a stronger theme from our data is that doctors are shaping the square peg of the evidence to fit the round hole of the patient's life. The nature of the conduit is determined partly by the doctors' previous experiences and feelings. These feelings can be about the patient, the evidence itself, or where the evidence has come from (the hospital setting). The conduit is also influenced by the doctor-patient relationship. The precise words used by practitioners in their role as conduit can affect how evidence is implemented. In some settings, logistical problems will diminish the effectiveness of the conduit.
>
> (Freeman and Sweeney 2001: 1100)

The tensions between evidence and practice are beginning to emerge. But even at the bedside or in the consulting room, it must be emphasized that evidence-based medicine is designed to answer real problems for real patients. The founding fathers of the evidence-based medicine movement are at pains to emphasize the patient-centredness of the activity, and to emphasize that people – not evidence – make decisions (Haynes *et al.* 2002).

The central importance of patient preferences is illustrated in the following quotations:

- 'Evidence based medicine is the conscientious, explicit, and judicious use of current best evidence in making decisions about the care of individual patients.' (Sackett *et al.* 2000)
- 'Evidence based clinical practice is an approach to decision making in which the clinician uses the best evidence available, in consultation with the patient, to decide upon the option which suits that patient best.' (Gray 1997)
- 'The practice of evidence based medicine is a process of lifelong self directed learning in which caring for patients creates a need for clinically important information about diagnoses, prognoses, treatment, and other healthcare issues.' (Straus and Sackett 1998)

The point is also made in the illustration used by Haynes, given in Figure 8.2.

Note that in Haynes's model there is no place for 'experience' in the construction of clinical expertise. This is a far cry from the practice

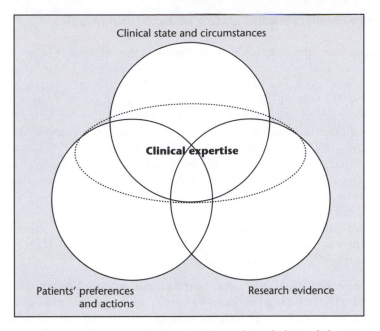

Figure 8.2 An updated model for evidence-based clinical decisions
(Haynes *et al.* 2002)

prevailing in the pre-Cochrane era, when experience was all. 'Grand
rounds', as they were called, were the opportunity for the medical
eminences to demonstrate their huge experience, often extending to
rarities which lesser mortals never encountered. Surgeons counted their
expertise in the number of times they had performed a procedure, and
anecdotal medicine was the order of the day. 'I saw a case of that once,
and she did awfully well on a large dose of . . .' is nowadays discounted as
an 'n=1 trial' in the language of evidence-based medicine.

However, experience is not entirely discounted by evidence-based
medicine practitioners. Sackett, for example, emphasizes that personal
experience heads the list of sources for estimates of pre-test possibility,
essential for any Bayesian interpretation (Sackett *et al.* 2000). That is
to say, unless you have an idea of how likely a patient is to have the
condition before you do the test, you cannot meaningfully interpret the
result of that test.

The role of evidence-based medicine in deciding treatment for an
individual was modelled scientifically by Glasziou and Irwig (1995).
Likewise, Sackett emphasizes the individual dimensions in determining
the appropriateness of a diagnostic test for a patient: 'Do patients who
undergo this diagnostic test fare better (in their ultimate health outcomes)
than similar patients who are not tested?' (Sackett and Haynes 2002).

Evidence-based medicine: getting research into practice

For the patient, the individual consultation is the important focus, but for those concerned with systematic health care, evidence-based medicine is failing if it does not affect the nature of practice across populations (Gray 1997). Making better use of research findings is a priority task for policy-makers (Haines and Donald 1998), and much research has gone into looking at the difficulties of implementing the evidence (Haynes and Haines 1998). There was early evidence of success in that one study reported that over half the patients admitted to a general medical ward at a District General Hospital received primary treatments that had been validated in RCTs (Ellis *et al.* 1995).

There have been some interesting 'swamplands' case studies looking at the difficulties in clinical practice. Lipman reported the attempt in a general practice partnership to enact an evidence-based policy on treating a common condition, urinary tract infections.

> We have described the often messy and uncoordinated process whereby we have tried to improve our practice. We are always busy, always have to get through the next surgery, and struggle to find time and effective ways to evaluate and improve our performance. Decisions must be made quickly using the best evidence and data, and we must often trade methodological rigour for practicability and speed.
>
> (Lipman and Price 2000: 1117)

In a commentary on this study, Greenhalgh describes the 'storyline':

> The hard liners for the evidence based agenda come to discover that their academic value system with its emphasis on experiment, rigour, precision, and reproducibility serves them poorly in the untidy and unpredictable environment of service delivery. Furthermore, the value system espoused by their service colleagues with its emphasis on using available data and information systems, maintaining harmony and job fulfilment among staff, responding flexibly to individual needs, and keeping the customer satisfied may be better able to initiate and sustain positive changes within the organisation.
>
> (Greenhalgh 2000: 1118)

Changing behaviours: the evidence base on evidence-based medicine

Guyatt *et al.* (2000) list two reasons why training evidence-based practitioners will not, alone, achieve evidence-based practice:

Firstly, many clinicians will not be interested in gaining a high level of sophistication in using the original literature, and, secondly, those who do will often be short of time in applying these skills.

(Guyatt *et al.* 2000: 954)

Controlled trials have shown that traditional CME (continuing medical education) has little effect on changing doctors' behaviour to become more evidence-based (Davis, Thomson *et al.* 1992; Davis *et al.* 1995). Guyatt emphasizes the underused potential of strategies that focus on behaviour change (such as restricted drug formularies) to achieve evidence-based care almost by default (Guyatt *et al.* 2000).

The predominance of guidelines in practice (Hibble *et al.* 1998) and the compelling evidence of their uselessness (Oxman *et al.* 1995; Bero *et al.* 1998) is a stark reminder that although policy-makers may be desperate to promote evidence-based medicine, they do not always practise it (see Figure 8.3)!

Muir Gray (1998) proposes the 'knowledge officer' as a means of making information more manageable at practice level.

The politics of evidence-based medicine

The fervour with which policy-makers have embraced evidence-based medicine has led to criticism that it may be a dangerous innovation – perpetrated by the arrogant to serve cost-cutters and suppress clinical freedom (see Anon 1995b).

There is always the risk that 'good practice' may become a rod with which to beat a profession, as has been the fear amongst the teaching profession, noted in Hammersley's chapter in this volume. A hint of this process came when a journal changed its title. In 1998, the *Journal of Clinical Effectiveness*, a journal about 'the application of **interventions** which have been shown to be efficacious to **appropriate patients** in a timely fashion to improve patients' **outcomes** and value for the use of resources' (Batstone and Edwards 1996) became *The British Journal of Clinical Governance*, a journal concerned with 'audit evidence-based practice, clinical guidelines, risk management and implementation of best practice health outcomes'.

Reviewing the problems of getting research findings into practice, Sheldon, from the NHS Centre for Reviews and Dissemination, and his colleagues from academia voiced some of the 'shoulds' in the medical paradigm (Sheldon *et al.* 1998). In evidence-based health care, purchasers, they state as a given, *should* be able to influence the organization and delivery of care, and the type and content of services. Policy-makers *should* ensure policies on treatment reflect research evidence, and that the

Figure 8.3   A pile of 855 guidelines in general practices in the Cambridge and Huntingdon Health Authority (Hibble *et al.* 1998)

incentive structure promotes cost-effective practice. They *must* ensure that there is an adequate infrastructure for producing, gathering, summarizing, and disseminating evidence. Perhaps these 'givens', which raised not an eyebrow politically in the letter columns of the *British Medical Journal* after publication, emphasize some of the differences between the prevailing cultures in medicine and education in Britain. Evidence-based medicine is entwined in the purchaser/provider culture and is accepted by practitioners in this context.

There has been little writing about the effects of this politicization on research, despite the potential to influence policy with the research endeavour. Most of what has been written concentrates on the huge amounts of money at stake for the pharmaceutical industry, sponsoring research (Moynihan *et al.* 2002) and their pleading that,

The rise of guideline led care around the Western world shows that far too many serious diseases are underdiagnosed and under-treated. Failure to put evidence based medicine into practice is quite legitimately addressed by the pharmaceutical industry.

(Tiner 2002: 216)

The time at which most doctors will have to answer for their evidence-based medicine strategies is at five-yearly revalidation (see Burrows *et al.* 2001; GMC and Health 2002). In preparation for this, peer appraisers are encouraged to raise the topic of evidence-based medicine at annual appraisal. Under-performance by doctors is judged in terms of the evidence base around clinical behaviours (Southgate and Dauphinee 1998; Southgate and Pringle 1999; Southgate *et al.* 2001a) and there is a new government body to characterize such evidence – the NCAA (National Clinical Assessment Authority, see Southgate *et al.* 2001b).

In the civil courts, as in the criminal, the definition of negligence is changing quietly to suit an evidence-based culture. Gradually the 'Bolam' test of what a responsible body of professional opinion might consider to be in the patient's best interests, is losing ground to codes of practice or court assessments based on 'Best Evidence'. This is the case in trials around consent issues (McCall Smith 2001).

The reach of evidence-based medicine often extends beyond the confines of medicine and into social care. A recent independent inquiry into inequalities in health emphasized the importance of the social environment and included sections on education and housing. Notwithstanding this, the evaluation group (exclusively medical) ultimately leant heavily on medical evidence, and as a result the recommendations were largely medical (see Laurance 1998). The reality may be that health differentials between social groups, or between poor and rich countries, are not primarily generated by medical causes and require solutions at a different level, and the medical evidence itself may be less valid.

The place for experience, intuition and tacit knowledge in an evidence-based culture

The extent to which beliefs are based on evidence is very much less than believers suppose.

(Bertrand Russell, *Sceptical Essays*, 1928: 11)

Grahame-Smith (1995) points out that in medical education there may be inadequate emphasis on the paradox whereby there is a positive impact of personal experience on the diagnostic art, but a misleading influence of personal experience in the appraisal of practice outcome. This is an example of the use of tacit knowledge (Polanyi 1959), a topic which is explored further in the context of evidence-based medicine by Wyatt (2001), and by several contributors to this volume in relation to educational practice.

Lilford *et al.* (1998) suggest that while the process of relating the results from a trial to a particular patient is usually an intuitive one for doctors, there is a place for decision analysis. They advocate the development of special algorithms that can be critiqued and improved, and argue that decision analysis provides a rational means of allowing health professionals to move from finding evidence to implementing it. They put it thus:

> Decision analysis depends on probabilities and values, neither of which can be measured with certainty. These problems are not lessened when health professionals approach them intuitively; decision analysis makes these uncertainties explicit. The attempt to make complex decisions intuitively inevitably results in gross oversimplifications because it is impossible to incorporate and consider several components of a decision simultaneously.
>
> (Lilford *et al.* 1998: 409)

Elsewhere, I have described a case study in synthesizing evidence to answer questions arising from intuition (Peile 2000). Health workers without counselling training wanted to know if encouraging an elderly person to talk about unresolved loss would cause more harm than good – it doesn't!

Towards practice-based evidence

The evidence presented so far in this chapter has been of an exponential acceptance of the new paradigm of evidence-based medicine throughout the medical profession over the past 30 years. The acceptance has been rapid, but we are now almost at the level of a cult or fashion, whereby the speed of uptake has exceeded the speed by which the evidence base for evidence-based medicine can be researched. Much energy has gone into the determination of relevant evidence. But there is scant conclusive evidence of the process by which the philosophy, skills and application of evidence-based medicine move downstream to make a difference at the level of patient experience or population health.

Evidence-based medicine was designed to help the individual doctor answer questions with, for and about the individual patient. Much of the attention to making the evidence base more useful in this situation has gone into making the databases wider and more easily accessible (Haynes and Haines 1998). There is still a lot of work to be done on the quality of the original research, so that the research output is capable of answering the questions to which practitioners and patients wish to know the answers (Haynes and Haines 1998; Freeman and Sweeney 2001).

This has been addressed in part by government sponsoring local research networks to generate practice-based evidence, and supporting these networks from academia to try to ensure that the research output is generalizable and useful (Carter *et al.* 2002). The value of generalizability in research is another 'given' in medicine, which may be more questioned in the world of education, where many researchers feel that the unique experience of one teacher and one group of students has validity unique to that situation. Cordingley discusses this in Chapter 6 of this volume.

At practitioner level, there is also interest in generating practice-based evidence in microcosm. The work of Richard Eve on 'PUNS' and 'DENS' has caught the imagination of many a doctor working on their personal development (see Eve 2000). In this exercise, the doctor records through-out the working day the Patient Unmet Needs (PUNS) which are encountered, and also the Doctor's Educational Needs (DENS). For the reflective practitioner, such exercises constitute a valuable component of educational needs assessment (Grant 2002).

The future threat to the paradigm of evidence-based medicine lies not in its complexity nor in its political implications (for, unlike teachers, the medical profession has accepted meekly the supposed benefits of an evidence-based culture). Rather, threats to it come from its failure to answer many of the questions which are important to individual patients. Only more practice-based evidence will preserve the positive aspects of the paradigm.

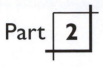

Part **2**

Evidence-based practice in practice

Section C: problems in practice

9

Educational research, philosophical orthodoxy and unfulfilled promises: the quandary of traditional research in US special education

Deborah J. Gallagher

> ... if social science does not present its findings in the form of law-like generalizations, the grounds for employing social scientists as expert advisors to government or to private corporations become unclear and the very notion of managerial expertise is imperilled. For the central function of the social scientist as expert advisor or manager is to predict the outcomes of alternative policies, and if his predictions do not derive from a knowledge of law-like generalizations, the status of the social scientist as predictor becomes endangered – as it turns out, it ought to be; for the record of social scientists as predictors is very bad indeed, insofar as the record can be pieced together.
>
> MacIntyre (1981: 89)

Special education in the United States, both as a field of research and an area of practice, finds itself in a great deal of turmoil. After years and years of research undertaken, articles published, and claims of effective practices made, things are just not turning out as hoped or expected. Special education researchers who have spent their entire careers in pursuit of scientific (empiricist) validation of evidence-based practices appear to be bewildered that serious issues have been raised about the knowledge generated by their research; and, in response to criticism that they have been unable to accomplish their goals, they feel both maltreated and embattled. The implication that their science has run its course with little to show for it has prompted some rather interesting responses.

A reading of the major US special education journals in the past decade or so reveals a combination of researchers' reactions that, taken together, form a rather incoherent tableau. Pronouncements of the extraordinary accomplishments of their scientific endeavours are combined with hand-wringing deliberations as to why so little progress has been made. One account for the lack of progress holds that they have produced effective treatments, but that these treatments are not being implemented by teachers. From their perspective, this 'research-to-practice gap' demonstrates a devaluation of science on the part of educators, policy-makers, and the general public. Hence, they suffer on the one hand from a dearth of good advertising in that they have neglected to make others aware of their accomplishments, an oversight for which they assume the blame. On the other hand, unjustified negative publicity inflicted by the media and, worse, by critics from within the academy, has had a deleterious effect on efforts to accrue public and institutional support for their work. The solution to this problem is twofold. First, they have worked harder to persuade the public and policy-makers to recognize their accomplishments. Second, they have made concerted efforts to silence the critics within the academy. Standing in stark contrast to the first account is another which cites problems with their research practices. These are problems that, in their view, are eminently resolvable once they buckle down and get to work on them. These methodological problems are not, as they see them, fundamental flaws in their science. Rather, they are simply the challenges presented to a scientific area of study on its way to becoming a mature science.

What follows is an analysis of these disparate accounts, one that reveals a misapprehension of the problem, and a corresponding misidentification of its solutions. I begin with the first account which claims that a coherent, scientific knowledge base of effective practices does indeed exist, but simply is not being used. The story here is one that portrays a case of neglect and abuse. The problem stems from a number of interrelated sources, including teachers, lack of public support and resources, unwarranted critique in the popular media, and, most virulent of all, 'hostile attacks' from within the academy. The proposed solution to the problem involves a concerted public relations programme geared towards educating those unaware of 'revolutionary' progress they have accomplished while simultaneously denouncing and silencing the critics within the academy.

I then turn to the second account of the problem – an admission that the knowledge base of effective practices is not all that adequate after all, in large measure because research practices have lacked a certain rigour. In this account, special education researchers' proposed solution is a concerted initiative to rehabilitate their research practices. The contradictory nature of these two accounts is in itself revealing, but more illuminating still are the methodological conundrums these researchers encounter while attempting to reinvigorate their research practices. Perhaps more effectively than their critics, special education researchers' rather agonized deliberations all but announce that fundamental flaws in their practices are, in the end, at the root of their quandaries over credibility. Failing to recognize the momentous implications of the obstacles they seek to rectify, they unwittingly affirm the very criticisms they consider so treacherously unjustified. Although it is perfectly legitimate for them to discuss the problems encountered (presumably because they believe them to be reparable), it is intolerable that other academic critics do so. I conclude with a portrait of mixed messages emanating from this group of special education researchers who continue to defend their philosophical orthodoxy while wondering aloud where the field will end up.

The scientific knowledge base: a case of neglect and abuse

In US special education journals, there are far more claims of scientifically grounded, evidence-based practices than actual recounts of what, exactly, these practices consist of (Brantlinger 1997; Heshusius, 2003). Recently, though, apparent efforts have been made to make these claims more explicit. These practices include most prominently: the commercial Direct Instruction Programs, self-monitoring, mnemonic instruction, strategy training, curriculum-based assessment, applied behaviour analysis (token economies and the like), functional assessment, medications, phonics-based approaches for teaching beginning reading, transition models, supported employment, and early intervention (see Fuchs and Fuchs 1995a; Forness, Kavale, Blum and Lloyd 1997; Hallahan and Kauffman, 1997; Hallahan 1998; Lloyd, Forness and Kavale 1998; Walker *et al.* 1998; Hockenbury, Kauffman and Hallahan 2000). These practices, it is claimed, have been validated by special education research, and have, according to Walker *et al.* (1998: 16), 'revolutionized practices and dramatically improved the quality of life for thousands of individuals and their families'.

Despite an insistence that 'best instructional practices for students with disabilities have been well-researched and documented' (Hockenbury, Kauffman and Hallahan 1999–2000: 9), Walker *et al.* (1998) offer the following observation: 'Perhaps in no field is there a more glaring disconnect between the availability of proven research-based methods and their effective application by consumers than in education' (p. 8). Teachers are accorded partial blame for the problem. For instance, they are criticized for ignoring best practices by instead choosing those based on 'ideological correctness' (Walker *et al.* 1998). Kauffman (1994) proposes that part of the problem is that special education has failed to recruit only the 'best and brightest' to teacher 'training' programmes. In an analogy that likens teaching to producing atomic energy (with teachers as the raw material), he admonishes, 'Remember that in making atomic energy, not just any uranium will do; you have to have the right kind of uranium' (Kauffman 1994: 615). Lest it seem that he is being unduly harsh with teachers, he adds that teacher education programmes have failed them and that schools have provided neither the material resources nor the professional support they require to do a good job. The bottom line, though, is that special education teachers are not doing a very good job.

Another charge is that the field of special education has become politicized to the point that ideological differences have damaged the credibility of the field and diminished public support (Kavale and Forness 1998; Walker *et al.* 1998; Mostert and Kavale 2001). Negative publicity from the popular press, for instance, is cited as having presented a formidable obstacle towards gaining and sustaining authoritative credibility. Prominent newspapers such as *The New York Times* and the *Wall Street Journal*, news magazines such as *U.S. News & World Report*, and television news programmes such as *60 minutes* have portrayed special education in the United States as being discriminatory to minorities and low-income students, inordinately expensive, and worst of all, ineffective (see Shapiro *et al.* 1993; Dillon 1994; Winerip 1994). Taking grievous exception to this negative publicity, Fuchs and Fuchs (1995b) announced that 'special education was mugged in a dark alley' by 'thugs' using the 'brass knuckles and tire irons' of 'half-truths and full-blown distortions' (p. 363). If deprived of public and governmental support, the entire field of special education is in danger of being, 'dismantled and hauled off to the town dump' (p. 364), along with, presumably, the entire special education research establishment.

More lamentable still are the critics within the academy. These critics are dangerous because in questioning the very foundations of special education's empiricist/positivist knowledge and the claim of scientific neutrality, they ultimately undermine the entire special education research enterprise. As noted by Heshusius (2003), when these critiques first appeared in the mid- to late 1980s, they were seen as an anomaly, and were accordingly viewed as puzzling but tolerably benign. Over the past decade, however, the opposition to critical scholarship has increased substantially, to the point where it is currently seen as posing, 'a significant challenge to our field' (Walker *et al.* 1998: 11). These internal critics are blamed for eroding public support for special education and for having elicited the damaging media attacks cited above (Walker *et al.* 1999–2000).

Other responses to this 'significant challenge' have likewise been interesting. Some of the same individuals who have been most outspoken about the damaging effect of this criticism also deny that there is any serious threat in the long run (see Walker *et al.* 1999–2000), while many others clearly evidence their ire towards these 'internal critics'. Glaringly misinformed characterizations have constituted a primary defensive tactic against the threat of critique. Those holding a position inconsistent with the empiricist/behavioural framework are invariably lumped together as being Marxists and postmodernists irrespective of their stated philosophical positions (see Kavale and Forness 1998; Walker *et al.*, 1998; Sasso 2001). Kavale and Forness (1998), for example, decry the 'Marxists' who question the scientific grounding of learning disabilities.

They allege that Marxist theories of social reproduction, conflict theories, social construction, and so on lack substantiation and are all but made up for the purpose of imposing progressive educators' wills on the rest of 'us'. 'Consequently, Marxist apologists are less inhibited by ignorance, but nonetheless possess an instinctual appeal' (p. 255). These authors also see 'Marxists',' critiques as a 'warping of reality' and guilty of 'fanciful distortions of history' (p. 258).

Ad hominem name-calling is another defensive tactic which reveals the 'revulsion' (Sasso 2001) the special education researchers experience in the face of anyone who challenges their framework. The following list of contemptuous shibboleths is not exhaustive, but provides a sufficient sample (for additional discussions of this, see Brantlinger 1997; Heshusius, 2003). Among other things, critics of traditional special education research and practices have been referred to as 'mules' who 'ignore rules', and as being 'shamelessly egocentric' (Kauffman 1999). Kavale and Forness (2000) assert that such critics possess, 'a significant ego preserve' and resemble 'a cult of ambiguity'. Sasso (2001) views 'postmodernists' as waging war against, 'White, male, heterosexual, Eurocentric Western society' (p. 179). 'PD lingo' is Walker *et al.*'s (1998) favoured term for referring to 'postmodernist/deconstructionist' writers who are self-indulgently busy doing 'what feels good'. Other appellations include 'charlatans', 'scam-artists', 'pied pipers' and 'peddling junk science and other frauds' (Kauffman 1999).

Hockenbury, Kauffman and Hallahan (1999–2000) offer the following regret: 'If only academics would spend more time researching and theorizing about effective special education practices rather than spending their energy crafting philosophical diatribes against special education, then perhaps the gap between research and practice will be narrowed' (p. 10).

Oddly enough, several special education researchers have assumed blame for leaving a void open for both media and internal critics by not doing a sufficient job of letting the world know of their accomplishments. For example, Walker *et al.* (1998) note that, 'it is also important that we prevent them from determining special education policy by our own default (i.e., by our failure to call attention to the reliability and value of the empirical evidence supporting our practices)' (p. 12). Hence, the obvious solution is to launch a public relations campaign to rectify the situation.

While condemning the politicized nature of their critics' arguments and 'might makes right mindset', special education researchers have apparently decided that the best defence is a good offence. This approach is demonstrated in calls to action designed to reassert the pre-eminence of scientific research. In his article entitled 'Campaigns for Moving Research into Practice', Carnine (1999) defines a campaign as 'any course of systematic aggressive action toward a specific purpose' (p. 3). In launching a campaign, he describes a militaristic strategy for suppressing any opposition.

Special education researchers' most concerted campaign to silence their detractors is, however, one that has been more private than public. This private campaign centres on controlling the US special education academic journals via the anonymous review process, thus ensuring that there are decisive limitations placed upon access to alternative perspectives. Heshusius (2003) summarizes the situation: 'Clearly, there is at present no such thing as a review process in the field of mainstream special education that accesses and fairly represents a broad base of the relevant discussions in contemporary scholarship.' Citing anonymous reviews shared with her by alternative thinkers in critical special education and disability studies, Heshusius portrays both the caustic and uninformed nature of reviews from these journals. Editorial commentary and reviewers' remarks indicate that they based their decisions to reject manuscripts on the grounds that they are, 'inflammatory', 'not data based', 'based only on personal experience' or 'personal testimony', 'manifestos', 'psychobabble', 'implicitly Marxist', and the list goes on and on. The upshot of all of these reviews was that the epistemological assumptions of empiricist science were beyond critique, and any other philosophical or conceptual orientation was both indefensible and unwelcome. Were the rejected works simply examples of poor scholarship, one might conclude that these comments make little difference in the end. However, while one paper was eventually accepted by a special education journal, the others were ultimately published in the most prestigious national and international academic journals outside special education.

Aspiring to repair the damaged credibility of special education (with particular emphasis on the sub-discipline of behavioural disorders), Walker *et al.* (1998) propose that rededication to empirical inquiry and use of collective expertise may 'achieve a degree of "macrosocial validation" for our efforts' (p. 7). Macrosocial validation is defined as the 'recognition, approval, and valuing of a field's professional activities by the larger constituencies affected by them, such as the general public, the US Congress, and policy-makers' (p. 7). Clearly, they believe, more respect (and governmental funding) is deserved than accorded. Yet, at the same time, these authors identify education (one must assume special education is subsumed under the heading of education) as an 'immature profession', a hallmark of which is 'the failure to develop and use cohesive knowledge bases in those contexts where it is possible' (p. 8). It does not require a deep analysis to apprehend the contradiction contained herein.

The self-doubt that lies beneath the surface of self-asserting bravado is further revealed by the spate of articles defending special education research with titles such as 'What is Right About Special Education' (Hockenbury, Kauffman and Hallahan, 1999–2000), 'What is Right with Behavior Disorders: Seminal Achievement and Contributions of the Behavior Disorders Field' (Walker, Sprague and Close 1999–2000), 'Counterpoint: Special Education – Ineffective? Immoral?' (Fuchs and Fuchs 1995c) and 'What's "Special" About Special Education?' (Fuchs and Fuchs 1995a). One might wonder why an area of scientific inquiry that boasts such amazing accomplishments feels so compelled to proffer such vindications. When was the last time anyone read an article entitled, for example, 'What's Right About Chemistry', in a respected journal in the physical sciences?

Aside from the sub-textual self-doubt of these public relations campaigns and other defensive measures, a more definitive sense of insecurity is expressed in published literature on the question of how, as Kauffman (1996: 59) expresses it, 'the work of practitioners can be informed by and *brought into line* with reliable research findings on instruction and management' [emphasis added]. He goes on to explain that one solution for ameliorating the problem involves 'getting researchers to do better research' (p. 57). If this is the case, a serious question might be raised about the current knowledge base if the research that produced it requires improvement.

Admissions, disclosures and methodological conundrums

In a recent article describing the five years of deliberations on how to improve their research practices, a group of special education researchers sought resolution to the dilemmas of conducting experimental and quasi-experimental research (Gersten, Baker and Lloyd 2000). Their key dilemma centres on the question of how to make their research relevant and more user-friendly for teachers and, at the same time, implement tightly controlled experiments to maintain scientific rigour. In attempting to resolve this dilemma, they allow that 'some traditional standards promulgated in textbooks must be adjusted if meaningful intervention research is to be conducted in these [classroom] settings' (p. 3). Admitting that it is unsatisfactory to do research 'by the book', they offer less experienced researchers the benefit of their 'craft knowledge' about how to get as close as possible to meeting the scientific criteria (to ensure internal validity) while remaining 'sufficiently flexible' (to ensure external validity) (p. 4). What follows is a list of problems and their recommendations for resolving them.

Operationalizing the independent variable

The difficulty researchers confront here is that, in order for their research to say anything definitive about the intervention tested, the independent variable has to be operationalized (that is, precisely defined in observable, quantifiable terms). But the more precisely it is defined, they state, the less flexibility it has in real-life classrooms because precise definition obviates teacher autonomy. To avoid this, teachers must be afforded the autonomy to define more flexibly the teaching technique. They recognize that, unfortunately, this solution raises a new problem because when teachers are afforded definitional autonomy, '. . . the intended intervention may only marginally resemble what is actually implemented' (p. 4). Put differently, at the conclusion of the study, the intervention that was supposed to be tested may not be the same one that teachers taught. Although these researchers acknowledge that this proposed solution inevitably presents problems for replication and synthesis of research, they reason that if the researcher is careful enough, this predicament can be addressed by using more precise descriptions of the actual instruction that took place. Nevertheless, how this resolves the issue remains unclear, as does the question of how precise is precise enough.

The gap between conceptualization and execution

No matter how well the teaching technique or intervention is operationalized, difficulty arises in making sure it is taught accordingly. So, in the end, it is hard to know exactly what it was they found to be *effective* or *ineffective*. Having pointed this out, they again recommend more careful description of the way the technique was actually delivered, assuming that (at least theoretically) everything that affects the dependent measure (outcome test) can be sufficiently pinned down.

Left unaddressed are some key questions: How, in the end, does the researcher know whether some crucial aspect of the lesson escaped his or her notice? How can he or she know whether the description was *accurate* or altogether misconstrued?

Measuring the independent variable

Here, the researchers cite further complicating factors related to the independent variable. It is, they explain, expensive to measure how consistently the intervention is implemented, in large part because the researcher has to be present every minute. They also advise that the researcher must be sure the comparison group is not implementing any part of the intervention. Further, this would obviously involve more than one researcher, or the lone researcher would have to be in two places at one time.

It goes without saying that increased research funding is the answer. But one further observation is in order: if this has been a concern for some time, and one must assume it has been, what does this imply about the quality of existing research and the integrity of the current knowledge base that has been so highly extolled?

Implementation fidelity

The question researchers raise here is – have the teachers been adequately 'trained' to deliver the intervention the way researchers intended, that is, does the intervention have 'implementation fidelity'? While they observe that most researchers do not report on this question, they recommend that researchers assess implementation fidelity using more sophisticated rating scales; but, they confess, this solution also has its limitations because with the use of these checklists, 'the more elusive aspects of superior implementation (e.g., the quality of examples used, type of feed-back provided), which are often at the heart of complex interventions, may not be captured by a checklist or rating form' (Gersten, Baker and Lloyd 2000: 6). Curiously, and without an apparent sense of irony, these patrons of 'scientific' research go on to suggest that qualitative research interviews with teachers can be used to assess implementation fidelity.

The nature of the comparison group

A researcher cannot know much about a tested intervention if he or she does not know what it is being compared to. Were the students in the comparison group more, less, or as *capable* as those in the experimental group? Was the teacher in the experimental group more *enthusiastic* or skilled than the teacher in the comparison group? These are difficult questions to pin down scientifically. Having raised these questions, the researchers suggest that the solution is to make sure the experimental and control groups of students and their teachers are equally matched in competence and that the teachers are equally as enthusiastic by counter-balancing teachers across experimental and control conditions. Avoiding relying on a single teacher for the experimental group is also helpful, they note. Finally, teacher effects can also be evaluated 'on a post hoc basis, using typical analysis of variance procedures' (Gersten, Baker and Lloyd 2000: 7). Potential problems with the *post hoc* evaluations (pertaining to their validity, reliability, and so on) are not discussed. How, after all, does one scientifically evaluate such factors as *teacher enthusiasm* without relying on one's own interpretation of enthusiasm?

In discussing the nature of the comparison group, these researchers allude to the problem that researchers in general are not much interested in putting their pet interventions up against a good comparison. They cite Pressley and Harris (1994), who state, 'To the extent that intervention researchers perceive studies to be horse races – that are either won or lost relative to other interventions – constructive communication and collaboration with workers representing alternative intervention is unlikely' (p. 197). There is certainly little doubt that good research depends upon researchers being self-disciplined enough to overcome their competitive impulses. In raising this point, though, they acknowledge (inadvertently one assumes) that the methods of science are incapable of purging researcher intent from the products of their labours.

Selecting, describing and assigning students to conditions

When conducting research on special education populations, how can the researcher know if the population is *sufficiently homogenous*? And how, in practical terms, does he or she procure a large enough sample that is homogenous (a particular problem for those studying students with low-incidence disabilities)? With regard to high-incidence disabilities such as learning disabilities, are all the students in the experimental/control groups really learning disabled (LD) or are some of them simply under-achievers? And if so, to what extent? Is there *comorbidity*? (Do some of them also have attention-deficit hyperactivity disorder, for example)? Should the researcher identify which students have these disabilities, or should he or she assume that the school identified them accurately in the first place? That the above questions are ones which still require deliberation is decidedly troubling; but, having raised them, the seasoned researchers suggest that the solution lies in developing more thorough descriptions of the sample's students, in addition to conducting a secondary analysis involving correlations between the pre-test and post-test measure. Yet, this solution fails to lay to rest the very questions they raise. Again, how thorough must the description be? And how can differences in the ways various researchers would describe their populations be accounted for?

Selection of dependent measures

The more narrowly designed the outcome measure or post test is, the more *valid* it is. Unfortunately, as these researchers point out, narrowly designed outcome measures are also more restrictive. Their answer is to use multiple measures; but, there is a caution: a researcher then needs to be careful to use the appropriate statistical measures to avoid inflating the possibility of finding significant effects. They further specify that using multiple measures also makes it difficult to account for the effect of the differing test formats. Moreover, there is the possibility that different tests of reading, for example, test different constructs of, say, reading comprehension. Readers are told that 'there is an art to selecting and developing measures' (Gersten, Baker and Lloyd: 12). Researchers, they also advise, have to use tests that are 'not heavily biased toward the intervention' (Gersten, Baker and Lloyd: 13). A suggested solution is to use a combination of tests. There is a problem here, though, in that 'experimenter-developed measures frequently do not meet acceptable standards of reliability', while standardized (broad) tests that avoid the pitfall of researchers' outcome measures may be 'insensitive to the effects of the intervention' (Gersten, Baker and Lloyd: 13). Perhaps the clearest message that can be taken from this discussion is that each successive solution offers new problems. If one were to conclude that the problems are irresolvable, would he or she be wrong? Further, if one were to conclude that all social and educational research is by its very nature interpretive, would he or she be wrong?

The above are only some of the dilemmas and problems subjected to rumination. Proposed solutions notwithstanding, the authors cannot escape a certain lack of coherence. They alternate between (a) acknowledging that 'the central problem with experimental designs is that efforts to control, manipulate, and understand a narrow and precisely defined independent variable rarely result in a deep understanding of classroom implementation' (Gersten, Baker and Lloyd: 8), and (b) recommending more flexible (less rigorous/partially qualitative) 'design/formative' experiments that allow for enhanced 'real world' insight. In turn, the results of these more flexible studies should subsequently be subjected to more rigorous experimental research, ostensibly to eliminate the subjective influences of the more flexible studies. What appears to escape their notice is that, in the end, they are left with irresolvable problems. The only way they can get their research methods to work is to exercise complete control, a condition they acknowledge is unachievable.

For years, critics have pointed out the flaws in their conceptual underpinnings and attendant methods (see, for example, Iano 1986; Poplin 1987; Heshusius 1989; Skrtic 1991). It is more than passingly ironic that the above deliberations, expressed in the special education researchers' own words and by their own lights, provide a more resounding critique of special education research orthodoxy than was ever offered by its dissenting critics. Unintentionally, one assumes, their attempt to locate solutions to their research problems essentially expresses the following – we cannot be sure what it is we are testing, the conditions under which it is tested, on whom it is tested, and what it all means in the end. Notwithstanding, they continue to make authoritative scientific knowledge claims even as they attempt to navigate their way through what Cronbach (1975) quite some time ago described as a 'hall of mirrors that extends to infinity' (p. 119).

The above quandaries do not appear to allow for the *scientific* findings that will lead to a robust technology of teaching and learning, much less rival the technological advances that have occurred in many areas of the physical sciences. Put differently, if the sciences that contribute to civil engineering were equally ambiguous, crossing the Severn Bridge or riding the lift to the top of the Sears Tower would be an exciting experience indeed.

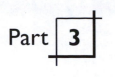

Part **3**

Questions

10

Some questions about evidence-based practice in education

Martyn Hammersley

The movement for evidence-based practice started in medicine in the early 1990s. It has grown in influence since then, and spread across many other fields, including education. This chapter will argue that while some aspects of it warrant support, others do not. Particular issues arise about the role that research is believed to play in relation to practice. One is that evidence from quantitative research, and especially randomized controlled trials, is prioritized, while that from qualitative studies is marginalized. Another problem is that research results are privileged against evidence from other sources. At the very least it is unclear how these results are to be combined with other kinds of evidence in making practical judgements. A third problem concerns the assumption that research can make practice transparently accountable. It will be argued that this is impossible in any full sense, and that the attempt to achieve it may be undesirable. Moreover, this is true even when accountability is interpreted in terms of democratic governance rather than managerialism. It is concluded that the movement for evidence-based practice makes some false and dangerous promises.

The movement for evidence-based practice, for enhanced use of research evidence in the work of the professions, started in medicine in the early 1990s. It has grown in influence there, and has spread across a number of other fields, including education (see Sackett *et al.* 1996; Gray 1997; Trinder 2000a; Davies *et al.* 2000; McSherry *et al.* 2002). Not surprisingly, it has taken a somewhat different form in each area; and has generated diverse reactions. So, while much can be learned from what has happened in medicine, and health care generally, we must also attend to the particular way evidence-based practice has recently been promoted and responded to in education, if we are to make a reasonable appraisal of it.

However, there is a generic problem with the notion of evidence-based practice which needs to be dealt with first. This is that its name is a slogan whose rhetorical effect is to discredit opposition. After all, who would argue that practice should not be based on evidence (Shahar 1997: 110)? In effect, there is an implication built into the phrase 'evidence-based practice' that opposition to it can only be irrational. In the context of medicine, Fowler has commented that the term seems to imply that in the past clinical practice was based 'on a direct communication with God or the tossing of a coin' (Fowler 1995: 838). Nevertheless, critics have managed to counter this implication by denying that practice can be based *solely* on research evidence. And the response, on the part of many advocates, has been to change from 'evidence-based' to 'evidence-*informed*' practice.[1] At face value, this suggests a more reasonable view of the relationship between research and practice. Yet it is at odds with the radical role that is often ascribed to research by the evidence-based practice movement. As a result, even more than before, we have a label that systematically obscures the grounds on which there might be reasonable disagreement with what is proposed.

In political terms, as a way of mobilizing support, the use of such opposition-excluding labels is no doubt a highly effective rhetorical strategy. However, it is a poor basis for rational discussion about the issues that the notion of evidence-based practice raises. Against this background, it is very important to emphasize that one can believe that research evidence is of value for practice without accepting much of what travels under the heading of 'evidence-based' or 'evidence-informed' practice; indeed, while rejecting substantial parts of it. So, let me say to start with that I *do* think that, on the whole and in the long run, practice would be improved if practitioners were more familiar with the results of research. I also accept that there is scope for more directly policy- and practice-relevant educational research. Furthermore, I applaud the emphasis within some accounts of evidence-based practice on the need for professional reflection and judgement about the validity and value of various kinds of evidence in making decisions.[2]

At the same time, there are problems and dangers with the evidence-based practice movement. These result from tendencies built into it, tendencies that have an affinity with other pressures in the current political environment. One is an over-emphasis on the capacity of quantitative research to measure the effectiveness of different types of policy or practice. Little seems to have been learned from the history of evaluation research, which began with an approach that was very similar in character to what is now being advocated on the model of the randomized controlled trial in medicine. The weaknesses of such an approach, particularly in seeking to evaluate social interventions, soon came to be recognized, and a variety of alternative strategies were developed (Norris 1990; Pawson and Tilley 1997). These included qualitative approaches, which were promoted on the grounds that they could take account of the negotiated trajectory of implementation and the diverse interpretations of a policy or programme among stakeholders, as well as of the unanticipated consequences that more focused quantitative evaluations often missed. It seems that here, as in successive recent governments' promotion of the role of educational testing, lessons from the past have been forgotten or ignored.

A second danger that arises from the evidence-based practice movement, which I will spend more time discussing, is the privileging of *research* evidence over evidence from other sources, especially professional experience.

The privileging of research evidence

The central claim of the evidence-based policy movement is that research can make a very significant contribution to improving the current state of policy-making and practice. One aspect of this is that 'evidence' is interpreted in a narrow way. In their introduction to *What Works? Evidence-based Policy and Practice in the Public Services*, Davies *et al.* comment: 'the presumption in this book is that evidence takes the form of "research", broadly defined. That is, evidence comprises the results of "systematic investigation towards increasing the sum of knowledge" ' (Davies *et al.* 2000: 3). In medicine, the movement has been primarily (though even here not exclusively) concerned with encouraging practitioners to make more use of the research evidence that is already available. Initiatives like the Cochrane Collaboration, concerned with producing and disseminating systematic research reviews, are seen as facilitating this; and the training of medical practitioners has, in many institutions, come to place more emphasis than previously on the skills involved in accessing and making use of research findings. By contrast, in other fields, most notably education, greater emphasis has been placed on a need to remedy the alleged absence of good quality research which could feed evidence-based practice (see, for example, Hargreaves 1996).

The idea that research can make a major contribution to improving practice stems to a large extent from the assumption that it is systematic, rigorous and objective in character. This is held to contrast with evidence from professional experience, which is portrayed as unsystematic – reflecting the particular cases with which a practitioner has happened to come into contact – and as lacking in rigour – in that it is not built up in an explicit, methodical way but rather through an at least partially unreflective process of sedimentation. Indeed, sometimes the contrast is presented in a form that can only be described as caricature, as with Cox's reference to teachers often relying on 'tradition, prejudice, dogma, and ideology' (quoted in Hargreaves 1996: 7–8).[3] Such caricature complements the already-mentioned rhetorical sleight of hand built into the very name of the evidence-based practice movement.

Moreover, this view of the role of research fits with an Enlightenment-inspired political philosophy in which evidence-based practice is seen as opposing the 'forces of conservatism' in the public sector, forces which are taken to represent entrenched interests. For example, Oakley claims that the medical profession, along with the pharmaceutical industry, have 'a vested interest in women's ill-health – in defining women as sick when they may not be, and in prescribing medical remedies when they may not be needed' (Oakley 2000: 51). These interests are seen as disguised and protected by the claim of professionals to a kind of expertise which cannot be communicated or shared with lay people, but which instead demands professional autonomy and public trust.[4]

In this chapter I will argue that we need to look much more soberly both at the features of research-based knowledge compared to those of knowledge deriving from practical experience, and at how research findings relate to professional practice.

The nature of research-based knowledge

Let me begin with what can be currently said about the character of research-based knowledge and its relationship to practice.[5] It is important to remember that research knowledge is always fallible, even if it is more likely to be valid than knowledge from other sources. Thus, we are not faced with a contrast between Knowledge with a capital K, whose epistemic status is certain, and mere opinion, whose validity is zero.[6] Furthermore, research knowledge usually takes the form of generalizations of one sort or another, and interpreting the implications of these for dealing with particular cases is rarely straightforward. A final point is that factual knowledge is never a sufficient determinant of good practice, in education or in any other field. One reason for this is that it cannot determine what the ends of good practice should be; or even, on its own, what are and are not appropriate means. Furthermore, the effectiveness of any practical action usually depends not just on *what* is done but also on *how* it is done and *when*. Skill and timing can be important. In other words, there are substantial limitations on what research can offer to policy-making and practice. This is not to suggest that it can offer nothing, but rather to caution against excessive claims about its contribution.[7]

The nature of professional practice

Built into some advocacy of evidence-based practice is not just an exaggerated estimate of the practical contribution that research can provide but also a misleading conception of the nature of professional practice. Very often, it is assumed that the latter should take the form of specifying goals (or 'targets') explicitly, selecting strategies for achieving them on the basis of objective evidence about their effectiveness, and then measuring outcomes in order to assess their degree of success (thereby providing the knowledge required for improving future performance).

This model is not wholly inaccurate, but it is defective in important respects. Forms of practice will vary in the degree to which they can usefully be made to approximate this linear, rational model.[8] And it probably does not fit any sort of professional activity closely. Reasons for this include: that such activity usually involves multiple goals which have to be pursued more or less simultaneously; that these goals cannot be operationalized fully in a way that avoids calling on professional judgement; that the same action has multiple consequences, some desirable and others less so, these being differentially distributed across clients; that there is frequently uncertainty surrounding the likely consequences of many strategies, even in a field like medicine where a great deal of clinical research is carried out; and that the situations being faced by practical actors frequently undergo change, requiring continual adaptation. As a result of these features, there can often be reasonable disagreement about what would be an improvement and about what sorts of improvement are to be preferred, as well as about how these can best be achieved. Moreover, sometimes it will simply not be sensible to engage in elaborate explication of goals, to consider *all* possible alternatives, to engage in an extensive search for information about the relative effectiveness of various strategies as against relying on judgements based on experience about this, or to try to *measure* outcomes. The linear rational model tends to underplay the extent to which in many circumstances the only reasonable option is trial and error, or even 'muddling through' (Lindblom 1979). Much depends on how costly and remediable the consequences are.

In this context, we should note that the very phrase 'what works', which the evidence-based practice movement sees as the proper focus for much educational research, implies a view of practice as technical: as open to 'objective' assessment in terms of what is and is not effective, or what is more and what is less effective. I would not want to deny that effectiveness, and even efficiency, are relevant considerations in professional practice. But the information necessary to judge them in the 'objective' way proposed will often not be available – even in principle, not just in terms of the costs involved in gaining it. And any such assessment cannot be separated from value judgements about desirable ends and appropriate means; not without missing a great deal that is important.

Furthermore, there is a significant difference between medicine and education in terms of the nature of professional practice. For whatever reason, much medicine is closer to the technical end of the spectrum, in the sense that there is less diversity in the goals and other considerations treated as relevant; and thereby in evaluative criteria. In addition, there seems to be more scope for identifying *relatively* simple causal relationships between treatment and outcome. Of course, it is possible to exaggerate these differences. In response to presentation of this argument on a previous occasion, Davies has claimed that 'medicine and health care [. . .] face very similar, if not identical, problems of complexity, context-specificity, measurement, and causation' to education (Davies 1999: 112). I do not deny that there are such problems in medicine; and that in some areas, for example mental health, they are very similar in scale and character to those faced in much education. What we are dealing with here is only a general difference of degree; but it is still a substantial and significant difference.

In short, in my view research usually cannot supply what the notion of evidence-based practice demands of it – specific and highly reliable answers to questions about what 'works' and what does not – and professional practice cannot for the most part be *governed* by research findings – because it necessarily relies on multiple values, tacit judgement, local knowledge, and skills. Moreover, this is especially true in the field of education. When pressed, advocates of evidence-based practice often concede one or other, or both, of these points. Yet those points undermine the claim that improved research, or a reformed version of professional practice which gives more attention to research findings, will lead to a sharp improvement in educational performance and outcomes.

The usability of research findings

It is also important to address the question of *how* research findings are to be used by policy-makers and practitioners. Let me mention two problems here. First, there is the issue of the transmission of research findings to these audiences. Some accounts of evidence-based practice imply that policy-makers and practitioners are expected to read all relevant research studies, and to engage in methodological assessment of them, before deciding what to do in each case they face. Thus, we have various books produced to aid medical practitioners in assessing research (see, for example, Crombie 1996 and Greenhalgh 1997). However, as a general model for accessing research information, this is simply unrealistic: medical practitioners are unlikely to have the necessary time and, often, the appropriate skills; and the same is true of teachers.

The alternative suggested by many advocates of evidence-based practice is the production of systematic reviews of research relevant to decisions faced by policy-makers and practitioners (see Davies 2000a). And this proposal certainly has the advantage that reliance is not placed on single studies, which often produce erroneous conclusions. However, reviewing multiple studies and condensing these into a set of practical conclusions is by no means a straightforward matter; nor is *using* such summaries.

The concept of systematic review shares some common elements with the notion of evidence-based practice. It portrays the task of reviewing the literature as reducible to explicit procedures that can be replicated; just as advocates of evidence-based practice see professional work as properly governed by explicit rules based on research evidence. Moreover, here too, questionable assumptions are made about the nature of research, and about the task involved; ones which have long been subjected to criticism as 'positivist'. It is not necessary to doubt the value of quantitative research, or even to believe that positivism was wholly mistaken, to recognize that these criticisms have some force and cannot be simply ignored. Yet the concept of systematic review does not take account of them. For example, it portrays the task of assessing the validity of research findings as if this could be done properly simply by applying explicit and standard criteria relating to research design. But validity assessment cannot rely entirely on information about research design. Much depends on the nature of the knowledge claims made, and assessment of them always relies on substantive knowledge as well as on specifically methodological considerations (see Hammersley 1998). The result of this mistaken approach to validity assessment is that systematic reviews are likely to exclude or downplay some kinds of study that may be illuminating, notably qualitative work, while giving weight to other studies whose findings are open to serious question (see Hammersley 2002a).

An illustration of the attitude underlying the notion of systematic review, and the evidence-based practice movement generally, is Oakley's recent adoption of what can only be described as a form of naive positivism.[9] This is surprising because she has been identified in the past as advocating qualitative methods, largely on feminist grounds. However, she is now a strong advocate of randomized controlled trials. She insists that she has never promoted qualitative method exclusively, and that she does not advocate quantitative method exclusively now. Nevertheless, in some parts of her recent book, *Experiments in Knowing*, she evidences a dismissal of qualitative work that is the obverse of her over-enthusiastic support for quasi-experimental research design. For example, she claims that the debate over Freeman's critique of Mead's anthropological study of Samoa is best read as an example of the 'untrustworthiness' of 'uncontrolled findings' (Oakley 2000: 57). The implication of this seems to be that all 'uncontrolled' findings are untrustworthy; a view that does not follow from Freeman's work and was not his position. Later she comments: 'Recent attitudes to evaluation in some quarters have been marked by a retreat into more "naturalistic" and theory-driven approaches to public policy evaluation, but these serve the interests of academic careers more than they promote the goals of either an emancipatory social science or an informed evidence base for social and policy interventions' (Oakley 2000: 323). Here we have dismissal of the views of those who disagree with her via the attribution of ulterior motives, and in the form of assertion rather than appeal to evidence. At one point she claims that anything else but randomized, controlled trials 'is a "disservice to vulnerable people" . . .' (Oakley 2000: 318; quoting Macdonald 1996: 21).[10]

A more general problem about how research can be used by practitioners concerns the funnelling process through which research findings need to be refined into summary statements that policy-makers and practitioners will have time to read. This almost always involves the paring away of most qualifications and methodological information. While such summaries may be a very useful representational device for those who have already read the whole review, or the whole study, they may be obscure or misleading for those who have not done this. In some cases, the summary may be difficult to understand without background information. This is true of all kinds of research review. For example, one of the key points of Gillborn and Gipps's narrative review of the educational achievements of ethnic minority children was that ' "colour-blind" policies have failed', but it seems clear that some audiences found this conclusion difficult to interpret (Gillborn and Gipps 1996: 80).[11] Alternatively, summaries of research findings in reviews may *seem* easily interpretable, but the interpretation given may be some distance from that intended; and/or the validity of the findings may be dismissed at face value. For example, a study which suggests that there is no positive, linear correlation between amount of homework done and level of pupil achievement may be interpreted as saying that homework should be abolished or is not important.[12] This stems from the fact that the interpretative frameworks within which policy-makers and practitioners approach research findings are often rather different from that of researchers; in particular these audiences are likely to be much more directly concerned with practical or political implications. It is also not uncommon for summary findings to be seen by policy-makers or practitioners as trivial, in the sense of repeating what is already known, because the actual contribution to current knowledge is only clear against the background of what can currently be taken to be known for research purposes (this, necessarily, being different from what policy-makers and practitioners take to be already well-established: see Hammersley 2002b: chapter 3).

This raises the issue of how research findings are to be related to what policy-makers and practitioners think they already know. This problem can be illustrated by David Blunkett's response to research findings about homework (see Note 12). He dismissed these on the grounds that they ran counter to his beliefs. He was wrong to dismiss them, and to believe that research which produces such findings must be unsound. However, he would not have been wrong to have approached those findings (like any others, especially those from a single study) with caution. And there is a genuine problem for practitioners about how to weigh contradictory evidence, especially when it has been produced in different ways. In his argument for evidence-based practice, Davies comments: 'There is no question of evidence replacing clinical judgement or experience, but of uniting these two dimensions of knowledge to provide a sound basis for action' (Davies 1999: 111). Yet conflicting evidence from different sources cannot be 'united' in any simple sense.[13] And evidence from professional experience cannot be assessed in the same way as research evidence; since the process by which it was produced is not documented. It is difficult to see what one can do, when faced with contradictory evidence from research and practical experience, other than either trust one's instincts, which is the Blunkett strategy, or assume that research evidence is always sounder than that from experience, which is what advocates of evidence-based practice sometimes seem to imply. Neither approach is satisfactory. What is perhaps required is that each source of evidence be subjected to internal scrutiny in its own terms: reflection on the sources, relations, and functions of particular beliefs, in the case of professional experience; and methodological assessment in the case of research. However, this is a time-consuming process; and it by no means guarantees that the result will be a satisfactory resolution of any contradiction between the two. Moreover, any resolution will itself necessarily rely on judgement that cannot be fully explicated.[14]

Up to now, I have looked at the role of research in relation to policy-making and practice in rather abstract terms, but it is important to locate the evidence-based practice movement, and reactions to it, in the current political context. This will be attempted in the next section.

Evidence-based practice and 'transparency'

The evidence-based practice movement is closely related to influential demands for 'transparent' accountability that are characteristic of what has come to be called managerialism, or the 'new public management' (Pollitt 1990; Ferlie *et al.* 1996; Clarke and Newman 1997; Mayne and Zapico-Goni 1997; Power 1997). As Davies *et al.* note: 'In contrast to the preceding culture of largely judgement-based professional practice, there has arisen the important notion of evidence-based practice as a means of ensuring that what is being done is worthwhile and that it is being done in the best possible way' (Davies *et al.* 2000: 2). Thus, it is assumed that research can 'ensure' that the best is being done; both by providing information about 'what works', and by documenting whether practitioners are actually following 'best practice'.[15] Moreover, research is believed to be capable of doing this because it is objective and explicit; what it provides is open to public scrutiny, in a way that professional experience and judgement are not.

The demand for 'transparent' accountability seems to have arisen from two sources, though my account of these here is rather speculative. The first source lies in the field of commerce and industry, and concerns the emergence of 'generic management'.[16] Where, in the first half of the twentieth century, managers had often worked all of their careers in a single sector, frequently moving up to managerial positions from within an individual firm, in the second half of the century there was increasing mobility of managers across sectors, and a growing tendency to define 'management' in terms of generic rather than sector-specific knowledge and skills.[17] Along with growth in the average size of firms (see Devine et al. 1985: 85–90), often as a result of mergers and take-overs, this led to the problem of how senior managers were to assess the performance of different parts of their organizations. The solution proposed was to find objective indicators of performance, in other words indicators that did not rely on direct observation of the work being done and whose interpretation did not demand detailed knowledge of what that work entailed. Over the course of the 1960s, 1970s and 1980s this reliance on performance indicators spread to the public sector (initially to the publicly owned utilities, for example in the energy field, later to health and education), on the back of arguments that this sector was inefficient by comparison with private enterprise.[18]

An equally important stimulus to the 'new public management', however, was recognition by the political Left of the force, and electoral appeal, of the argument that citizens had a right to know that their taxes were being well spent. Public accountability of this kind now came to be seen as central to democracy, on the Left as well as on the Right. But, of course, most citizens were in exactly the same position as the generic manager, in that they did not have direct knowledge of what was involved in the work of public sector agencies. What they did have was some differentiated experience as clients of those organizations; and access to others' anecdotes about failures in service, which were elaborated by media campaigns against the 'inefficiency' of the public sector. Here, too, the solution proposed was objective performance indicators; indicators that would allow politicians and the general public to judge what was happening and whether it could be improved. Indeed, the new public management portrayed government ministers as managers of the public sector, and therefore as responsible for monitoring performance and intervening to improve it. Furthermore, in the context of the New Labour Government, politicians began to suggest that their *own* performance should be judged by whether promised improvements in the work of public sector organizations took place, as measured by performance indicators; an extension of transparent accountability encouraged by the media, for whom the results of such indicators constituted a useful source of news.[19]

More generally, criticism of the public sector for failing to 'deliver' a satisfactory level of service, and portrayal of it as inferior to the private sector, arose out of widespread attacks, in the second half of the twentieth century, on professionalism and on the role of the state. Once again, these came from both sides of the political spectrum, and also from social scientists.[20] The claim of professional occupations to be governed by a service ethic, which justified their having autonomy in performing their work, was challenged on the grounds that they had misused this autonomy to serve their own interests. There was some evidence for this; but the charge also reflected a change in the prevalent vocabulary of motives, whereby any claim to motives other than self-interest was subjected not just to suspicion but to disbelief. From the Right, in particular, it was insisted that people would only do what was in the general interest if circumstances were arranged in such a way that it was in their self-interest to do it. The market was regarded as the model in this respect; a fact which fuelled not just privatization but also the application of 'market discipline' within the public sector.

The assumption was that markets provide consumers with all the knowledge they need in order to assess the relative value of the goods on offer. As a result, consumers' purchasing decisions reward efficiency and punish inefficiency. However, to a large extent, this is simply a myth. It does not even hold true where conditions of perfect competition are approximated, a situation which is very rare. This is because consumers do not usually have easy access to *all* of the information they would need to judge effectively the value of what is on offer. Reliable and comparable information about the relative quality of different products, even different products from the same supplier, is often not available.[21] Moreover, most consumers would probably not have the background knowledge or the time necessary to make use of that information were it available. In fact, the tendency is for consumers to rely heavily on one kind of information, that which is most easily accessible and open to assessment – price. And this tendency distorts the production process, since it often leads to the lowering costs being given priority over ensuring quality.[22]

Of course, the attempt to introduce transparent accountability into the public sector is not in any simple sense a process of marketization. Instead, efforts are made directly to measure the quality of services; and not so much as a basis for consumer decision making (though this is sometimes the case, as with school league tables) but so as to allow the public to judge whether the public services are meeting satisfactory standards of performance and providing 'value for money'. However, for the reasons explained in the previous section, these performance indicators do not usually measure what is important effectively; and, indeed, advocates of transparent accountability will often acknowledge this, while insisting that they provide the best evidence available. Yet, ironically, the severe problems associated with such performance indicators were demonstrated long ago in the attempts of Eastern European governments to control centrally the production of goods and the provision of services. Here, even attempts to specify industrial production targets and measure performance for relatively simple goods failed (Nove 1980: chapter 4).[23]

Moreover, this parallel shows that efforts to render people accountable in terms of performance indicators distort the production process at least as much as does the emphasis on lowering cost and price which is characteristic of the private sector. This is because it encourages, indeed to a large extent forces, individual practitioners to adopt an instrumental orientation in which scoring highly on the indicators becomes more important than doing a good job in terms of their own judgement. Indeed, they may even lose the confidence to exercise such judgement.

Where the focus is professional services the problems are especially severe, because of the level of specialized expertise and knowledge on which these services rely. Furthermore, what they involve is not a determinate process. For example, even the best surgeons do not succeed in all cases; and, to the degree that they deal with more difficult cases than their colleagues, their failure rates may be relatively high. Similarly, schools vary considerably in how amenable their pupils are to the sort of education that schools are required to offer, and this variation cannot be easily measured. In this context, it is not just a matter of judging a product or service in terms of whether it meets requirements, or meets requirements better than others – which is hard enough – but judging whether the best that could have been done has been done. In the field of education this task is further complicated by the fact that teachers deal with children in batches, not on a one-by-one basis. So, here, judgement has to be according to whether what was done was the best for all concerned, which may involve trading benefits for some against costs for others.

The application of transparent accountability to medicine, education and other areas has been premised on the assumption that explicit information can be provided about all the factors relevant to judging the quality of professional performance in these fields. And research is seen as playing a key role in this: the belief is that it can show what works and what does not work, thereby providing a standard against which the practice of professionals can be assessed. Moreover, it is assumed that research is itself transparent, that it simply documents how things are in an objective fashion. However, for reasons already explained, research is unable to play this role. Furthermore, efforts to make it play such a role seem likely to have undesirable consequences. In relation to practice, the appeal to research findings on all significant issues may undermine the value of practical experience and common sense, and thus erode practitioners' confidence in their own judgements. While it is sometimes claimed that evidence-based practice represents an enhanced professionalism, its devaluing of professional experience and judgement relative to accountability in terms of externally produced research findings seems likely to lead to a weakening of professionalism, in most senses of that term. Equally important, the attempt to make research serve this function has the effects of privileging practical against academic or scientific research, and of eroding the distinction between research and the work of management consultancy, audit and inspection agencies.[24]

There is no doubt that evaluations of professional practice can be valuable; and that some professional practice, in all fields, is poorer than it could be, for all manner of reasons. However, not only is the notion of transparent accountability a myth, but it relies on a version of perfectionism which implies that failures and risks can be avoided, or at least can be progressively reduced in number and seriousness. So, it is assumed that performance can and should *always* be further improved; and that measures can be taken to ensure that any failures that have occurred in the past do not recur in the future. In promising this, transparent accountability encourages a climate in which clients demand that their needs and wants be fully met, while practitioners are increasingly concerned simply with protecting themselves from likely criticism (not to mention possible legal action). And, given that the indicators do not measure performance effectively, especially not across the whole range of each profession's activities, this could worsen rather than improve the quality of performance.

Advocates of evidence-based practice often deny that there is any link between this and attempts to introduce 'transparent accountability' into the public sector. Yet the current government sees each as serving the other, and is acting on that basis in seeking to bring about 'reform'. It views research as playing a major role in this – hence the current attempt to bring educational research under increased central control, co-ordinating and concentrating funding on issues directly relevant to policy and practice (see NERF 2000b; and Hodkinson 2001).

Conclusion

In this chapter I have argued that while few would disagree that professional practice could be improved if practitioners had better access to the products of a large body of relevant, good-quality research, the evidence-based practice movement is not likely to lead to a dramatic improvement in educational performance. In fact, my argument suggests that it could even produce a reduction in the quality of service. The reasons for this lie in misconceptions about the nature of both research and practice which are built into the assumptions on which it operates. Its advocates have too much confidence in the validity of research findings, especially those coming from research of specific kinds; both in abstract terms and in comparison with knowledge deriving from professional experience. And they assume that research could play a much more direct role in relation to practice than it usually can. They tend to treat practice as the *application* of research-based knowledge, neglecting the extent to which it necessarily involves uncertain judgement. Moreover, there are some serious difficulties involved in the use of research evidence by practitioners. One relates to problems in interpreting this evidence without background knowledge about the studies from which it arose. Another concerns the question of how contradictions between research evidence and professional experience are to be resolved.

Finally, I pointed to the close contemporary association between the evidence-based practice movement and the 'new public management', with its efforts to make the public sector transparently accountable and thereby to improve its performance substantially. I argued that this notion of accountability is built on a mythology of the market that does not accurately capture how markets work, and that is peculiarly inappropriate to the case of providing services that necessarily rely on a good deal of specialized expertise. I suggested that the search for transparent account-ability is a futile enterprise, and one which is likely to have negative consequences for both professional practice and research. It offers a false hope of dramatic improvement in quality, while at the same time under-mining the conditions necessary for professionalism to flourish. The entanglement of the movement for evidence-based practice with these developments means that it should be treated with the greatest caution.

Notes

1 Davies *et al.* have added two even weaker formulations: 'evidence-influenced' and 'evidence-aware' practice (Davies *et al.* 2000: 11).
2 An example of such an account is Sackett *et al.* 1997.
3 Other examples include Oakley's claim that the generalizations of 'well-intentioned and skilful doctors [. . .] may be fanciful rather than factual . . .' Indeed, she goes so far as to refer to 'the largely unscientific character of modern medicine', appealing to Illich's notion of 'medical nemesis' (Oakley 2000: 17). Another caricature is Greehalgh's contrast between evidence-based decision-making and 'decision-making by anecdote' (Greenhalgh 1997: 4).

And Evans and Benefield, advocating systematic reviews in the field of education, suggest that previously even when health practitioners used research
evidence they relied on 'idiosyncratic interpretations of idiosyncratic selec-
tions of the available evidence (rather than objective interpretation of all the
evidence) (Evans and Benefield 2001: 531).

4 Interestingly, Oakley extends this argument to researchers, claiming that
'most research proceeds from the interests of researchers because researchers
generally have more to gain from the research process: publications, external
research grant income, points in academic research exercises'. She excepts
experimental research from this charge, on the grounds that it is 'in a somewhat special category, in that its purpose is to arbitrate between competing
interventions, and thus to work towards a solution which is as much (if not
more) in the interests of the researched as of the researchers' (Oakley 2000:
285). Here, aside from special pleading, there are signs of the anti-academic
attitude that underlies much recent promotion of the role of research in relation to policy-making and practice. An even more influential exponent of
this was the previous Secretary of State for Education, David Blunkett: see
Blunkett 2000; and, for a discussion, Hammersley (2000).

5 For more extended discussion, see Hammersley (2002b).

6 Cochrane often seemed to come close to this view in his advocacy of evidence-
based practice in medicine: see Cochrane (1972: 30). For a useful discussion of
problems that have arisen even where randomized controlled trial methodology has been extensively applied, from a perspective that is sympathetic to
the movement, see Hampton (1997).

7 It is also important to avoid too *narrow* an interpretation of that contribution,
see Hammersley (1997).

8 In many respects, this model amounts to taking a positivist conception of
research as the pattern for all forms of rational action. This perhaps explains
why evidence-based practice is sometimes closely related to the idea that professionals should themselves engage in research (see, for example, Hargreaves
1996 and 1999a). This amounts to another version of what I have referred to
elsewhere as researcher imperialism, see Hammersley (1993).

9 Oakley is director of the of the Evidence for Policy and Practice Information
Co-ordinating Centre (EPPI-Centre), which has been given responsibility
for developing systematic reviews in education. See its website: http://
eppi.ioe.ac.uk/

10 Some recent accounts of the role of research in relation to evidence-based
education are more sympathetic to qualitative research: see Davies (1999) and
Fitzgibbon (2000). However, it is striking that Fitzgibbon devotes only two
paragraphs of her article to discussing it, giving by far the greatest attention to
quantitative research. And while Davies (2000b) seeks 'to redress any such
demeaning of qualitative research and evidence' (p. 292), he fails to recognize
the sharp conflict between the orientation of some kinds of qualitative work
and quantitative method; and the difficult questions that even more moderate
versions of a qualitative approach raise for some of the fundamental assumptions of evidence-based practice; on which see Hammersley (2002: chapter 4).
For an account which takes more account of the distinctiveness of a qualitative
approach, see Popay *et al.* (1998).

11 For a discussion of how this review was represented in the mass media in diverse ways, see Hammersley (2003).

12 I am referring here to the response of a previous Secretary of State for Education, David Blunkett, to the findings of one study of the relationship between homework and achievement; in which he accused the researchers of double standards, of being unwilling to extend to other children the benefits their own children have had. See S. Farrow 'Insulted by Blunkett', *The Guardian*, Wednesday 21 July, 1999. In his speech to the CBI Blunkett also included the following comment: 'Some researchers are so obsessed with "critique", so out of touch with reality that they churn out findings which no one with the slightest common sense could take seriously' (Blunkett 1999, quoted in Pring 2000: 76). Mr Blunkett's response was similar to research which suggested that eviction laws were being applied over-zealously by some local authorities. His comment was: 'If this is what our money is going on, it is time for a review of the funding of social research', BBC News web page for 20 November 2000. His criticism of these two studies was repeated in his speech to the ESRC: Blunkett (2000).

13 In the context of evidence-based medicine, Sackett *et al.* talk of 'integrating individual clinical expertise with the best available external evidence from systematic research' (Sackett *et al.* 1996: 72). But 'integrating' is no better than 'uniting': it is a fudge which covers up a serious problem.

14 For the argument that even natural scientific research cannot be reduced to explicit procedures, see Polanyi (1959 and 1966).

15 This is an example of what Oakeshott referred to as 'the politics of perfection' Oakeshott (1962: 5–6).

16 For the background to this development, see Burnham (1941), and Chandler (1977 and 1990).

17 This was closely associated with the rise of management education, and of the accounting profession. The whole process was, of course, simply a further stage in the development of what Marris calls 'managerial' capitalism, initiated by the invention of the public, joint-stock, limited liability company in the late nineteenth century (see Marris 1971).

18 As far as one can tell, the arguments for the superiority of the private sector rested on economic theory and anecdotes about 'over-manning', 'bureaucracy', and so on in the public sector; rather than on objective empirical evidence.

19 Performance indicator results have many of the key characteristics of newsworthiness: they are about the government, they offer apparently clear-cut and authoritative findings, and they often suggest serious failings. For a rather different, but not incompatible, account of the developments I have sketched here, see Aucoin (1990). Aucoin stresses the role of public choice theory and managerialism, portraying them both as anti-bureaucratic, and argues that there are tensions between the two, especially in relation to centralization/decentralization and control/delegation.

20 One aspect of this was criticism of state regulation of industry. For an account of this in the United States, and of the pendulum swings towards and then away from regulation over the course of the twentieth century, see Vietor (1994: 312 and *passim*).

21 This was why the Consumers' Association began to publish *Which?* magazine: see Sargant (1995: 190–2). However, even that publication cannot provide everything one would need to know in order to make the best choice of many kinds of product. The sheer number and diversity of products is too large, and subject to too frequent change.

22 It is not clear that quality is given emphasis even where fashion, technical hype, or snobbery will support relatively high prices.

23 Nove writes that in the Soviet Union 'many of the functions of government ministers and senior party officials can be regarded as a form of senior management, in some respects analogous to those of the senior directors of a big Western corporation' (Nove 1980: 88). He continues: 'how can the centre issue instructions in a form which does not give rise to ambiguities and contradictions? How can it encourage initiative, new techniques, the flow of desired and undistorted information? By what standards and in what way can we evaluate performance? Around these issues one finds grouped many of the most serious weaknesses of Soviet micro-economics. This is where many things go wrong' (Nove 1980: 89). Indeed it is, and not just in the old Soviet Union!

24 Thus, in *What Works?* Davies *et al.* comment that: '[. . .] the majority of research evidence considered in this text is the output from more formal and systematic enquiries, generated by government departments, research institutes, universities, charitable foundations, consultancy organisations, and a variety of agencies and intermediaries such as the Audit Commission, or Office for Standards in Education (Ofsted)' (Davies *et al.* 2000: 3). For a useful discussion of the relationship between research and Ofsted inspection, see Smith (2000).

The relationship between research, policy and practice
Phil Hodkinson and John K. Smith

Introduction

In the arena of learning and teaching/training, the relationship between research, policy and practice is currently high profile. At UK government level, David Blunkett, the Secretary of State for Education and Employment in 2000, gave a widely reported speech to the Economic and Social Research Council (ESRC) calling for better research that could help improve policy and practice (Blunkett 2000). The ESRC's Teaching and Learning Research Programme (TLRP) at around the same time received a far larger budget than any previous research programme involving learning, and has the explicit goal of improving learning quality.

However, despite interest and willingness from many quarters, there is confusion and/or disagreement about what sort of relationship is possible or advisable between research, policy and practice. The dominant message is 'answerism' (Avis *et al.* 1996). That is, research should produce findings that help us to do things better/more efficiently/more effectively. This often assumes a linear relationship between research and its users. The essence of the argument is that

(i) we need high-quality, 'safe' research that is relevant to the needs of potential research users;
(ii) we then need a better process to inform the users of what the research findings are (Hillage *et al.* 1998; and
(iii) mechanisms to help them 'transform' the findings, in ways that will embed them into the users' own beliefs and practices.

(Desforges 2000a)

This is sometimes paralleled by a second rather different track, currently more prominent with regard to schools and Further Education (FE): the engagement of practitioners as researchers themselves, so that they can use their own research findings, and those of their peers, to improve the quality of their practice. This has roots in the long-established tradition of action research (Stenhouse 1975; Carr and Kemmis 1986; Elliott 1991). It can be seen, for example, in the scheme by the Teacher Training Agency (TTA) to fund small-scale research by practising teachers, which was then disseminated to the profession as a whole. Both the TTA and the TLRP are attempting to combine both approaches: 'The intention is . . . to conduct research to solve immediate practical problems whilst at the same time obtaining basic understanding of fundamental processes, an understanding necessary to the rapid, practical generalisation of solutions to similar problems' (Desforges 2000b: 12).

Despite their obvious popularity, there are fundamental problems with the former approach, and with the supposedly unproblematic combination of the two. In this paper, we explore some of these problems, and then advance a rather different way of understanding the potential value of research to policy and policy-makers, and to practice and practitioners. The problems can be examined by focusing upon three areas: the nature of research and knowledge; its relationship with policy; and its relationship with practice. We spend rather more time on the first, because it is fundamental to understanding the others.

Research, knowledge and endemic uncertainty

A conventional, deeply embedded view of research is that if it is carried out correctly, it can get closer to truth than other forms of knowledge development. Rigorous, objective research practices can separate fact from value, and establish what is real from what is subjectively believed. Such 'safe' knowledge is always provisional, in the sense that it can always be superseded by a better understanding or a superior grasp of truth, but it is inherently superior to other means of improving knowledge. In many ways, the ideal form of research, from this perspective, is the controlled experiment (Oakley 2000). Here, all variables are held constant except the one under investigation. Ideally, this one variable is deliberately changed, in two exactly parallel situations as, for example, when a new medical drug is tested against a placebo. If a difference is noted, rigorous tests are conducted to minimize the chances that it is coincidental. Laboratory experiments are repeated, to ensure the results always turn out in the same ways. When involving human populations, inferential statistics are used to determine the probability of a coincidental result. This is the view of research that lies at the heart of the evidence-informed practice movement, and of the TLRP.

Over the last 30 years in particular, this view of research, and knowledge, has come under attack in three areas. They are:

(i) philosophical questioning of pure objectivity and the separation of researcher as subject from the object under investigation;
(ii) arguments that knowledge is increasingly produced outside academe in everyday practices; and
(iii) in the argument that social life is inherently complex and reflexive, and understanding is to be found in the ways numerous variables interact with and reconstitute each other.

We examine each of these, in turn.

Epistemological uncertainty

The names of those associated with what is often called post-empiricism, or the interpretive turn in the philosophy of science and social science, are well known: Hanson (1958), Winch (1958), Kuhn (1962), Rorty (1979), Taylor (1980), Putnam (1981) and Bernstein (1983) are a few among many. The most crucial idea advanced by these people was that there was no possibility of theory-free knowledge or theory-free observation. No matter how the point was argued, all agreed that observers/researchers were not neutral spectators of the world, but participants in that world. This was the core idea that led, for example, Kuhn to talk about Gestalt switches in the natural sciences, Giddens (1976) to advance the idea of the double hermeneutic, Nagel (1986) to dismiss the possibility of a view from nowhere, Goodman (1978) to tell us about ways of world making and Winch, writing directly about social inquiry, to say that the concepts central to scientific prediction are fundamentally at odds with the concepts important to our understanding of social life.

For the last 30 and more years, researchers have attempted to come to terms with the implications of this idea of no theory-free knowledge for our understanding of the nature, purposes and possibilities of social research. This era has produced numerous arguments and variations on arguments and variations on variations on arguments about who we are and what we do as researchers. These arguments and variations have marched behind numerous banners – transcendental realism, scientific realism, constructivism, interpretivism, hermeneutics, pragmatism, fallibilism, critical theory, postmodernism, and on and on. In all this intellectual turmoil, two distinctive approaches can be discerned: neorealists and relativists.

The neorealists begin with a commitment to the idea of a real world out there independent of our interest in, or knowledge of, it. This is a reality that can be known, at least in principle, as it really is. Neorealists also accept, as did their empiricist predecessors, that the metaphors of finding and discovering are appropriate, even essential, to the research process. Where they part company from their predecessors is that the neorealists attempt to combine their ontological realism with an epistemological fallibilism. That is, they have given up on the hope for certitude, a direct correspondence theory of truth, and accept that knowledge, at least in part, is socially constructed. Post-empiricism has left them no choice but to accept that any claim to knowledge must take into account the perspective of the person making the claim. However, for many neorealists, an independently existing social and educational reality, accessible through our inquiries, sets limits upon what can be accepted as warranted, plausible, credible, and so on.

Relativists, of whatever disposition, have no quarrel with the assumption that there is reality out there, certainly a physical one, that is independent of our interest in, or knowledge of, it. However, they argue that this assumption cannot do the work desired of it by neorealists, because, as even the neorealists accept, we can never know if we have accurately depicted that reality. Put differently, if one accepts that there is no theory-free observation and continues to assume that reality can validate our interpretations, then one must be able to specify, in the case of any claim to knowledge, where theory-laden observation leaves off and reality begins. For relativists the assumption about an independent social and educational reality is all well and good, it is just that it is an assumption that cannot be cashed in, in order to discriminate among differing interpretations of the motivations, intentions, experiences, actions, and purposes of people – in the workplace or elsewhere.

For relativists, the metaphors of discovery and finding must give way to the metaphors of constructing and making. In shifting these metaphors, they have found one of their most difficult tasks is to answer the charge that they are relativists of an 'anything goes' variety. Their critics routinely charge that once one abandons a serious conception of the real as the test for truth, the only possibility is the void of all things equal. The relativists' response to this criticism, taking their cue from Rorty (1985) and Gadamer (1995) among others, is to argue that they are not anti-foundationalists, but rather nonfoundationalists. For them nonfoundationalism means nothing more than that we are finite human beings who must learn to live with uncertainty and contingency and forgo the hope that something can be called upon, something that stands beyond interpretation, that will allow us to transcend our human finitude.

This issue of the definition of relativism warrants further comment because it is the point at which many discussions between researchers go past each other. For the critics of relativism, the term is almost always defined as anything goes, everything is equal, or that no differentiated judgements can be made. This is to be feared because, the critics believe, such a stance would mean the end of rationality, reason, and even research itself. For relativists, however, the term *relativism* only refers to our inescapable condition of human finitude and does not at all imply that anyone considers all things equal. We all make judgements and prefer some things to other things and will continue to do so for as far as anyone can foresee. It is, in fact, impossible to imagine any serious concept of personhood in the absence of judgement and preference. The only point relativists make here is that we do not have access to an extra-linguistic reality, to brute facts or givens, that would allow us to ground our judgements and thereby sort out our differences.

In an excellent book on criteria, Chisholm (1973) paraphrased Montaigne as follows:

> To know whether things are as they seem to be, we must have a procedure for distinguishing appearances that are true from appearances that are false. But to know whether our procedure is a good procedure, we have to know whether it really succeeds in distinguishing appearances that are true from appearances that are false, And we cannot know whether it does really succeed unless we already know which appearances are true and which are false. And so we are caught in a circle.
>
> (p. 3)

Neorealists, as discoverers of that which is outside of us, must hold that there is a way out of this circle. Relativists, as constructors of knowledge, must hold that while certainly the circle of our interpretive discourse may expand and deepen and become more interesting or even more useful, there is no way out.

For these reasons, at the current point in time, there is little agreement within social research communities about what the criteria for good research might be. Many contrasting lists are advanced. They overlap, but also differ. In this context, there is no universally agreed or foundational way to determine that, for example, controlled experiments are superior to interpretive case studies, or vice versa. Nor is there universal agreement about what might determine better or worse examples of many particular research approaches, perhaps especially those using predominantly qualitative methods. In this context, the identification of 'safe' research, which entails an unambiguous separation from that which is 'unsafe', could be seen as little more than the expression of preferences for particular methods or research approaches.

The growth of 'Mode 2' knowledge

Gibbons *et al.* (1994), in a widely cited and influential text, argued that in the contemporary, increasingly globalized world, academic, scientific and research-based knowledge (mode 1), especially that which is grounded in separate academic disciplines, is being superseded. The greater complexity of the (post)modern world, the rapid speed of change, the ways in which technology has opened up access to information and to communication, changed forms of commercial activity and production and so on mean that mode 1 knowledge is being challenged by knowledge that is constructed outside the universities and research institutes, in the everyday social practices of governments, employers and other organizations. Their main argument was that universities would have to change their practices, become much more inter-disciplinary, focus much more of their work on problem-solving and, in effect, become integral parts of the mode 2 knowledge society.

This analysis has been challenged, for example by Usher (2000), who argued that the distinction between mode 1 and mode 2 was too sharply drawn, and that mode 2 knowledge had a much longer history than Gibbons *et al.* suggest. Nevertheless, their work alerts us to the fact that research and researchers are not the universal sources of knowledge, whether it be seen as useful, true or both. Hager (2000) makes a similar point in a different way. Without referring directly to Gibbons *et al.*, and in ways that suggest he has much more sympathy with a neorealist than a relativist position, he argues that knowledge and knowledge formation are not merely processes of the mind. Academe, he argues, predominantly operates as if the Cartesian separation of mind and body, and in that separation the superiority of mind, were unproblematically valid. He argues that, rather, all knowledge and knowledge formation is embodied. Reason and rationality remain, but they are not and cannot be pure. He further argues that one way of seeing mind and body as synthesized is through viewing knowledge as an ongoing process of judgement-making. He further argues that embodied knowledge is inherently superior to that where the attempt was made to separate out intellectual reason from these deeper, more practical and emotional dimensions. This sort of analysis lends itself to further extension: that knowledge and knowledge production are not only embodied, they are also essentially social and cultural.

If we apply this sort of thinking to the distinction between mode 1 and mode 2 knowledge, the distinction blurs, as Usher suggested, and the linear relationship between research and policy or practice disintegrates. For it can be argued, following the sorts of analysis of learning advanced in a Vygotskian tradition, for example by Lave and Wenger (1991), Billett (1998) or Engestrom (2001), that both modes or knowledge production are cultural, social and embodied. From this perspective, researchers ply their trade, not through pure rationality and reason alone, but through a conscious and rigorous partial, or pragmatic rationality (Hodkinson *et al.* 1996), that is grounded in their embodied persons, and located as part of an academic community of practice. What is more, this community of practice is fragmented or, perhaps more accurately, is a collection of overlapping communities of practice. Each of these communities contains its own, partly tacit modes of behaviour and rules of procedure. The nature of these procedures, or practices, often only becomes apparent when two communities, with partly but significantly different practices, meet or come together. This often produces failed understandings, as they talk past each other, finding it difficult to identify where the point of misunderstanding lies. This frequently happens when groups of researchers mix with groups of, say, policy-makers or employers, but also when two different groups of researchers come together. It happened to one of us, recently. Within our interpretivist community of practice (Smith 1989), a fundamental assumption is that though good research must be focused, it is essential not to pre-judge what might be discovered/constructed, so as to maximize the chances of finding significant factors that had not been expected. Indeed, such researchers often view the latching on to the unexpected, with associated changes in direction and of research question, as normal, and even a sign of success. One of us had extreme difficulty, in the recent past, when trying to explain this approach to a colleague with a fundamentally different view, drawn from a different community of practice. For he argued that research had to be directed at precise questions, that the evidence needed to answer those questions had to be identified in advance, and robust instruments adopted to accurately assess the extent of their existence. Without this sort of precision in advance, he argued, good research was not possible. The ensuing conversation was extremely difficult for both parties.

The view of knowledge creation as an embodied social practice changes the ways in which we view the relationship between research, policy and practice. From this perspective, the task becomes that of sharing/integrating/blending (or contrasting, contesting and disputing) the knowledges produced in different communities of practice. Hager's notion of embodied judgement can be seen as central in this process, for such an integration or inter-communication entails making some very difficult decisions about what knowledge is safe/valid/useful/moral. It is important to remember that such decisions are judgements that cannot be entirely grounded in reason – not matters of incontrovertible fact.

Complexity or simplicity?

The model of research, which lies at the heart of empiricism and evidence-informed practice, is essentially reductionist. It assumes that the best way to understand complex phenomena is to isolate all the significant variables and test their effects, in order to construct a better understanding of the whole: to reduce complexity to measurable parts. To use a simplistic analogy, knowledge is like a wall, where the quality of the whole is determined first by the quality of each brick, then of the mortar, and then of the way they have been put together. But a wall is not reflexive. That is, the quality of the brick does not change because of the ways in which the wall is put together, and the quality of the mortar does not change the quality of a brick. In the world of learning, as with other human relations, the situation is different. Even in a formal classroom, we know that the ways in which teachers and pupils behave are influenced by the ways in which they reflexively react to each other (Delamont 1976; Bloomer 1997), and that the learning of students is strongly influenced by things that happen outside school or college (Bloomer and Hodkinson 2000). In workplace learning, the situation is even more complex. This complexity has led an increasing number of researchers to focus explicitly on the inter-relationships between reflexively related variables, for example through in-depth case studies. Sometimes these are ethnographic (Lave and Wenger 1991), sometimes based on interviews (Hodkinson *et al.* 1996; Eraut *et al.* 1998, 2000).

When such research is compared to the more scientific, analytical approach of separating out variables, we are faced, once more, with competing belief systems and practices. Though many arguments can be and indeed are marshalled to legitimate the superiority of either over the other, there is no foundational basis upon which either can be declared inherently superior. We are once more in the territory of Hager's embodied judgements. Rationality or reason alone cannot provide us with the answer. What is broadly agreed is that, thus far, there are very few 'safe' scientific truths about learning that have been currently produced. Where, for example, is the learning equivalent of a cure for polio? However, the reasons for this absence, and the recommended remedy, look different from different positions. A currently dominant argument in the UK research policy discourse is that this is because our science has been too poor, too small scale, and insufficiently rigorous (Reynolds 1998). The counter-argument is that complex, reflexive social behaviour cannot be reduced to isolatable, measured variables. From the latter perspective, the things science can tell us are trivial, and what matters has to be researched in other ways.

Research and policy

In this section, we are drawing extensively upon Kogan (1999). He has produced a seminal analysis of the problematic nature of the relationship between research and education policy, and much of his argument stands if the centre of gravity is shifted to focus on work-based learning. In a recent seminar one of us attended, John Woolhouse, the ex-director of the Technical and Vocational Education Initiative (TVEI), made the comment, drawn upon his long experience working in and with government, that politics was not rational. By this he meant that policies were not made through the careful examination of what is known about, say, youth training provision. Often, he argued, ministers did not know much, and did not want to know much. To use Hager's term again, they were making embodied judgements, where the prime focus was on electability, the correct ideological and political message for their party, the need for a big idea upon which to build a career, and a strong desire to bring about rapid and lasting change, in ways that fitted their sometimes deeply held beliefs about what could and should be done.

Two examples illustrate this process. Gordon Brown announced Labour's 'New Deal' policy, prior to the election in 1997. No doubt much thinking had gone into the construction of the policy, and some research may have been influential in that process. But vast tracts of research, about unemployment, disaffection, the state of the UK labour force and its weak training/learning infrastructure, were either ignored or, more plausibly, not even known about. A trawl though even a small fragment of the relevant research, such as that on vocational education and training (Brown and Keep 1999), reveals two uncomfortable truths. Firstly, a significant part of it throws serious doubt on some of the central planks of the new policy. Secondly, parts of the research corpus are at least partly contradictory, and taking all or most of that research seriously would have made it more, rather than less, difficult to come up with a vote-catching big idea. Once the policy was in place, criticism of its fundamental parts would have been singularly unhelpful to policy-makers. Huge resources had already been committed, and promises made that could not be reversed without huge political damage. At this point in time, the only research that was helpful to the politicians and those tasked to carry out their bidding, was that which confirmed the policy was right and showed how to do it better.

The second example is the creation, in England but not Scotland, Wales or Northern Ireland, of the new Connexions Service. This is intended to help bring the educationally excluded back into education and employment and, almost as an afterthought, provide a holistic guidance service to all young people between the ages of 13 and 19. The origins of this policy are well documented (Watts 2001). Essentially, the Social Exclusion Unit drew upon some earlier think-tank ideas, as part of its influential report, *Bridging the Gap* (Social Exclusion Unit 1999). This report used a significant volume of research, mainly upon the patterns of social exclusion, and the correlations between exclusion and unemployment and a wide range of other factors, including poor educational success. The report also examined the well-known problem of fragmented agency provision for disaffected/excluded young people, and picked up on the think-tank suggestion that a single guidance service, with a new profession of holistic guiders or personal advisers, should be a major part of the solution. The

Connexions Service was announced, almost as soon as the report was published.

But large, relevant bodies of research were again overlooked or ignored. For example, the compilers of the report said nothing about racism or gender prejudice, as influences on educational and employment success, and appeared unaware that the pattern of universal one-off careers guidance interviews to all 16-year-olds was a recent imposition of the government upon the newly privatized Careers Services. At best, the thinking in the report, upon which the Connexions Service was initially based, was controversial and contested (Colley and Hodkinson, 2001).

It would be easy to use this example to blame those involved for not doing their homework thoroughly enough, or researchers for not having their relevant findings readily available. But drawing out the lessons from complex bodies of research is not easy, takes a long time, and can most easily be done with hindsight. This causes major problems for the political process. Given the contemporary world of media-hyped instant solutions, and oppositional attacks and retaliations, how feasible would it have been say, for the report to be published, the ideas to be critically scrutinized, research to be trawled for evidence of implications, and a root and branch reformulation of policy to have taken place? And how much more difficult would this have been if, as is likely, different researchers were giving different advice, based on different research findings and ways of viewing the world?

As both these illustrations show, no matter what policies are produced, part of the job of researchers is to provide independent external critique, as well as, where relevant, providing assistance to bring the policies into being and to improve their effectiveness. But doing either or both can be messy. Above all, the relationship between research and politics is itself political. It cannot often be linear, and neither should be subsumed into the other.

The relationship between research and practice

The relationship between research and practice is every bit as problematic as that between research and policy, for partly different reasons. It is increasingly understood that practice is a cultural and social phenomenon. Some of the arguments advanced around mode 2 knowledge are directly relevant here. There is a wealth of research, some of which has already been cited, suggesting that what people learn at work is constituted in the culture and practices of the workplace. Furthermore, learning is often located in practical consciousness, or tacit. Study after study show that workers find it hard to articulate how they learn. What is more, the prime purposes of workplaces are seldom learning. Things are being made, services provided. Learning, paradoxically, is omni-present, while being peripheral to the main business, what ever that is. Like other social settings, workplaces are also sites of conflicting interests, unequal power relations, struggle and contest, as well as co-operation and teamwork. Workplace learning often has a communal, as well as an individual, dimension. How can research figure in improving these complex processes?

In principle, it should be able to provide insights that might be valuable to those who manage, organize or support learning, or to those who are being organized. But their practices are also culturally bounded, and part of that culture may be specific to the particular employer or place of employment. In the current UK context, the link between practice and research is configured in two different ways. On the one hand, some practitioners might engage in a little action research themselves. There are two different sub-variations. Within school-teaching, there is a long tradition, complete with its own traditions and communities of practice, with a focus on the ways research conducted by a practitioner (alone or with others) can bring to that same practitioner greater understanding of their own practice. Such research, though ideally rigorous, is intentionally subjective. In the second variant, practitioner research is centrally located in workplace problem-solving, often at the behest of the employer, or line manager. This can be seen, for example, in the growth of the work-based learning movement in higher education (Boud 1998; Symes and McIntyre 2000). Both forms of practitioner research are largely idiosyncratic, aimed at improving the practices of a particular workplace, or a particular practitioner, or both. They are not designed to be scientifically safe or generalizable, and therefore fail a significant part of Desforges's (2000b) intention, already cited.

The other broad approach is to tell practitioners what 'safe' research has discovered, and look for mechanisms to help them take ownership of the findings, by somehow transforming them into part of their own practice. There are several problems with this. Trivially, even reading the summaries of safe findings takes time, and the transformation of those findings into changed practices takes longer. Yet, in many workplaces, time is the one commodity that is in shortest supply. Next, if most practice is internalized and/or tacit, how is the practitioner to identify which published safe findings are relevant, in order to begin the process of transformation? Or, even more difficult, how can the publishers of safe research know how to describe their work in ways that will relate to the practical consciousness of particular practitioners or communities of practice? Thirdly, research may well be safe as defined by the evidence-based practice process, but seem anything but safe, within a particular community of practice. There may well be good reasons why even the best research findings, however that 'best' is defined, should be ignored in a particular context. For example, an employer or human resource development manager may know from research (Hewison *et al.* 2000) that time for learning is a particular problem for female employees, but reject acting on the knowledge, because in her/his community of practice, reducing working hours or finding additional learning leave may be culturally and/or economically unacceptable.

As this example illustrates, just as with politicians, the identification of which research to transform and make use of, will often have little to do with its 'safeness'. In English Further Education (FE), the learning styles inventories of Honey and Mumford (1986) have recently become almost ubiquitous. The questionnaires are routinely administered to thousands of students, so that teachers can identify their preferred learning styles, in order to match teaching to them. But, within the literature about learning, the assumptions that people have inherent learning styles, that the Honey and Mumford instrument accurately measures them (there are numerous rival instruments and configurations, such as Kolb 1984; Riding 1997), that they do not change, and that they are a significant determinant of learning success, are all contested. None of these assumptions is either scientifically safe, or supported by research into the nature of learning. So why have the instruments been so widely adopted? A plausible explanation is that current FE inspection regimes require tutors to provide evidence that they are meeting the individual needs of all the learners in their classes. The use of the questionnaire is an easy means of demonstrating that they are taking this requirement seriously.

Again, there are two reactions to this situation, apart from a defence of learning styles as safe knowledge. The current policy assumption would be that we need to use research to find the knowledge about learning that *is* safe, so that practitioners can be told, and Honey and Mumford's approach disappears into the annals of FE history, or is confirmed as scientifically legitimate. The alternative reading, which we prefer, is that the story shows that choice of research evidence by practitioners is every bit as non-rational as that by politicians, and for similar reasons. They identify and utilize findings that fit with their existing cultural practices and beliefs, or which appear to help meet a current need, almost regardless of the quality of the research itself – however that is judged. Demonstrating that meeting individual students' needs is complex, and that learning styles approaches do not work, would be very unlikely to make much difference to their widespread adoption.

Using research to raise levels of understanding

When we look at these various sets of factors, about the contested and uncertain nature of research findings, about the political nature of the relationship between research and policy, and about the practices entailed in using research to influence practice, it becomes clear that the dominant linear model of safe findings, which inform policy and/or are transformed into practice, is extremely unlikely to work. In its place, we advance an alternative configuration: that researchers, some policy-makers and some practitioners can usefully work together to construct a better understanding of work-based learning.

In that better understanding, there is no clear hierarchy. Knowledge from what Gibbons *et al.* (1994) call mode 1 and mode 2 can be usefully blended, but research knowledge is not inherently superior to all other forms. Central to this process is the need to raise the capacity to make better judgements about practice, about policy and about research. This links directly with a part of the TLRP approach that we have not previously described. For the programme is also focused upon increasing research capacity. At times, this appears to mean the capacity for people to conduct high-quality research. Perhaps more profitably, it could also be taken to mean the capacity to understand better what research can and cannot do and the capacity to make more informed judgements about which research could be useful, how and why. Of course, such increased understanding would also make it easier for those who had it to engage in higher quality research themselves, either action research, or some other form.

There are various ways in which such a blending of policy, practice and research knowledge could be enhanced. One is through an increasing number of fora, where knowledge and expertise can be shared, and thinking advanced. The *Working to Learn* seminars (see footnote to this chapter) have tried to do that. The VET Forum, in the University of Warwick in the early 1990s, did it rather more substantially, drawing on greater financial support. Another way, which is also present in the TLRP, is involving some practitioners and policy-makers in all stages of the research process, so that mode 1 and mode 2 understanding are increasingly mingled. Yet another way is through appropriate masters or doctorate-level programmes of study, where practitioners and policy-makers can step back from the day-to-day pressures of work, and engage with new ideas and ways of understanding problems. Such programmes need not, of course, lead to a qualification to achieve the desired purpose. It is the level of engagement that is significant. Another strand is practitioner or policy-maker research, which can help those involved understand not only the complexities of the problems they are investigating, but of the nature of research, and the judgement processes about research. However, such understanding does not follow automatically from any form of research engagement. Research approaches that abstract techniques from understanding, and conceal the deeper problematics of research and of knowledge construction, will contribute little, and may actually undermine the development of better judgement-making.

There would be major problems. It would be difficult, in the present climate, to get either time or funding in adequate amounts for these sorts of developments. The impact would be patchy, depending upon who has the will and resources to get involved. The impact upon performance would often be impossible to measure, as it would seldom be possible to separate out the impacts of such processes and those from other, parallel practices.

But what some might see as the most serious problem, could also be described as a strength. For such a process would open up to more practitioners and policy-makers, the fragmented, uncertain and contested nature of research knowledge, for example in relation to learning. It would similarly open up to some researchers, the professional understanding of those engaged in the work-based learning field. Such a process would seldom produce scientifically safe answers, though some individuals or groups might take pointers from it to help guide future actions. But it might help construct better questions, and engender a climate where there was a much deeper understanding of what research can and cannot do, as well as a greater understanding of the nature of work-based learning, and how it can be enhanced. Above all, it would raise the capacity of the work-based learning community to make informed judgements, about their own work and that of others. Research and researchers have a valuable role to play in such a community of practice, not least because they have more time and independence to stand back from the immediate contexts and pressures of policy and practice in the field. With others, they can, for example, help retain critical perspectives in the discourse, and ensure that lessons of recent past experiences are not entirely forgotten.

Note: This chapter is an adaptation of a paper presented in a *Working to Learn* seminar at the London Institute of Education, 15 June 2001.

12

Making evidence-based practice educational
John Elliott

Redirecting educational research in the service of outcomes-based education

According to some current commentators, like David Hargreaves, educational research needs to be redirected towards the systematic development of a body of knowledge that is capable of informing the practical judgements of teachers. The idea of 'evidence-based practice' is central to this redirection. Hargreaves (1997: 413) argues that: '. . . research should provide decisive and conclusive evidence that if teachers do X rather than Y in their professional practice, there will be a significant and enduring improvement in outcome'.

More recently, Hargreaves (1999b), has displayed an increasing sensitivity to accusations of 'positivism' (see Hammersley 1997). He qualifies the idea of 'evidence-based practice' by suggesting that 'evidence-informed practice' is a less ambivalent expression. It more clearly indicates that relevant research *informs* rather than *displaces* the judgement of teachers. He also appears to qualify the injunction that research evidence should be *decisive and conclusive* for practice. Such evidence does not presume the existence of universal causal laws as a basis for generating means–ends rules that are beyond doubt.

Hargreaves sees the future of educational research to require more experimental studies and randomized controlled trials, in search of *what works* in practice to produce improvements in outcome. These studies investigate 'some "reasonably stable relationships" ' (1999b: 247) but are open to revision in the light of exceptions and changing circumstances. Their generalizable findings deal in statistical probabilities only.

Moreover, in discussing the relationship between research and policy-making, Hargreaves acknowledges that practical decisions are context-bound. He argues that they need to be based on a wider range of considerations than 'relevant research'. Knowledge derived from research 'serves as a supplement to, not a substitute for, the policy-maker's existing knowledge' (1999b: 246).

By attempting to uncouple educational experiments into *what works* from positivistic assumptions, Hargreaves (1999b) aims to strengthen the case for an 'engineering model' of educational research, as opposed to an 'enlightenment model'. The former he contends aims to exert a direct influence on educational action in the areas of policy and practice, by generating evidence of *what works*. The latter in contrast aims only to shape the way people think about situations and the problems they raise. The influence of such research on their concrete decisions and actions is at best indirect. Hargreaves acknowledges that 'enlightenment research' can in the longer-term indirectly impact on policy and practice by permeating the prevailing climate of opinion. However, this 'uncontentious fact', he argues, is no excuse for a *hermit stance*, 'in which the researcher withdraws from the messy world of short-term, practical problems into intellectual obscurities masquerading as profundities whilst dreaming of ultimate recognition' (1999b: 243). Indeed, Hargreaves claims that the transmission of theories and ideas alone to 'enlighten' professional practitioners is a dangerous enterprise. By way of example, he points to the intellectual monopoly social scientists in education have, 'until recently', exercised over the initial training of teachers. In the process they have purveyed the ideas of researchers like Piaget, Skinner and Bernstein (1999b: 244) in distorted forms. Arguably, he contends, this has done 'untold damage' to teachers' professional practices.

Hargreaves portrays the 'enlightenment model' as an oppositional stance to an 'engineering model' framed by naive positivistic assumptions. By uncoupling the 'engineering model' from such assumptions, he aspires to disarm the opposition in the academy, and to reinstate it at the core of social science research generally and educational research in particular. In this way the future of social and educational research can be redirected to generating *actionable knowledge* for both policy-makers and practitioners.

Has Hargreaves succeeded, in his latest writing, at finally uncoupling his endorsement of an 'engineering model' of social and educational research from the charge that it presumes a crude and naive positivism? Has he thereby exposed, as mere rationalization, the grounds for opposing such a model? I would argue that Hargreaves has only partially succeeded.

From the standpoint of social philosophy, his arguments are not exactly novel ones. They echo in some respects those developed by Alasdair MacIntyre (1981) in Chapter 8 of his seminal text entitled *After Virtue*. Discussing *The Character of Generalizations in Social Science and their Lack of Predictive Power*, MacIntyre identifies the discovery of statistical regularities as an important source of predictability in human behaviour. He argues that generalizations of this kind, couched in terms of probabilities rather than strict causal laws, do not entail explicability in terms of such laws. This point is echoed by Hargreaves (1997) in his rejoinder to Martyn Hammersley's (1997) contention that many educational researchers would perceive his account of 'evidence-based practice' as positivistic. MacIntyre also argues that knowledge of statistical regularities plays an important role in informing human choices between alternatives, in terms of their chances of success and failure. They constitute what Hargreaves calls *actionable knowledge*. However, unlike Hargreaves, MacIntyre does not view the existence of exceptions to constitute a platform for improving the predictability of research findings and therefore their utility as *actionable knowledge*.

According to Hargreaves (1999b) educational research evidence about *what works* in classrooms should be cumulative and based on a process of continuously investigating exceptions (pp. 247–8). He appears to assume that such exceptions constitute counter-examples in the sense that they expose deficiencies in the original generalizations which need to be improved upon by further research. However, MacIntyre argues that the probabilistic generalizations of social science are different in kind from those which obtain in natural science fields like statistical mechanics. Unlike the former, probabilistic generalizations in such natural science fields do not merely consist of a list of instances to which there are exceptions. Rather they 'entail well-defined counter-factual conditionals and they are refuted by counter-examples in precisely the same way and to the same degree as other law-like generalizations are' (1981: 91).

Given this difference, Hargreaves's assumption that exceptions to social science generalizations can function as counter-examples, and thereby constitute a basis for cumulative research which improves the actionability of its findings, is an erroneous one. MacIntyre emphasizes Machiavelli's point, that in human life people may act 'on the best available stock of generalizations' and yet, when faced with unpredicted exceptions, see no way to improve them or reason to abandon them (p. 93). Relatively speaking, such generalizations are predictively weak. Hargreaves's belief that they can be improved upon, rather than simply added to or changed, in a way which leads to a progressive diminution of unpredictability in human affairs, suggests that he has not entirely shed the assumptions of positivism.

However much Hargreaves has modified his position on evidence-based practice in response to accusations of 'positivism', there is a consistent theme running through his writing since the TTA lecture he delivered in 1996. It is that the major task of educational research is to improve the *performativity* of teachers with respect to the outcomes of their teaching. At first sight this view of the aim of educational research appears to be a matter of common sense and not open to question. Teaching is an intentional activity directed towards bringing about learning outcomes for pupils. What is more open to dispute (see Stenhouse 1970, 1975) is a thread of ideas which originally stemmed from Bloom *et al.*'s *Taxonomy of Educational Objectives* (1956) and Bloom's research into *Mastery Learning* (1971). In the 1980s these ideas were further developed under the name of *outcomes-based education* (OBE). Within the thread of ideas that make up OBE are the injunctions that learning outcomes should be the same for all students, operationally defined as *exit behaviors*, and progress towards them measured against *benchmarks*. The terminology employed tends to shift over time and context but its meaning remains constant. Hence, within the UK National Curriculum, framework specifications of *outcomes for all students* are referred to as 'standards', *exit behaviors* as 'targets', and *benchmarks* as 'attainment levels'.

One of the attractions of OBE is that it appears to provide a framework of practical rules for designing teaching interventions and measuring teaching effectiveness. In applying these rules to instructional design, the outcomes of teaching are conceived as measurable *outputs*. As such they are specified in a form which renders them predictable and amenable to technical control by the teacher. Within the OBE framework 'evidence-based teaching' can be characterized as a means of improving teaching as a form of technical control over the production of learning outcomes, thereby rendering them increasingly predictable. In spite of various adjustments Hargreaves has made to his accounts of 'evidence-based practice', and the role of educational research in relation to it, they continue to embrace and endorse the control ideology of OBE. In this respect they remain open to the charge of positivism.

In what follows, the phrase 'outcomes-based education' will be used to refer to the particular strand of ideas sketched above. In so doing I in no way wish to deny the truism that teaching involves the intention to bring about worthwhile learning outcomes for students. What I would deny is that teaching, to become effective, has to take on the particular ideological baggage of OBE. The truism referred to does not necessarily entail that the teacher should have the same outcomes in mind for all students, or that s(he) should specify outcomes in the form of exit behaviours or outputs, or assess the effectiveness of his or her teaching by measuring students' progress in learning against benchmarks. Hargreaves's account of the role of educational research can be interpreted as an attempt to reposition it as the hand-maiden of OBE and the educational policies which are increasingly shaped by the ideology which underpins it.

I will return to the question of what constitutes *actionable knowledge* in the context of social practices like education shortly. First, I want to explore Hargreaves's view of the role of *educational research* in the prevailing policy context. I shall do so in the light of MacIntyre's account of the use of social science generalizations in the management of society.

The policy context of educational research

Hargreaves endorses political interventions to shape pedagogical practices in school classrooms so long as they are informed by research evidence rather than ideology. He writes:

> In England and Wales policy-makers were formerly limited, or limited themselves, mainly to decisions about the structure of the education service; the internal activities of what teachers did in classrooms, even the curriculum itself, was largely left to the discretion of teachers enjoying a high level of professional autonomy. Today a new link is being forged between what hitherto have been mainly distinct areas [of policy and practice] and marks the end to the convention by which ministers remain distant from classroom practice.
>
> Policy-makers' interventions in classroom activities will, I suspect, increase, especially if the national literacy and numeracy strategies succeed in raising levels of students' measured achievement. Ministers now recognize that standards of teaching and learning are unlikely to be raised by policy action that never penetrates classrooms. This is less dangerous than it initially appears, as long as ministers retain some distance by a pragmatic attention to 'what works' and by an acknowledgment that the discovery of 'what works' is more a matter of evidence, not just ideology or of political preference.
>
> (Hargreaves 1999b: 246)

From MacIntyre's point of view Hargreaves's optimism about the uses of educational research in the policy context, as depicted above, would appear to be ill-founded. MacIntyre argues (pp. 106–8) that the claims of politicians and bureaucrats to expertise in the 'social engineering' of society is a masquerade for a histrionic imitation of scientifically managed social control. Such claims, he argues, arise from 'the dominance of the manipulative mode in our culture', but which 'cannot be accompanied by very much actual success in manipulation' for 'our social order is in a very literal sense out of, and indeed anyone's, control'. MacIntyre concludes that it is 'histrionic success which gives power and authority in our culture' and not scientific evidence about how to manipulate/ engineer the social order to achieve certain purposes. In doing so he anticipates a likely response from social managers and bureaucrats that interestingly echoes Hargreaves's account of the role of educational research:

> We make no large claims [to expertise] – We are as keenly aware of the limitations of social science generalizations as you are.

We perform a modest function with a modest and unpretentious competence. But we do have specialized knowledge, we are entitled in our own limited fields to be called experts.

(p. 107)

MacIntyre argues that these modest claims do little to legitimate the possession and uses of power 'in anything like the way or on anything like the scale on which that power is wielded' in bureaucratic systems. He sees them as an excuse for continuing 'to participate in the charades which are consequently enacted'. His account of how political and managerial power is generated in our culture seems credible. In such a case, Hargreaves's account of the significant, if modest, contribution of educational research to the production of *actionable knowledge* in the current policy context is based on a fiction about the capacity of such research to inform and shape policy interventions. It is a fiction which nevertheless provides an excuse for an unprecedented extension of the operation of political and bureaucratic power to regulate the pedagogical activities teachers engage their students in within classrooms. Hargreaves it appears, from this point of view, has cast educational researchers for a role in the histrionic production of the power and authority of the state and its officials over the processes of education. MacIntyre 'reminds' educational researchers that they also will need to be good actors when he writes: 'The histrionic talents of the player with small walking-on parts are as necessary to the bureaucratic drama as the contributions of the great managerial character actors' (p. 108).

I would contend that in giving the 'engineering model' of educational research a central role for the future, Hargreaves takes for granted a set of prevailing assumptions about the nature of social practices, like 'education', and their relationship to desirable social outcomes. These assumptions are embedded in a climate of opinion which currently surrounds the formation of social policy in the post-industrial nations and the systems of quality assurance associated with the process. In the field of education, such assumptions are embedded in the notion of *outcomes-based education* outlined earlier. They can be summarized as follows:

1. Social practices are activities which need to be justified as *effective* and *efficient* means of producing desirable outputs.
2. Means and ends are contingently related. What constitutes an appropriate means for bringing about the ends-in-view needs to be determined on the basis of empirical evidence.
3. The determination of means requires a clear and precise pre-specification of ends as tangible and measurable outputs or targets, which constitute the *quality standards* against which the performance of social practitioners is to be judged.

The prevailing policy-context in education, as in other areas of social policy, tends to reflect these assumptions, inasmuch as it prioritizes *target-setting* and forms of evaluation and quality assurance which measure the *performativity* (efficiency) of practices against *indicators* of success in achieving the targets. In other words it is a context in which practices are treated as manipulative devices (technologies) for engineering desired levels of output.

Hargreaves's vision of the future of educational research neatly fits this policy-context and he apparently sees no problem with it. He clearly assumes that restrictions on the autonomy of teachers by the interventions of policy-makers to shape classroom practice are justified, so long as they are informed and disciplined by empirical evidence of *what works* to produce a given level of output. What he fails to consider is MacIntyre's point that such evidence can never provide 'the managers of society' with the amount of predictive power that is commensurate with the concept of *managerial effectiveness*. Such a concept for MacIntyre is a moral fiction (pp. 106–7). If we accept his line of argument, then, in a policy-context characterized by 'managerialism', empirical evidence about statistical regularities is only *histrionically useful* as a masquerade for arbitrary preferences. In this case, Hargreaves's vision, of government ministers distancing themselves from their ideological preferences and pragmatically attending to evidence of *what works*, is somewhat fanciful and no basis on which to sanction restrictions on teacher autonomy. Indeed the fact, evidenced by the limited forms of empirical generalizations produced by the social sciences, that human life is accompanied by a high degree of unpredictability as a permanent condition, is a good reason for giving teachers a measure of autonomy from political and bureaucratic control. Trusting in their capacities to exercise wisdom and judgement in the unpredictable circumstances, which they regularly encounter in the course of their activities is the wise policy.

We need a third vision of educational research as an alternative to either the 'enlightenment' or the 'engineering' model, one which places the judgement of teachers at the centre of the research process. It is the articulation of this third vision that the rest of this chapter is devoted to.

The concept of education and the role of educational research

Hargreaves's vision of the future of educational research ignores a tradition of thinking about social practices, such as education, which goes back to Aristotle and is exemplified in contemporary thought by MacIntyre's *After Virtue*. According to MacIntyre this philosophical tradition defines a social practice as:

any coherent and complex form of socially established cooperative human activity through which goods internal to that form of activity are realized in the course of trying to achieve those standards of excellence which are appropriate to, and partially definitive of, that form of activity, with the result that human powers to achieve excellence, and human conceptions of the ends and goods involved, are systematically extended.

(p. 187)

From this *ethical perspective* goods internal to a practice are distinguished from external goods because one cannot specify them independently of the activities and processes the practice itself consists of. They are norms and values which define what are to count as the worthwhile activities and processes which make up the practice, and not some extrinsic goods which may result from participating in it. Moreover, unlike the latter, goods internal to a practice can only be identified and recognized 'by the experience of participating in the practice in question' (see MacIntyre 1981: 189).

In the field of education such a perspective constituted in the 1960s and early 1970s a major resource for two highly influential and inter-linked bodies of work. I am referring to Richard Peters's work in establishing the philosophy of education as a major discipline in education (see *Ethics & Education 1966*, 'Aims of Education – A Conceptual Inquiry' 1973) and Lawrence Stenhouse's use of Peters's work in developing research-based teaching as a coherent and integrated form of educational practice (see Stenhouse 1970b, 1975, 1979, 1979b). In fact, the linkage between Peters's educational theory and Stenhouse's work in placing the idea of 'research-based teaching' at the core of the curriculum development process in schools, as exemplified by his Humanities Project (1970b), is not sufficiently acknowledged by either philosophers of education or educational researchers. Yet it provides a significant exception to Hargreaves's contention (1999b: 244) that the transmission of theories of education have not been accompanied in the past by a sound body of empirical evidence related to teachers' routine practices (see, for examples, Stenhouse 1970b, 1977, 1979b; Ford Teaching Project Publications 1974; Elliott and MacDonald 1975; Stenhouse, Verma, Wild and Nixon 1979; Ebbutt and Elliott 1985; Elliott 1991).

Peters was a member of the Humanities Project's Steering Committee, and Stenhouse viewed this project as an example of curriculum development grounded in a well-articulated philosophy of education. Consistently with this Stenhouse sent a member of his team (myself) to study the philosophy of education under Peters, on a part-time basis, at the London Institute of Education.

In this section I shall revisit Peters's work on the aims of education and their relationship to educational processes, and argue that its implications for educational research and evidence-based practice are very different from Hargreaves's position. In the final section I shall sketch out Stenhouse's vision of the relationship between educational research and teaching and indicate its congruence with the educational theory of Peters.

For Peters, *educational aims* do not refer to ends which 'education might lead up to or bring about' (1973). From his point of view economic ends like 'providing students with jobs' and 'increasing the productivity of the community' are goods extrinsic to education. *Education*, Peters argues (1966: 27), is not 'a neutral process that is instrumental to something that is worthwhile which is extrinsic to it'. Such extrinsic ends are more appropriately referred to as *purposes* rather than *aims of education*. The latter refer to norms and values which define what it means for a person to become *educated*, and what is to count procedurally as a worthwhile *educational* process for realizing such a state. They define 'goods' that are intrinsic to *education* as a process. A process which is solely directed towards *extrinsic* ends such as economic ones, Peters (1966) argues, is best described in terms of *training* rather than *education*. However, people can be taught a body of knowledge, such as science, or a practical skill, like carpentry, for both 'their own intrinsic value and because of the contribution which they make to extrinsic ends' (Peters 1966: 29). *Education* and *training* are not necessarily discrete processes.

According to Peters the norms and values which define the intrinsic goods of education fall into two closely connected clusters (1973: 18–24). First, there are those which provide general criteria of education when it is viewed as an achievement. Peters claims that success at becoming an educated person involves:

- coming to care about an activity for 'what there is in it as distinct from what it may lead onto' e.g. 'the pursuit of truth' or 'making something of a fitting form' (p. 18).
- possessing 'depth of understanding' by grasping the principles which underpin an activity.
- not being narrowly specialized but able to see the connection between an activity one cares about and understands and a 'coherent pattern of life'. Peters calls this ability, to make connections between specific human activities (e.g. science, history, or engineering) and a wider pattern of meaning in life, *cognitive perspective*.
- having one's way of looking at things in life generally, one's *cognitive perspective*, transformed by what one has learned in pursuing specific worthwhile activities.

The implication of such an analysis, of what it means to be *educated*, is that becoming such a person involves a process that is qualitatively different from one which involves merely learning bodies of knowledge and skills that are valued solely in terms of their relationship to extrinsic economic and social purposes. *Education*, for Peters, involves the transformation of a person's way of seeing the world in relation to him or herself. It is a holistic process. He argues that a person is never *educated* 'in relation to any specific end, function, or mode of thought' (1966: 34). The acquisition of specific competencies in these respects is more appropriately described in terms of *training*. Nor do people become *educated* additively, by virtue of the sheer amount of knowledge and skills they acquire. Knowledgeable or omnicompetent individuals are not necessarily *educated*. From this we might conclude that our government's current project of 'driving up standards' in schools has little to do with improving the quality of *education* within them, since the acquisition of specific competencies are not in themselves *educational achievements*. The latter refer to the *manner* in which people learn and involve qualitative transformations in their general outlook on life, the conditions of which can be specified by the kinds of general criteria Peters has drawn our attention to. His purpose, in attempting to clarify aims which are intrinsic to the process of becoming educated, is 'to clarify the minds of educators about their priorities' (1973: 21). The need for such clarification is perhaps greater now at a time when the educational policy context is being driven by economic imperatives in an age of globalization, and teachers at all levels of the education system are being held to account in terms of standardized learning outputs which are believed to posses *commodity value* for the labour market.

The second cluster of aims cited by Peters refers to procedural values and to principles rather than the achievement aspect of education. Some of these aims, he argues, are linked to the claims of the individual in the process of education, and draw attention 'to a class of *procedures* of education rather than prescribe any particular content or direction to it' (1973: 22). Aims like 'self-realization' and 'the growth of the individual' imply principles of procedure such as 'learning by discovery', 'inquiry learning', 'autonomous learning', 'learning by experience'. Other procedural aims refer to the rules or standards that are built into *educationally* worthwhile activities, such as respect for reasons and evidence (1973: 25). Procedural aims and principles are emphasized, Peters argues, 'when the educational system is either geared towards the demands of the state – or when individuals are being molded relentlessly in accordance with some dull and doctrinaire pattern' (1973: 23). Under these conditions there is a point in stressing the need, for example, to respect the individuality of learners by allowing them a measure of self-direction and control within any *educationally* worthwhile process. There may also be a point in emphasizing the intrinsic value of procedural standards built into an activity, such as 'respect for evidence', in contexts where the activity is in danger of being valued only for its instrumentality as a vehicle for producing goods which are extrinsic to *education*.

If, for Peters, general aims function to remind educators of their priorities with respect to what they should be trying to achieve in *educating* students as opposed to merely training them, then procedural values and principles function to remind them that their methods should be consistent with both the standards that define and discipline *educationally* worthwhile activities, and the moral claims of individuals as learners. Procedural principles based on the latter remind educators of the ethical limits *education* as a task places on the pedagogical methods they employ to structure students' learning.

According to Peters, procedural values and principles cannot be characterized independently of his characterization of education as an achievement. Although they specify criteria which characterize those processes 'by means of which people gradually become educated' (1973: 15), they do not, Peters argues, specify 'efficient means for producing a desirable end' (1973: 15).

The connection between *educational* processes and becoming an *educated* person is a conceptual rather than a contingent one. Why, he asks, are values and principles embedded in *educational* procedures treated as *aims* of education? The answer he argues: 'is connected with the impossibility of conceiving of educational processes in accordance with a means ends model and of making any absolute separation between content and procedure, matter and manner, in the case of education' (Peters 1973: 24).

Peters here is not denying that considerations of instrumental effectiveness, in achieving specific educational outcomes, are pedagogically relevant. What he is denying is their relevance to judging the *educational quality* of pedagogical methods. This is because, for him, both the achievement and procedural criteria of education characterize different aspects of the same process of *initiating* people 'into a public world picked out by the language and concepts of a people and structured by rules governing their purposes and interactions with each other' (1973: 26). The achievement criteria characterize *educational outcomes* in a form that renders them inseparable from the process of *becoming educated*. They characterize *qualities of being* which are manifested *in* a process of *becoming educated* and cannot be described independently of it. Such a process, Peters argues, is inconsistent with both the view of teachers as operators who shape minds 'according to some specification or "top them up" with knowledge' and the view that their function is simply to 'encourage the child to "grow" ' as if s(he) were an 'organism unfolding some private form of life' (1973: 26). The function of procedural criteria, according to Peters, is to act as a guide to teachers in helping learners, viewed as active and developing centres of consciousness, 'to explore and *share* a public world whose contours have been marked out by generations which have preceded both of them' (1973: 26). The central pedagogical problem for teachers as educators, Peters claims, is the procedural one of how to get students to enter into this public world and enjoy their public heritage. Procedural values and principles articulated as *aims of education* remind them that this can only be achieved by methods that acknowledge both the internal standards which govern the activities that people are being initiated into, and the moral standards appropriate to their status as 'developing centres of consciousness'.

Since there are multiple criteria for judging both what it means to become *educated* and what are to count as *educational* methods or procedures it is obvious, Peters argues, that some will be emphasized more than others at particular times, 'according to the defects and needs of the contemporary situation' (1973: 20). The demand for aims in education serves to focus attention on a neglected priority. The existence of multiple criteria, for Peters, means that educators can be pulled in different directions by conflicting educational priorities, and that such dilemmas cannot be resolved by the formulation of a single over-all aim of education which everyone could agree about. Which aim(s) should be emphasized in any particular circumstance must be left to the discretion and practical wisdom of the teacher(s) concerned (1973: 27–9).

Let us now briefly explore the implications of Peters's theory of education for a future direction of educational research that is very different from the one enunciated by Hargreaves.

Hargreaves's account of the sort of research evidence which can be used to inform pedagogical development confines itself to evidence of 'instrumental effectiveness'. However, from Peters's account of the procedural aims and principles implicit in the concept of education alone, one might argue that educational research, if it is to inform *educational* practice, should prioritize the gathering of empirical evidence which can inform teachers' judgements about the ethical consistency of the teaching and learning process with the procedural values and principles that define what is to count as a worthwhile process of *education* (see Elliott 1989). The primary role of *educational* research, when understood as research directed towards the improvement of *educational* practice, is not to discover contingent connections between a set of classroom activities and pre-standardized learning outputs, but to investigate the conditions for realizing a coherent *educational* process in particular practical contexts.

Both the indeterminate nature of educational values and principles, and the context-dependent nature of judgements about which concrete methods and procedures are consistent with them, suggest that *educational* research takes the form of case studies rather than randomized controlled trials. The latter, via a process of statistical aggregation, abstract practices and their outcomes from the contexts in which they are situated. Such case studies entail close collaboration between external researchers and teachers on 'the inside' of an educational practice. As Alasdair MacIntyre points out, the identification and recognition of goods which are internal to a practice depends on the experience 'of participating in the practice in question' (1981: 189). In the context of research directed towards the improvement of *educational* practice, teachers need to be involved in prioritizing their *educational* aims in a given situation, in defining what is to count as relevant evidence of the extent to which they are being realized and interpreting its practical significance for them. In other words *educational* research, as opposed to simply research *on* education, will involve teachers in its construction and execution and not simply in *applying its findings*. Teachers *engage* in *educational* research and not simply with it.

The implications outlined above, of Peters's educational theory for educational research, are highly consistent with Stenhouse's *process model* of curriculum development and the central role of *research-based teaching* within it.

Stenhouse on research-based teaching

Stenhouse drew on Peters's work in *Ethics and Education* (1966) to develop his *process model* of curriculum and pedagogy in opposition to the emerging 'objectives model', which forged the basis of what has now become widely known as 'outcomes-based education'. In demonstrating the process model in practice through *The Humanities Curriculum Project* Stenhouse saw himself to be addressing the issue: '. . . can curriculum and pedagogy be organised satisfactorily by a logic other than the means-ends model?' (pp. 84–5).

He derived this alternative logic substantially from the arguments Peters sketched out in *Ethics and Education*.

> Peters (1966) argues cogently for the intrinsic justification of content. He starts from the position that education 'implies the transmission of what is worthwhile to those who become committed to it' and that it 'must involve knowledge and understanding and some kind of cognitive perspective, which are not inert' (45). Believing that education involves taking part in worthwhile activities, Peters argues that such activities have their own in-built standards of excellence, and thus 'can be appraised because of the standards immanent in them rather than because of what they lead on to'. They can be argued to be worthwhile in themselves rather than as means towards objectives.
>
> (Stenhouse 1975: 84)

Stenhouse was emphatic that the intrinsic 'standards of excellence', which Peters links to the development of 'knowledge and understanding', could not be specified as 'objectives'. The term 'process objectives', used by some curriculum theorists, to refer to standards intrinsic to the learning process, was also misleading (1975: 39). In selecting content to exemplify 'the most important procedures, the key concepts and criteria and the areas and situations in which the criteria hold' (p. 85) one does not designate objectives to be learned by the students.

> For the key procedures, concepts and criteria in any subject – **cause, form, experiment, tragedy** – are, and are important precisely because they are, problematic within the subject. They are the focus of speculation, not the object of mastery. – Educationally they are also important because they invite understanding at a variety of levels. – It is the building of curriculum on such structures as procedures, concepts and criteria, which cannot adequately be translated into the performance levels of objectives, that makes possible Bruner's 'courteous translation' of knowledge and allows of learning which challenges all abilities and interests in a diverse group . . . The translation of the deep structures of knowledge into behavioral objectives is one of the principal causes of the distortion of knowledge in schools.
>
> (Stenhouse 1975: 85–6)

For Stenhouse, the dynamic nature of the procedural standards and principles that structure intrinsically worthwhile activities implies that they constitute *resources for thinking* about experience, and leave space for students' *individuality, creativity and imagination*. They structure thinking in ways which open rather than close the mind to new ways of interpreting the world. Stenhouse claims that 'the principles which obtain for knowledge within a field are problematic within that field' and therefore pedagogically should always be treated as 'provisional and open to debate'. This echoes Peters's view that procedural principles refer to both standards internal to an activity and the claims of individuals as learners participating in it.

I have argued elsewhere (Elliott 1988: 51 and 1998, chapter 2) that the translation of the structures of knowledge into objectives through the English National Curriculum was a considerable error, and has denied students in schools that 'courteous translation of knowledge' that is a condition of giving them equality of access to our cultural heritage. I predicted that it would result in widespread disaffection from schooling, and this now appears to be manifest, even to policy-makers. The Secretary of State's proposals for revising the National Curriculum acknowledged that it 'was failing to engage a significant minority of 14–16 year olds, who were as a consequence becoming disaffected from learning' (see Elliott 2000).

Stenhouse did not discount the appropriateness of an objectives model of curriculum design in particular contexts. He argues (1975: 80) that education in a broad sense comprises at least four different processes; *training, instruction, initiation* and *induction*. Training is concerned with the acquisition of specific skills, such as speaking a foreign language or handling laboratory apparatus. The use of an objectives model in this context is quite appropriate, Stenhouse argues. Instruction is concerned with the retention of information e.g. learning the table of chemical elements, dates in history, the names of countries, German irregular verbs, and cooking recipes. In this context too the objectives model is appropriate. Contrary to Peters, Stenhouse views initiation as 'familiarization with social values and norms' leading to a capacity 'to interpret the social environment'.

As a process it appropriately takes place as a by-product of living in a community and operates in schools as the 'hidden curriculum'. Induction, according to Stenhouse, appropriately describes the introduction of people to the thought-systems of the culture and is concerned with developing their 'understanding'. This is 'evidenced by the capacity to grasp and to make for oneself relationships and judgments'. For Stenhouse induction is at the core of any *educational process*. Within such a process both training and instruction have important but subsidiary functions, for 'skills and information are often learned in the context of knowledge, which is, in one of its aspects, an organization of skills and information'. It follows that in designing an educationally worthwhile curriculum there is a place for specifying objectives in terms of the information and skills to be learned. The danger, for Stenhouse, lies in extending its scope to include the most important aspect of education; namely, the process of inducting students into the thought-systems of our culture. Its scope, he argues, should be confined to designing subordinate units within the curriculum that play a service role to the induction process.

One pedagogical implication of Stenhouse's account of the relationship between 'process' and 'objectives' models of curriculum design is that technical means–ends reasoning about the most *effective* and *efficient* training and instructional methods has a place, albeit a subsidiary one, in teachers' decisions about how to improve teaching and learning in an *educational* situation. His account does not deny the value of a form of research aimed at discovering statistical correlations between teaching and learning processes and the acquisition of specific skills and information. Such studies might play a subordinate role in informing the judgements of educators. I will explore Stenhouse's views on this point a little later. For the moment I want to examine his central arguments for research-based teaching.

Stenhouse's idea of 'research-based teaching' is linked to a 'process model' of curriculum design. This, in turn, rests on the belief that the structures of knowledge into which students are to be inducted are intrinsically problematic and contestable, and therefore objects of speculation. This implies that teachers ought to cast themselves in the role of learners alongside their students. Stenhouse argues (1975: 91) that:

> Either the teacher must be an expert or he must be a learner along with his students. In most cases the teacher cannot in the nature of the case be the expert. It follows that he must cast himself in the role of a learner. Pedagogically this may in fact be a preferable role to that of the expert. It implies teaching by discovery or inquiry methods.

For Stenhouse, the teacher who casts him or herself in the role of a learner alongside his or her students, must have 'some hold on, and a continual refinement of, a philosophical understanding of the subject he is teaching and learning, of its deep structures and rationale' (1975: 91). It is this depth of understanding in relation to the subject-matter that makes the teacher into a learner with something to offer to students; namely, a research stance towards the content they teach. From such a stance they model how to treat knowledge as an object of inquiry. Stenhouse argues that a teacher who casts him or herself in the role of expert, representing knowledge as *authoritative* and therefore beyond doubt and speculation, is misrepresenting and distorting that knowledge. His major objection to the use of the 'objectives model' to map learning in the fields of knowledge, is that it reinforces authoritative teaching, and in the process compounds error.

For Stenhouse *research-based teaching* is an implication of a theory of education that places induction into knowledge structures at its centre, and then characterizes them as *objects for speculative thought*. This theory of education implies a logical framework for a teaching and learning process. At the centre of this framework is a pedagogical aim that he characterizes in the following terms: 'to develop an understanding of the problem of the nature of knowledge through an exploration of the provenance and warrant of the particular knowledge we encounter in our field of study' (1979: 7).

As an aim for all learners, Stenhouse was aware that some would doubt its realism. However, anything less would consign many children to a permanent condition of educational disadvantage, for 'we are talking about the insight which raises mere competence and possession of information to intellectual power of a kind which can emancipate'. Such an aim, for Stenhouse, implied certain procedural values and principles governing methods of teaching and learning, for example 'inquiry' or 'discovery' learning, and 'teaching through discussion'. 'Research-based teaching' can also be regarded as a procedural principle implied by the aim, in as much as it characterizes the personal stance to knowledge the teacher must adopt in support of the other principles of procedure.

As I indicated earlier Stenhouse did not view his methodology of induction to be incompatible with instruction. He argues that in order to cover the curriculum we need instruction and 'text-books too'. The key to the relationship between, say, 'discovery' or 'discussion' methods and instruction, he argues, lies in the pedagogical aim.

> The crucial difference is between an educated and an uneducated use of instruction. The educated use of instruction is skeptical, provisional, speculative in temper. The uneducated use mistakes information for knowledge. Information is not knowledge until the factor of error, limitation or crudity in it is appropriately estimated, and it is assimilated to structures of thinking – which give us the means of understanding.
>
> (1979: 8)

Stenhouse was concerned to transform teaching in the state educational system, from one in which the great majority of children experienced their teacher as *an authority* on the content of education to one in which the teacher was *in authority* with respect to the process of *education* and the maintenance of procedures that are consistent with his or her pedagogical aim as an educator. This involved inquiry in particular contexts into how to effect such a transformation in practice.

He casts the problem in a form that turned it into an agenda for *educational* research: 'The problem is how to design a practicable pattern of teaching which maintains authority, leadership and the responsibility of the teacher, but does not carry the message that such authority is the warrant of knowledge' (1979: 7).

The major task of educational research is to show how teaching and learning can be made more *educational*. For Stenhouse such research produced *actionable evidence* as a basis for teaching, but included evidence of a rather different kind to that envisaged by Hargreaves. It is evidence that is relevant to the problem of how to make the concrete activities of teaching and learning more *ethically consistent* with the criteria that define what it means to become educated (for example, those cited by Peters). Evidence that is relevant to simply making teaching and learning a more effective and efficient process for the production of specific learning outputs is not sufficient as a basis for inducting students into the deep structures of knowledge. Indeed the ethical requirements of the latter may impose limits on the strategies the teacher employs to secure specific instructional or training outputs.

Educational research of the kind Stenhouse envisages, as a basis for teaching, implies a similar stance from the teacher to the one he describes in relation to his or her subject-matter:

> Just as research in history or literature or chemistry can provide a basis for teaching those subjects, so educational research can provide

a basis for teaching and learning about teaching. Professional skill and understanding can be the subject of doubt, that is of knowledge, and hence of research.

(1979: 18)

Stenhouse's view of educational research implies *doing* research as an integral part of the role of the teacher, just as teachers who *use* research into their subject as a basis for teaching imply that they *do* research into the subject *through* their teaching. In this respect, both dimensions of research-based teaching are similarly conceptualized in terms of their relationship to educational practice. Neither implies that research, whether it be in history or in education, can only be carried out by 'insiders' who are actively engaged in educational practice. However, for Stenhouse *educational* research does imply that 'outsiders' engaged in such research need to collaborate with educational practitioners. His reasons for this are clearly stated. *Educational* research is a form of *action research* and this means that:

> ... real classrooms have to be our laboratories, and they are in the command of teachers, not of researchers – the research act must conform to the obligations of the professional context. This is what we mean by action research. It is a pattern of research in which experimental or research acts cannot be exempted from the demand for justification by professional as well as by research criteria. The teacher cannot learn by inquiry without undertaking that the pupils learn too; the physician cannot experiment without attempting to heal. – Such a view of educational research declares that the theory or insights created in collaboration by professional researchers and professional teachers, is always provisional, always to be taught in a spirit of inquiry, and always to be tested and modified by professional practice.

(1979: 20)

Stenhouse would agree with Hargreaves about the limitations of an 'enlightenment model' of educational research. He argues (1979: 18) against 'the received doctrine' that 'has been at the core of education for teaching' since the 1950s; namely, that it should be based 'in the findings of research in the 'contributory disciplines' of philosophy, psychology and sociology'. Stenhouse proposes an alternative to the constituent disciplines approach, which was 'to treat education itself – teaching, learning, running schools and educational systems – as the subject of research' (see also Elliott 1978). In this respect Hargreaves appears to echo Stenhouse in a common aspiration for educational research directly to inform the concrete activities of education rather than studying them for the contribution they can make to the development of theory within a particular discipline. However, as I have indicated, their ideas about what constitutes *actionable evidence* from research are somewhat different.

Stenhouse claims that his alternative proposal does not imply a neglect of the disciplines, because research in education draws eclectically upon them, particularly with respect to 'methods of inquiry and analysis together with such concepts as have utility for a theory of education'. In relation to the very last point I have attempted to show how Stenhouse's idea of 'research-based teaching' is informed by Peters's theory of education as a process. What distinguishes his idea from Hargreaves's idea of 'evidence-based teaching' is that 'what counts as evidence' is not simply evidence about the instrumental effectiveness of the strategies employed to secure certain learning outcomes, but evidence about the extent to which teaching strategies are ethically consistent with *educational* ends. What characterizes Stenhouse's view of educational research is its focus on the problems of realizing a form of teaching in particular contexts of professional practice. He writes:

> The problems selected for inquiry are selected because of their importance as educational problems; that is, for their significance in the context of professional practice. Research and development guided by such problems will contribute primarily to the understanding of educational action through the construction of theory of education or a tradition of understanding. Only secondarily will research in this mode contribute to philosophy, psychology or sociology.
>
> (1979: 19)

Here Stenhouse is alluding to the inseparability of developing a theoretical understanding of educational action and doing educational research into the practical problems of education. If educational research focuses on the problems which arise in trying to realize a form of *educational* practice then it will pose questions both about which actions in the context are constitutive of such a practice and about the educational criteria employed in deciding this. Educational research, on Stenhouse's account, is a process which involves the joint development of educational practice and theory in interaction.

In another paper entitled *Using Research Means Doing Research*, Stenhouse (1979b) explicitly examines the usefulness to teachers of the kind of evidence that Hargreaves advocates as a basis for teaching; namely probabilistic generalizations. He does so in the context of his own research into teaching about race relations in schools which compared the effects of two teaching strategies on student attitudes. The research was undertaken in the wake of the publicity surrounding Stenhouse's Humanities Project. In this project some teachers were asked to adopt a 'procedurally neutral' role in handling race relations as a controversial issue within the school curriculum. Some members of the public objected to an open-ended pedagogy in this area, on the grounds that it was the role of the teacher to inculcate 'positive attitudes' in students towards the members of other races by adopting an anti-racist stance in the classroom. They persisted in doing so in spite of evaluation evidence which showed that procedurally neutral teaching did not harden racist attitudes in students, and indeed appeared to shift those of girls in the direction of greater tolerance of racial differences in society. In this context Stenhouse felt that the effects of an open-minded teaching strategy aimed at 'understanding issues' needed to be compared with one that was explicitly aimed at combating racism. If the latter proved to be more effective in this respect then the former would be inappropriate, however defensible it might appear to be on purely *educational* grounds. Hence, the follow-up research Stenhouse carried out in the form of an experimental trial.

Having gathered and analysed the evidence statistically, he tried to imagine how it might inform a teacher's decision about which strategy to adopt. His imaginary teacher had been adopting a 'procedurally neutral' stance (strategy A) within the research project. Others had been experimenting with a strategy that was explicitly anti-racist (strategy B).

In the scenario Stenhouse depicts, the statistically significant discriminations 'when presented through means and standard deviations' suggests that 'strategy B does not look markedly superior from strategy A'. The imaginary teacher concludes that 'I don't seem to need to change my teaching style.' However, s(he) then examines another page of the research report which presents the same data in a different form 'to show the situation in individual schools'. This complicates the issue for the teacher. The analysis of variance for both strategies show that in a number of schools the results of each strategy are either doubtful or alarming. Also when the pupil data is examined in detail it looks as if 'the same teaching style and the same subject matter make some people worse as they make other people better'. The teacher concludes that: 'what I have to find out now is whether teaching about race relations by Strategy A is good for **my** pupils in **my** school' (1979b: 6).

What Stenhouse does, through this scenario, is to show that psycho-statistical research is no substitute for teachers undertaking *case studies* of their own teaching. However, it can inform teaching as a source of *hypotheses* for teachers to test through systematically conducted experiments in case study form. Stenhouse would not deny Hargreaves's contention that probabilistic evidence of statistical regularities can inform teachers' decisions and constitute actionable knowledge. What he does is to describe the conditions under which teachers can make the best use of such evidence to inform their decisions. This involves the adoption of a research stance towards their teaching and gathering case study evidence about its effects. Stenhouse's *Teaching about Race Relations* research combined both statistically based experimental trials and case studies, in which teachers collaborated with professional researchers.

In *Using Research Means Doing Research*, Stenhouse appears to be providing us with an account of research-based teaching that is not simply concerned with the extent to which teaching strategies are ethically consistent with *educational aims*. In a context where teachers are expected to produce specific outcomes for the benefit of society they are presented with the problem of whether they can teach in ways that are both ethically consistent with their *educational* aims and instrumentally effective. Such a problem can be defined as an *educational* one, since educational values and principles are put at stake by the demand that teaching and learning serves purposes that are extrinsic to education. This introduces a third dimension to *research-based teaching*. Whether, and how, socially mandated learning outcomes can be brought about through an educationally worthwhile process of teaching and learning is a problem for research-based teaching to address. In making a wise and intelligent response to the problem teachers need to base their teaching on evidence about both its *instrumental effectiveness* and its *ethical consistency* with educational aims and procedures.

Although Stenhouse excludes *educational* considerations from his imaginary scenario of a teacher exploring the findings of an experimental trial, it is clear from his paper that the research design was informed by educational values which the public reaction to the 'neutral teacher', as a strategy for teaching about race relations, had put at stake.

In his imaginary scenario about the usefulness of probabilistic evidence to a teacher, Stenhouse (see 1979b: 11) argues that a condition of a teacher making good use of such evidence is that s(he) engages in case-study research that requires a qualitative analysis of meaningful actions and interactions in particular situations. Hence, *using* research means *doing* research. The latter will be largely qualitative because it involves the study of *meaningful actions*, that is actions that cannot be defined simply on the basis of observed behaviour 'without interpretation of the meanings ascribed in the situation by participants'. Although, Stenhouse argues, such situational analysis can draw on probabilistic generalizations, in addition to intuitive organizations of experience and theory, they cannot provide the sole evidential basis for teaching. Teachers themselves, Stenhouse believed, had a critical role to play in constructing an evidence-base for informing professional judgements. He writes:

> Given that by participating in educational settings, he is in a position to interpret meanings in action, he is not able to fulfill his professional role on the basis of probabilistic generalizations but on the contrary is expected to exercise his judgment in situational analysis.
>
> (1979b: 11)

Taking Stenhouse's work on 'research-based teaching' as a whole it is clear that the situational analysis he refers to can involve a teacher in an examination of both learning outcomes and the *educational* quality of classroom processes in contexts of meaningful action. Such an analysis will be based on evidence about the complex transactions between the teacher and his or her students, and between both and 'contextual actors' (parents, principals, other teachers and so on). Such evidence will include evidence of both the observable behaviour of participants and the meanings they ascribe to their own and others' behaviour in the situation (see Stenhouse 1979b: 11).

From Hargreaves's writing, the extent to which he would go along with Stenhouse's view that *using* research means *doing* research is not entirely clear. He acknowledges the limits of probabilistic generalizations as evidence on which to base practice. Hence, the notion of 'evidence-informed practice'. He also acknowledges the significance of *reflection* about the practical situation as a link between evidence and judgement. However, for Hargreaves, 'reflective practice' does not satisfy the conditions for it to be called 'research'. He tends to redefine Stenhouse's teacher-researchers as reflective practitioners. Perhaps the major difference between them is one of perspective. Whereas Hargreaves is primarily concerned with *defining research as a 'basis' for practice*, Stenhouse is primarily concerned with *defining practice as a basis for research*.

Concluding remarks

In this chapter David Hargreaves's ideas about the nature of evidence-based practice and the future direction for educational research have been explored in the light of the work of Richard Peters, on the aims of education, and of Lawrence Stenhouse, on curriculum design and 'research-based teaching'. This has involved revisiting a body of once influential thinking about the nature of education and educational research respectively.

Central to both Peters's and Stenhouse's work is a view about the relationship between educational aims and processes which is neglected in Hargreaves's account of the role of educational research in informing educational practice. The explanation appears to lie in Hargreaves's unquestioning commitment to an outcomes-based view of education. I have tried to show how Stenhouse drew on Peters's educational theory to construct a comprehensive view of *educational* research as 'research-based teaching'.

What is lacking in the contemporary discourse about the future direction and practical utility of educational research is any consideration of the contribution of educational and curriculum theory to conceptualizing its aims and processes. The current discourse is uninformed by any theory about the nature of *educational* practice, and therefore excludes any consideration of the implications of such a theory for educational research. In rectifying this situation we could make a beginning by revisiting the work of Richard Peters and Lawrence Stenhouse. This chapter is a contribution to that 'beginning'. In drawing attention to work that shaped 'a new direction' for both teaching and learning *and* educational research in the recent past, I have tried to demonstrate that its potential as a resource to draw on in conceptualizing links for the future has not yet been exhausted.

13

Using action research to generate knowledge about educational practice

Harry Torrance

Introduction

The debate about evidence-based policy and practice begs many questions of definition and intention. Who could be against evidence-based policy? Who would wish to advocate superstition-based practice? The government's push for evidence-based development of the public services, and particularly education, is at the rhetorical level at least, irresistible. But exactly what is meant by evidence-based practice remains a contentious issue. The government's focus on 'systematic reviews' of current research findings, being conducted according to a particular set of procedures, and produced as irrefutable evidence of the efficacy of a particular policy, seems to be based on a classic centre-periphery research, development, dissemination (RDD) model which has attracted much criticism over many years for its rigid conceptualization of the process of change (for example, Schön 1971; Havelock 1973). The specific operationalization of such reviews can also be problematic since the procedures are drawn so narrowly that sometimes little relevant research can be discovered on a particular policy issue (Evans and Benefield 2001). The research community may or may not be culpable here, but if new research is then commissioned, it certainly means policy-makers will have a long wait for the dissemination phase. If such a model ever was appropriate, it would hardly seem to be so now, given the pace of change that is being engendered in our social and economic life and which in turn is required of our public services. The current imperative would seem to for much more responsive forms of research and development conducted at local level, though this in turn begs questions of how more formal public knowledge of problems and effectiveness might be built.

In education, the idea laid out in David Hargreaves's 1996 Teacher Training Agency (TTA) Annual Lecture 'Teaching as Research-based

Profession', seemed very close to the RDD model whereby research would produce an 'agreed knowledge base for teachers' (p. 2) which 'demonstrates conclusively that if teachers change their practice from x to y there will be a significant and enduring improvement in teaching and learning . . .' (p. 5). Some teachers were envisaged to be at the centre by Hargreaves, helping to define the research agenda, but most were conceived of at the periphery – receiving and implementing the results of such research in schools. More recently Hargreaves has been drawn to a much more local model of research-based practice, the 'Knowledge Creating School' (Hargreaves 1998), whereby teachers would 'tinker' (p. 7) with 'what works' in the mould of engineers working in high-technology businesses. The TTA and Department for Education and Skills (DfES) have been similarly ambivalent in the short time that evidence or research-based practice has had some resources put behind it. They sponsored small- scale research and development work via TTA Research Consortia and the DfES 'Best Practice Research Scholarship' scheme, which were very much in the 'tinkering' mode, yet also aspired to formal knowledge production, through reporting and dissemination mechanisms, including putting BPRS reports on the DfES/BPRS website (http://www.teachernet.gov.uk/ Professional_Development/opportunities/bprs/; see also Cordingley 2000a, and Cordingley's chapter in this volume).

The dilemma, then, seems to be that 'evidence' has to be well-founded and seen to be well-founded, but it also has to be useful and timely if it is to help to improve practice. Thus we seem to be faced with a dichotomy between the pursuit of formal, propositional, *theoretical* knowledge about education, which is the subject of intense debate but nevertheless reasonably well-understood methodological strictures (method to follow from the nature of the problem, findings to be subject to public scrutiny, and so on); and the pursuit of timely, useful, *practical* knowledge which might not be subject to such methodological imperatives and scrutiny. Moreover, while the criticism of public knowledge is that it can become too divorced from practice, too theoretical, and can take too long to be disseminated in classic RDD fashion, the criticism of local knowledge is precisely the reverse – it can be trivial, context-bound and, crucially, unable to conceive of asking fundamental questions about the nature of the problem which tinkering might ameliorate.

A different version of research or evidence-based practice is also available to us, however – the application of research *methods* rather than research findings to educational endeavours and problems. Revisiting Stenhouse (1975), Elliott (2002, and see also his chapter in this volume) refers to this tradition. Drawing on Stenhouse's idea of a curriculum being a hypothesis about knowledge to be tested through practice, Elliott (2002) reminds us that, similarly, substantive research findings can be produced by professional researchers and teachers alike, but they should be treated as hypotheses to be *tested* in the classroom by practitioners, not simply accepted as conclusions to be implemented. Validity and reliability of the knowledge claim is warranted as much by the test of practice, as by the methodological sophistication of the original research design. Indeed, Elliott argues, relationships between producers and users of research should be included in any definition of the methodology of applied research. In this respect, action research, often conceived of as a rather narrow and empiricist approach to professional development and problem-solving in the classroom, can be seen as a more public enterprise and '. . . is best interpreted more generally as a form of applied research aimed at generating actionable knowledge' (2002: 10).

'Primary Response': investigating and developing formative assessment in the primary school

It was with ideas such as these in mind that a colleague, John Pryor, and I designed an action research project to investigate and develop formative approaches to pupil assessment in primary schools – the 'Primary Response' project as it came to be known in the project team.[1] We had completed an earlier, more 'basic' research project exploring how teachers conducted routine, every-day assessments in early years' classrooms. This research indicated that the effectiveness of classroom assessment in helping children to improve their work could not be assumed, and that there were great differences between children in the same class, dependent on their perceptions of the implicit social rules of the classroom and their orientation to achievement goals. Teachers often did not make the purposes of classroom tasks clear, nor indeed the processes by which they could be completed. Far less did they make clear the criteria by which classroom tasks might be *successfully* completed – that is what counted as 'good work'. Interesting examples of more explicit and positive approaches to classroom assessment were also reported, but the research as a whole concluded that attention to the social construction and accomplishment of classroom assessment was a prerequisite for any systematic attempt to improve the quality of interaction and the positive impact of assessment on learning (Torrance and Pryor 1996, 1998).

When reporting our work in conferences and seminars the data were found to be intriguing but also rather frustrating – 'how could such problems be overcome?' was the often asked question. How might one work with classroom teachers to develop effective, formative, classroom assessment? The original research project also produced a dichotomous typology of formative classroom assessment contrasting 'convergent' and 'divergent' approaches to formative assessment (see Torrance and Pryor 1998) which we thought might be the basis for further work – putting the conclusions of basic research to the test of practice in an action research design. Would teachers recognize the validity of the concepts of 'convergent' and 'divergent' assessment, and would they be able to use the concepts and their implications for practice to develop their own classroom assessment strategies? It was with questions such as these in mind that we developed the second more 'applied' action research project design (Torrance and Pryor 1999, 2001).

We were interested in investigating through collaborative action research whether, and to what extent, teachers could develop their classroom assessment practices and integrate them into a more self-consciously articulated model of classroom pedagogy, in order to test the claims of formative assessment in ordinary classroom settings. We also wanted to explore whether and to what extent an 'action research' approach could help to accomplish the process of development.

Methodology and design

More substantive accounts of the project's findings are reported in Torrance (2001) and Torrance and Pryor (2001). This chapter focuses on the methodological origins and implications of the project. The research team comprised teacher researchers (TRs), conducting research on their own classroom practices, and university researchers (Torrance and Pryor) who combined additional interviewing and classroom observation with the orchestration of overall team development and direction. The 'action research' approach involved discussing with the TRs their implicit theories of learning and assessment while also supporting them in investigating practice within their own classrooms and thus developing knowledge about particular events and practices. Thus the project sought to explore the extent to which such an approach to professional development and knowledge creation could be utilized in this field (Elliott 1991, 1994; Altrichter *et al.* 1993).[2]

A team of 11 teacher researchers were recruited in collaboration with a neighbouring Local Education Authority (LEA). A 'flyer' was sent to all primary schools in the authority, resulting in an initial meeting which included two teachers who had been involved with the previous basic research project and wished to continue to be involved. The only selection criteria were the TRs' interest in the project and their headteacher's support: thus the team comprised a group of what one might term very 'ordinary' primary school teachers (ten female, one male) in terms of their qualifications and career development, though of course they were volunteering to become involved in a research project.

The work developed through two cycles or phases, in 'classic' action research design terms: phase 1, reconnaissance; and phase 2, intervention for development. Data were gathered by the TRs through the audio and video recording of assessment interactions in their classrooms and by keeping research diaries and examples of students' work. A 'core' of seven TRs completed seven initial investigations of their classroom assessment practices (phase 1) and five of these went on to explore specific interventions and new approaches (phase 2). Thus, of the eleven TRs originally recruited, five completed two cycles of research activity resulting in project reports; two completed one cycle and report; while four withdrew during the first eight months of the project without producing any written reports – either through pressure of work at school (such as promotion) or through ill health.

A central part of the methodological approach was that the development of the TRs' 'practical arguments' (Fenstermacher 1986) should be enabled and facilitated through the introduction of key theoretical resources. In particular the concepts of convergent and divergent assessment were to comprise the core resources. However, phase 1 of the project contributed to the further development of these resources, which were then able to be tested and further developed in phase 2. During phase 1 the university researchers were also working on the manuscript of a book of the previous project (Torrance and Pryor 1998). Partly as a result of phase 1 discussions, we used the data from the basic research project to develop a descriptive and analytic framework of the processes of formative assessment which formed a significant part of the concluding chapter of the book. At the same time as the TRs' first reports were circulated to all team members, the final manuscript of the book was also made available to TRs. The analytic framework was then used by team members to describe and analyse their own practices. Although subsequently viewed more critically, especially with respect to how it was necessary to reintegrate aspects of the framework into a more holistic model of classroom assessment, the utility of this framework became one of the key findings of the overall project. Thus the team used, tested and modified both the original concepts of convergent and divergent assessment and the analytic framework. Subsequent modification of the framework represented a key aspect of the transformative process from classroom research to more self-conscious and theoretically-informed classroom practice. (See Torrance and Pryor 1998, and Torrance and Pryor 2001 for a detailed account of the descriptive and analytic framework of the processes of formative classroom assessment.)

Developing 'actionable knowledge'

As the TR team began to study their own classroom assessment practices, a significant discovery in the reconnaissance phase was that in many cases their teaching seemed to close down opportunities for exploring pupil understanding rather than opening them up. A second consistent finding in this opening phase, was that very little of the purpose of classroom activities was made clear to pupils, far less what would count as success in terms of quality. The TRs were surprised to discover how little they focused on learning goals as opposed to behavioural goals and classroom management. And this is a particularly intriguing issue for the development of practice since it revealed a discontinuity between theory and practice – the TRs knew that they should focus on learning goals, and thought that they were, but discovered that, in practice, they were not. Thus another key finding of the overall project is that teachers need the opportunity to monitor and reflect on their own classroom practices – to investigate them in detail – before being ready then to think about how best to develop more principled intervention strategies.

From this opening phase certain key concerns were identified for investigation in the second cycle of action research:

(i) the need to make more explicit what was the purpose of certain activities and what would count as doing them well (i.e. task and quality criteria);

(ii) the need to respond more flexibly to students in the classroom and think about developing a more 'divergent' approach to formative assessment; in particular this was manifested in a concern to develop different approaches to questioning, observation of the students at work, and feedback.

The first phase had heightened the TRs' awareness of the complexity of classroom interactions, and a great deal of what they routinely did was now called into question. The framework introduced at the beginning of phase 2 provided an analytic account of the range of possible activities included in formative classroom assessment, and a vocabulary with which to interrogate, express and organize their data and subsequent ideas for development. Conceptual distinctions, such as that between 'task criteria' and 'quality criteria' came to be regarded as important analytic tools. They not only provided a means to describe and explain the areas of their practice on which they had already focused, but also brought into the open other elements of their intuitive and implicit practice. Thus the framework was used in parallel with data which the TRs had themselves gathered in their own classrooms, as a device for disinterring their practice and subjecting it to detailed analysis in identifying the frequency and importance of each of the different processes.

Here it is important to note that the TRs began to use the vocabulary (and, by implication at least, the embedded conceptualizations) of convergent and divergent assessment, and of the framework for formative assessment itself. They very explicitly subjected their own practice to analysis in these terms, although subsequently became dissatisfied with the detail of the framework, and thus generated an (at least implicit) critique of the overly detailed conceptualization contained within it.

The following transcript demonstrates an attempt to focus on 'communication' issues and then use one example to illustrate task and quality criteria to the class. The processes of formative assessment, summarized and italicized by the TR in the final paragraph, derive directly from the vocabulary used in the framework.

I am moving around the class looking at the children working. Children put their hands up or come up to me as and when they require help and advice. Rebecca approaches me with a draft copy of the book that she is working on with Selena.

T: This is what I like to see! Where are you sitting, Rebecca?

I follow Rebecca back to her table and open the book.

T: Right *(reads)* – Looking After Dogs. Number 1 – Types. You can get lots of sorts of dogs like black labradors, spaniels, golden retrievers. Food and drink, meat, water, dog biscuits it might be useful there to ask – find out how many times a day a dog needs to be fed because they don't have breakfast, lunch and dinner do they? . . . Either try and look it up some where or perhaps ask somebody who knows . . . somebody like Daniel – he's got a dog hasn't he? Also you need to take a dog for a walk every day – sometimes twice a day, some big dogs.

I continue reading.

Grooming – for grooming you need a brush, and brush the dog. Why? Why's that important?

R: To keep it clean.

T: To keep it clean – that's right, to get rid of insects and um – to keep it healthy [. . .] and Training. To train a dog you have to make it sit and jump over things. Why's it important that they learn how to do as they're told? You need to explain perhaps a little bit but apart from that it's absolutely brilliant.

S: Shall we use the books over there?

Points to Reference book section of book shelves.

T: Yep. You can go to the library as well if you want.

(To the class) Can everyone stop! I know you're not all doing books like this and you don't all want them set out like this but this is the sort of point where they can start making this into a book now. It's excellent – they've got their cover, with the title and it's obvious what it's about isn't it? [continues]

This may appear to be a lengthy extract of transcript but in fact it was less than three minutes of interaction. Yet within it seven different strategies of formative assessment can be identified. Initially

I examine Rebecca and Selena's work to *gain understanding* of what they have been doing; then I ask *principled questions* (asking them to consider why it's important) in order to gain insight into their knowledge and understanding and I also try to *communicate task criteria* by suggesting that they need to extend their information; I then assign a *judgment* to the work by referring to it as 'brilliant' before *reinforcing the task criteria to the whole class*; by exemplifying the structure of the book I demonstrate quality criteria; then finally suggest what needs to be done in order to get to this stage.

(TR 5)

Of course one might argue that this teacher researcher is simply reporting what she thinks she ought to report – the classic 'performance goal' response to assessment rather than a 'learning goal' response (Dweck 1989). But much other evidence from this TR and others in the team demonstrates critical engagement with the concepts; and in fact the key issue from the above extract for the argument here is actually that 'it was less than three minutes of interaction'. Ultimately, while the framework was helpful in analysing and thinking about practice, that is it helped to produce 'actionable knowledge' (Elliott 2002), it was not a directly useful prescription for action, which is sometimes what the evidence-based practice lobby seems to want research to produce.

A further example, shown in Table 13.1, makes this even more clear, as TR 1 refers, almost in passing, to the 'real life' of the classroom:

'F' often follows 'E' in the 'real life' of the classroom: Questioning/Eliciting/Clarifying is part-and-parcel of routine teacher–pupil interaction. This identifies children's understanding of the knowledge they have gained. Its effectiveness depends on the quality of questioning by the teacher. In my experience, this fluctuated according to my energy levels. The information gained from this type of questioning can provide more information for planned changes in the child's development.

The next brief conversation clearly shows an example of how I ask for clarification about what has been said. It is not a pseudo question, it genuinely engages the pupil's interest while also providing a further opportunity for using the answer to reiterate the task and the criteria which I wanted the children to use. The simple question 'why?' is both principled and clarificatory so long as it is related to communicating criteria.

Abe: I think it sounds cool.
   T: Why?
   Abe: Because I like ghosts.
   T: Right, so therefore it does sound interesting to you. Now, what about describing how the characters actually feel, which is the actual point on the check list.

(TR 1)

Table 13.1 A Teacher researcher uses elements of the framework to analyse her teaching and feedback to pupils

E: Questioning/Eliciting

Description	Possible teacher intentions	Possible resultant effect for pupil
C T asks principled question, (seeks to elicit evidence of what P knows, understands or can do). P responds	Insight into P's knowledge, understanding or skills.	Rehearsal of knowledge, understanding, or skills; articulation of understanding to realize understanding.

F: Clarifying

Description	Possible teacher intentions	Possible effect for pupil
F T asks for clarification about what has been done/is being done; P replies	Gain in understanding of what P has done.	Re-articulation of understanding; enhanced self-awareness and skills of summary, reflection, prediction, speculation

Here, the TR refers to a 'checklist' of points for structuring and making a story interesting which she had developed through a previous activity with the class – attempting to make task and quality criteria explicit by discussing them at length and getting the class to agree a checklist to which they could all refer. More important for the discussion here how-ever, is the reference to 'real life' and the transitory contexts in which instant judgements about 'principled' interventions in learning must be made. 'Tinkering' might describe what this teacher is doing, but it is tinkering with a purpose and informed by considerable prior thought and discussion – with colleagues in the Primary Response team and with her class.

Although engagement with the framework seemed to constitute an important prerequisite for the improvement of practice, it did not in itself represent or provide a direct guide to action. Rather, although the TRs became aware of the conceptual distinctions between the different processes of formative assessment, and could relate them to examples of their own practice, they emphasized that, in classroom situations, these processes were often embedded one within another, or occurred in linked sequences or progressions. Thus key elements of the analytic categories became reintegrated into new, more self-consciously theorized practice. The categories of the initial framework were a useful device for conceptualization and mental referencing, but the actual accomplishment of formative assessment involved movement within more holistic and permeable categories. Figure 13.1 attempts to represent this dynamic process, reintegrating into a practical classroom model the analytic categories included in the original framework. It does so using language generated by the TRs ('helping' as well as 'testing' questions). In particular, it places clarity of criteria at the core of classroom practice, but established dynamically, through the interaction of questioning, observation and feedback, rather than simply being stated or asserted, as through a more sequential or transmission-oriented model.

Thus the framework provided a vocabulary for analysis, but did so in the context of the TR's own perceived need for making sense of what they had experienced through their reconnaissance phase. Exploratory data collection combined with extensive team discussions had encouraged them to examine their own tacit theories of learning and assessment and resulted in a change in their understanding of formative classroom assessment. Having begun by thinking about exploring the validity of convergent and divergent assessment, and being struck by just how convergent their current practice was, the framework (which was itself developed in dialogue with them) enabled them to reappraise their practices and provided them with a catalyst for further classroom development. Unlike a catalyst however, the framework did not emerge unscathed from the (re)action. It required significant modification to become more of a representative model of action. Similarly, while the TRs

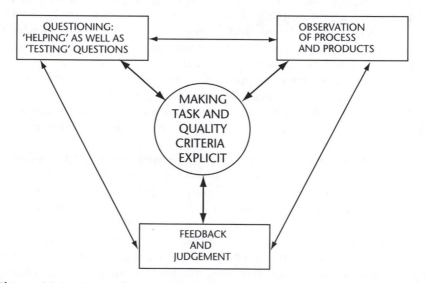

Figure 13.1 Formative assessment in practice
(Source: Torrance and Pryor 2001)

wished to explore and develop the 'divergent' approach to assessment more thoroughly than the 'convergent' approach, they nevertheless still argued that convergent approaches were important, and indeed inevitable given the convergence of the curriculum and constraints on teacher time. They came to understand that they could develop and use a 'repertoire' of assessment strategies and practices and did not have to 'implement' something completely new. They used the concept of divergent assessment as a heuristic device with which to explore and expand the boundaries of their classroom practice.

Thus the second phase of the action research involved the development and implementation of new classroom practices where analysis was less important than the need to integrate and synthesize new understandings and the various categories of the framework. The result was changed, more self-consciously theorized ways of approaching formative assessment, which were informed by the convergent/divergent model and the framework but which in practice conformed more to the process shown in Figure 13.1. An important contention here, however, is that simply starting with the more integrated model presented in Figure 13.1 would not be so productive, since it would hide as much as it revealed of the complexity of the process. Conducting the action research and generating the model was an important transformational act in moving from theory to practice.

Drawing on Elliott (1991, 1994, 2002), Fenstermacher (1986) and others, the collaborative research relationship can be represented as in Figure 13.2.

Although this model of collaborative research makes clear that the TRs had an impact on the conceptualizations of the university-based researchers as well as the researchers on the TRs, and in this sense played an important part in the generation of new knowledge, it has been the university-based researchers (including myself, of course, in this chapter) that have 'garnered' this knowledge and transformed it into communicable public form.

From actionable knowledge to knowledge about action

Where then, does this leave us in relation to the issue of developing evidence-based practice? The structure and sequence of collaboration between the university researchers and the TRs comprised:

- introductory input by the university researchers, raising issues of assessment and learning;
- discussions of the logic and methods of action research;
- design of specific investigations in individual classrooms;

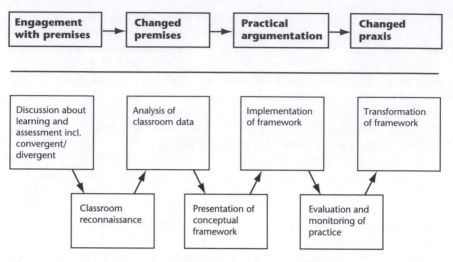

Figure 13.2   Model for collaborative action by university and teacher researchers.
(Source: Torrance and Pryor 2001)

- reporting of progress and discussion of data;
- presentation of emerging findings – both substantive and method-ological – and more explicit interrogation of the problems and possibilities of formative classroom assessment.

Clearly the TRs developed their practice on the basis of evidence, evidence supplied by the university researchers and by their own investigations. In turn, the collaborative applied research has resulted in the production of theoretical categories, an analytic framework and a more informed understanding about how these might interact, heuristically, with practice. But this developed practice and these better understandings have been produced as a result of significant research investment and the commitment to knowledge production of the university-based researchers. The significant questions were raised in the first instance by theory and the prior basic research project. Turning these into actionable knowledge required focused work by the TRs, but turning that back into knowledge-about-action has required further reflection on theory. While the TRs were integrated into a supportive team, they remained immersed in their own projects, developing 'actionable knowledge' about their own classrooms. The project allowed TRs the opportunity to 'problematise their educational practices by reflecting on their underlying meanings' (Elliott, MacLure and Sarland 1996), but the generation of public know-ledge, that is the distillation of findings, establishment of an overview and theorization at a meta-level, remained the province of the university researchers. An important element of this public knowledge, however, is confirmation that teachers do indeed need to 'do research in order to use research' effectively (Stenhouse 1979). Investigating and reflecting upon their own classroom practices was crucial to developing an understanding of theory-in-practice. Thus the 'findings' of the research are as much about the methodology of implementing evidence-based practice as they are about the substance of developing effective assessment practices.

Overall, successful collaboration was an outcome of the fact that neither TRs nor university researchers would have been able to accomplish what they did without each other. This would seem to be a realistic form of collaboration to aspire to in the future, but it is also a much more theoretically informed and resource intensive collaboration than is apparently envisaged by many current developments of evidence-based practice. In the course of the action research schools and teachers came under increasing performance and accountability pressures – league tables, target-setting for the improvement of national test results, Ofsted inspections, the introduction of the National Literacy and Numeracy strategies. It was difficult to sustain the work given these other pressures on the TRs. Of the original team of 11, three withdrew because of work pressures and one because of ill health. Of the remaining core team of seven, all had Ofsted inspections during the course of the project. That the work was sustained and brought to any sort of successful conclusion is a testimony to the determination of the teachers involved, and to the intellectual rewards that such work can bring to a professional group working in an environment that they feel is increasingly utilitarian and hostile. However, these pressures (and resource issues) beg severe questions about the feasibility of teachers to be involved in research as both conductors of investigations and users of results.

Similarly, close relationships with the collaborating LEA, although sustained, did not bring as much benefit as might have been anticipated because the primary school policy agenda had moved on from implementing formative assessment to implementing the Literacy and Numeracy strategies and target-setting. Although the LEA intended to use the teacher researchers as a 'cadre' of excellent teachers with respect to classroom assessment, this has not happened as the LEA's policy attention (and key personnel) have had to shift elsewhere.

As noted earlier the TRs could be described as a very ordinary group of primary school teachers: representing a range of age and experience and even, perhaps, under-qualified in traditional higher education terms, for example, for entry to Masters-level work. For the most part they produced excellent investigations and reports under difficult circumstances and demonstrate what can be achieved with good resourcing and support. However, the whole process of 'going public' seemed remote from their professional priorities as well as hard to accomplish within their very crowded professional lives. My involvement in other initiatives, such as mentoring BPRS holders, providing consultancy to Training Schools and so forth, albeit with less systematic attention to methodology than reported here, similarly indicates that without addressing issues of central policy prescription and system micro-management, initiative overload and the terms and conditions of teachers work, much of the current rhetoric about developing evidence-based practice will remain just that – political rhetoric which is likely to undermine the activities of educational research *per se*, rather than being a meaningful contribution to the reconstruction and improvement of the research endeavour overall. Work will be produced which might be claimed as 'research' (certainly as 'evidence') and which will trade on the legitimacy of research as a systematic form of inquiry, while actually producing little more than anecdotal accounts of constrained policy implementation. Producing actionable knowledge in schools requires the provision of significant theoretical resources and the use of research methods to test and modify their utility in action. Producing knowledge about practice requires systematic investigation of practice and the time and space to reflect on the significance of problems and incongruities, and of associated institutional constraints on action. Evidence-based practice must necessarily involve that dialectic.

Notes

1 Supported by the Economic and Social Research Council (ESRC: R000236860; 1997–99).
2 Seven TRs produced the data and written reports on which we draw here: Julie Collins, Jane Cowley, Janice Gill, Margaret Maiden, Sandie Piper, Susie Round and Sally Turner. We are extremely indebted to all the hard work and intellectual contribution made to the project by the teacher researchers.

14

Conclusion: evidence-based policy and practice

Richard Pring

Introduction

The idea of 'evidence based health care', when it first came to be articulated, and indeed became the basis of a Masters course at the University of Oxford, struck me as odd to say the least. It came as a surprise to learn that decisions over the most appropriate form of medical treatment were not necessarily based on evidence – for that seemed to be the implication. Medical prognosis and treatment, I had taken for granted, would be based on scientific research. Indeed, to qualify as a doctor required a rigorous background in the relevant science.

However, the Cochrane Centre in Oxford, under the leadership of Sir Ian Chalmers, did not have such confidence. Much practice was, as it were, 'inherited wisdom'. Other practice, apparently based on evidence, competed with other practices based on other evidence. Anyone who has sought medical help for back problems will know what I mean.

In many respects, this should not be surprising. A merely superficial acquaintance with the philosophy of science makes it clear that science grows from constant (and often successful) attempts to negate the current state of scientific knowledge. All such knowledge is, as it were, provisional – to be accepted until such time as it is refuted and replaced by more comprehensive and better-corroborated scientific propositions. But such development in science, such gradual 'approximation to the truth', depends on the application of rigorous scientific methods whereby error is to be eliminated. The Cochrane Centre believed that such rigorous methods were often lacking in the arrival at medical 'truths' which informed and shaped medical practice.

Such methods required strictly controlled experiments, with very large control and experimental groups, so that one might see clearly the difference which a particular intervention might make. But this in turn required extremely careful articulation of the hypotheses to be tested, and that in turn required a sophisticated process of refining the felt problem (felt as often as not by the patients as much as by the medical researchers) into a testable set of hypotheses. Furthermore, such large-scale experiments would have to take into account the research which others had conducted in similar areas. But that required putting together pieces of research which, more often than not, were based on different samples or which made slightly different assumptions. Hence, an important part of refining the evidence lay in the systematic review of existing research, rejecting that which did not meet rigorous experimental criteria, ignoring that where the data and method were less than clear, reconciling where possible the different bases for the samples, identifying where further research was needed to fill the gaps in our scientifically based knowledge. These systematic reviews and the subsequent meta-analyses of available research (which are described by Davies, Gough and Andrews in this volume) were difficult and time-consuming. They required co-operation across continents. They required an explicitness of, and openness to, the problem, the hypotheses, the sampling process and the data. They encouraged open and critical debate, and the constant refinement of the conclusions in the light of that critical debate and new data. Indeed, 'evidence based', so conceived, had a thoroughly Popperian ring to it.

Such has been the success of the Cochrane Centre's work that people in other areas of the public services have looked for the lessons which can be learnt from it. The Campbell Collaboration, based in the United States, but with regional centres in Canada and Denmark, has extended the work to other areas of social life – for example, education and criminology. This is described very well by Davies in this volume. Both the Secretary of State for Education and the Home Office saw the approach of Cochrane and Campbell to be what was required to improve the quality of research to inform both government policy and professional practice. And this was seen to be necessary because of the criticisms of that research, certainly in education. The criticisms were several, but they might be summarized as saying that the research was: too fragmented (too little of the large scale and 'bold' hypotheses thoroughly tested); based on different assumptions, samples and data; often less than rigorous in method; not unambiguously addressed to a specific question to which the policy-maker or the practitioner needs an answer.

The reaction to the transfer, to the field of education, of the evidence-based approach of Cochrane and Campbell has varied from the hostile to the welcoming. That is reflected in this volume. But the essence of these criticisms and of the differences between them is philosophical. It concerns the nature of research, and that in turn the nature of knowledge. What counts as evidence for a particular kind of knowledge claim? In this paper I shall briefly outline what I think are the key philosophical difficulties, not simply in the adoption of evidence-based policy and practice, but also in some of the criticisms of it.

These philosophical issues are: first, the nature of 'evidence'; second, the extension of the methods of the natural sciences to understanding of human beings; third, the adoption of a means/end model of educational planning and decision-making.

Evidence

A lot depends on how one interprets the word 'evidence'. There are many different kinds of evidence, depending on the type of claim being made. Evidence that water boils at 100 degrees Centigrade at sea level would be very different from the evidence to indicate that a rock face is 100 million years old or that Caesar really did cross the Rubicon or that Saddam Hussein's regime was evil or that Freddie has been a good boy. There are different forms of discourse, each characterized by different ways of looking at the world, different kinds of truth claim, different ways of investigating the truth. What counts as evidence will depend upon the kind of discourse one is engaged in. Historical evidence is different from that in science, and even within science there are different sorts of discourse, each characterized by differences in what is deemed to constitute evidence. Hence, there is a danger of criticizing a piece of evidence because it does not meet the standards of evidence in a quite different form of discourse. Indeed, that is the cause of certain problems within the arguments 'for' and 'against' evidence-based policy and practice within education. Some, who advocate 'evidence-based', do so by blurring the boundaries between scientific and non-scientific forms of discourse, thereby rejecting certain claims as without foundation. On the other hand, certain critics, by identifying evidence-base with only one sort of evidence, reject entirely the idea of 'evidence-based' as irrelevant to the complex problems of educational policy and professional practice. Furthermore, 'evidence' must not be confused with proof. I have evidence that John told a lie, but I cannot prove it. One can gradually build up the evidence for a belief but gradually proving it seems a little odd. On the basis of evidence, it may be *probable* that something is the case – although there may be counter-evidence which is less persuasive.

These comments are by no means irrelevant to the educational debate. Often politicians seem to advocate an evidence-based policy as though one should only act when one can demonstrate that a particular course of action is *proven* to be the correct one. They feel let down when the research, on the basis of which a particular policy is adopted, turns out to be less than adequate. But all one can say, as a result of research, is that in the light of all the evidence, and balancing the evidence both 'for' and 'against', one course of action seems to be the most rational one to adopt. And, indeed, that may well be the case, until such time as contrary evidence is discovered. Furthermore, the evidence upon which one acts can be weak or strong, and, very often, one has no alternative but to act on weak evidence. The teacher, faced with a quick decision over the treatment of an offender, has no time to find conclusive evidence. 'Deliberation', followed by 'judgement', requires a quick survey of different kinds of often weak evidence before action is swiftly taken – proximity to the scene, previous record of similar behaviour, a *prima facie* motive. Indeed, evidence here is much more like the notion of evidence in a detective novel than it is in scientific research. And notions of 'deliberation' and 'practical judgement' (which goes beyond the available evidence) cannot be avoided.

Furthermore, educational discourse is eclectic. It draws upon different kinds of evidence – scientific certainly, but also personal insight, historical, psychological. What is to count as evidence in any one situation will depend on the particular educational judgements being made, and generalizations will always be negated by particular cases – a point which I shall develop in the next section. Thus, educational practice requires judgements about 'achievement' as well as about the 'ability to achieve' and about the 'capacity to have the ability to achieve'. It requires judgement about intention as well as motivation. But no amount of observed behaviour, though logically related in normal circumstances to having certain intentions (for example, to complete one's homework) or to being motivated in a particular way (for example, to please one's parents), proves or means that such *is* the intention or the motive for action. There is always a logical gap between the conclusion and the evidence for the conclusion.

These preliminary remarks on the concept of evidence precede a discussion of the more philosophical issues arising out of the papers in this volume. For at the heart of the understandings of evidence-based policy and practice, and indeed of the arguments about the importance we should attach to it, are philosophical issues about the nature of evidence, of proof, of knowledge within the social sciences and of educational discourse and judgement.

Philosophical issues

I want to pick out three interconnected philosophical issues which, in one way or another, arise in the various contributions. These are:

1. the logical unpredictability of all the consequences of a particular course of action or a particular policy;

2. the irreconcilability of scientific discourse (and thus the social sciences within a particular tradition) with that concerned with persons;
3. the logical separation of educational 'ends' or 'goals' from the 'means' of achieving them.

Unpredictability

The first issue concerns the difficulty in predicting what will happen if . . . in complex social situations. (It is an argument developed very effectively by Luntley (2000), in connection with the proposal for performance-related pay.) Thus, the government, in the light of evidence, believes that a particular policy will have certain predictable results. And, indeed, from the government's point of view, research should be indicating what consequences will follow from certain policies. What practices are most effective in achieving the desired results? However, there are two senses in which this cannot be the case.

The first sense is that the agents, whose actions are being predicted by the adoption of such a policy, change the context in which the predictions are made once they are aware of what is being intended. Once the pupils are aware of the rationale for the emphasis upon literacy strategies (for example, raising the scores of the school and thus the position of the school in the league table) so they are able, and might be willing, to subvert the policy. Such changed consciousness and its effects could not themselves be anticipated in the development of the strategy, however evidence-based that was in the light of previous practice. The second, and connected sense, is this. According to Luntley (p. 17),

> classrooms (and other educational units) share a common structural feature with other social and natural systems – namely, non-linearity. Ignore this and you get a faulty logic of understanding of the system at issue.

Within very complex systems of interacting elements, especially when those elements are endowed with intelligence and where the interactions are consciously engaged in, the full impact of all these millions of inter-actions cannot be predicted with accuracy. And the impossibility of so doing is not just a matter of size and complexity. Rather it is a logical matter, for one interaction changes the nature of the situation such that the effect of x upon y will not be the same the second time round. The many different elements in the situation are interacting with each other in a way that cannot be controlled from the centre, and they are thus chan-ging the context which the centre wishes to control and influence. In economics, the countless interactions in the marketplace constantly change the context in which macro-economic management is meant to take place. The tax changes also 'tax' the imagination of those who seek

new and unpredicted ways of dodging the taxes, thereby creating a different economic and social situation, which in turn makes unpredictable
demands upon the economy.

Given this necessary unpredictability of complex social situations, there
is a limit to how far the accumulation of evidence can ensure certain
consequences will follow from carefully considered interventions.

Explaining human behaviour

Educational policy and professional practice are ultimately about getting
people (usually young people) to learn something – and something which
is deemed to be of value. To educate is to develop the capacity to think,
to value, to understand, to reason, to appreciate. These are states of mind,
mental capacities, distinctively human qualities. One feature of such
states of mind is that they constitute a different kind of 'reality' from that
which is the subject matter of the natural sciences. I can observe tables
and chairs; I cannot observe in the same way intentions, motives and
thoughts. The hand raised is seen by everyone, but may well be interpreted very differently – a wave to a friend, a request for attention, the
signalling of a revolution, an expression of exasperation. The understanding of that behaviour depends on knowing the intention – and the
motivation for so intending. Thus, the request for attention (the intention
of raising the arm) could be motivated by boredom or by excitement at a
discovery or by the wish to annoy. Explaining human actions requires
reference to intentions and motives, not to causes (generally speaking).

Furthermore, those intentions and motives presuppose a social context
of rules whereby the intended behaviours are going to be interpreted by
others in a particular way. It is no good signalling a revolution if the fellow
revolutionaries do not understand the gesture. To explain human actions
requires a grasp of the social rules through which social intercourse is
able to take place. Furthermore, such social rules will change from social
group to social group – indeed, a social group is partly defined in terms
of the social rules through which they engage with each other. There
is a set of expectations among allotment owners which shapes their
behaviours in a way which would not be fully understood by those who
have never been apprenticed to this form of life. And no doubt these rules
and expectations vary from one allotment to another as populations and
economic circumstances change. (Candlelight dinner parties are held by
some allotment holders on our patch, but none the less within a social
context which inherits certain expectations from previous allotment
holders.) Explanation, without reference to such social rules and context
and without recognition of their variability according to different social
and economic circumstances, is not an explanation of the *human* world
we inhabit.

Certain consequences about evidence-based policy and practice are drawn from these considerations – some valid and some not so. First, the distinctive nature of human explanation must set logical limits to large-scale explanations of behaviour, whether educational or not. Such large-scale explanations cannot be sensitive to the complexity and variability of social rules and expectations through which decisions and actions are made intelligible. The significance of being numerate or literate, the value of higher education, the respect for the teacher, an interest in literature, and so on will be different from one social group to another – whether such groupings are determined by ethnicity, religious tradition, economic affiliation, social class, regional history or family allegiance. What might 'work' in one context might not do so in another, and the reason might be partly explicable in terms of the social rules and the institutional framework (of family, of religious faith, of civic custom) within which the agents are making sense of the world, finding value in some activities rather than others or developing relationships of a particular kind. That is why evidence-based practice needs to look carefully at the particular contexts (the implicit rules and expectations which shape behaviour and which are sometimes embodied within the institutions the learners belong to) in which professional judgement and decisions are to be made.

However, a second consequence is often falsely drawn from these considerations. Such importance is attached to the intentional explanation of human behaviour and activity, and indeed to the variability of social context, that the large-scale explanation of educational practice is rejected entirely. A sharp contrast is drawn between the kind of evidence which pertains to the explanation of physical events (and included in that would be the successful intervention of drugs in the treatment of diseases) and the kind of evidence which pertains to the explanation of human behaviour. Favoured by the former, but not by the latter, would be the large-scale and carefully matched experimental and control groups, in which a particular intervention within the experimental group (all else being held equal) would demonstrate its causal significance. Certainly, such large-scale experiments are seen to be the way forward by some in advancing our knowledge of educational improvement. And there are examples of such interventions in research into early learning (see Sylva and Hurrell, 1995, into the effectiveness of Reading Recovery and the phonological training of children with reading problems). However, the critics point to the failure of such evidence to address the particularities of the social situations which are meant to be explained. And that failure is seen to be at base philosophical – the adoption of what are often referred to as *positivism* which has no place in our understanding of human beings and social institutions. There can be no 'science of man' – the title of a paper by the once most prominent logical positivist, A.J. Ayer.

This is surely a mistaken conclusion. It commits what I refer to as the 'uniqueness fallacy'. It is correct to point to the uniqueness of each individual, since he or she is defined partly in terms of the particular way in which the world is seen and appreciated (no one can have exactly my thoughts and feelings). Similarly, it is correct to point to the uniqueness of each social group or society, reflected in the social rules and expectations which distinguish that group. But although each person or each society might be unique in some respect, it is not the case that each is unique in every respect. I am unique in that no one shares the same life history, but I am not unique as an Englishman, as a university professor, as a writer, as an allotment holder. And, in all these things, I can, within certain parameters, be predicted, under normal conditions, to behave in a certain way. Furthermore, what enables me to understand (if only to some extent) people within very different societies from my own is that all human beings, whatever their differences, have certain propensities, desires, needs and wants in common. There is such a thing as a recognizable human form of life which enables us to make predictions, even though in particular cases the predictions may be wrong – the person consciously bucks the trend. But even the exceptions can be understood in the light of further explanation that helps us to make sense of the situation. And 'explanations', by their very nature, put the unique case into a wider framework in which the uniqueness diminishes somewhat. A person fails to act as predicted because he was ambitious for a specific acknowledgement, but 'ambition' is a recognizable human motive. To say that someone acted out of ambition is to place his actions within a wider explanatory framework.

Therefore, to contrast so starkly the large-scale explanations of human behaviour, characterized by predictors of what will happen (having arrived at such a position through randomized control experiments), with the uniqueness of the individual human condition, which escapes any such pigeon-holing, is a false dualism. Much is predictable about human behaviour. And key interventions can be identified which, generally speaking, will lead to certain consequences. To draw different conclusions is to commit the uniqueness fallacy.

But of course one needs to be very careful in spelling out the conditions in which the intervention is likely to make a difference. Such conditions might refer to the particular kind of institution or social arrangement. An intervention in a highly selective system of schooling might have little effect in a non-selective system. The literacy hour might be effective in certain teaching environments and not in others. The Cochrane ideal was not to determine professional practice but to inform it. The teacher, aware of what generally speaking is likely to be the case, may well exercise professional judgement about the circumstances, which are judged to be sufficiently different from the norm as to create an exception to the general rule.

Means and ends

The concern for evidence-based policy and practice arises within a climate of 'improvement', 'raising standards', 'making schools more effective'. Knowledge is required of 'what works'. To do this, so the argument goes, there is a need to set targets, as specific as possible. These are the goals to be aimed at, the ends to be striven for. It seems plausible to argue that you cannot be very effective until you know exactly where you are going. Only then can you focus your energy and effort on reaching your goals. Having established those targets, the school or the local authority or the government can then discover (by the most appropriate empirical inquiry) the way in which those targets can be met. Such investigation relies upon unambiguous and clear targets. And it requires rigorous research into the most effective means of hitting those targets.

Within such a climate, there has been in the last decade a massive expansion of research into school effectiveness – the characteristics of a school and its leadership which will ensure 'success'. Success is spelt out in terms of very precise targets (such as a given proportion of students attaining grades at GCSE and A Level). Similarly, effective teaching (clearly essential to the effective school) is defined in terms of pupil performance, which can be precisely measured. With systematic gathering of evidence, one might develop a science of effective teaching (see, for example, Reynolds 1998). Once the government or whoever is assured, on the basis of rigorously conducted experiments, of the right interventions to make, then it will put in place the right mechanisms for ensuring higher performance against the agreed standards. And, indeed, teachers will then receive payment which is performance-related.

It is within this climate that a major authority on evidence-based education policies (Slavin 2002) confidently writes about 'transforming educational practice and research' and refers with approval to the various government initiatives which have adopted 'experimental-control comparisons on standards-based measures'. For example, the Bush administration's 'No Child Left Behind' mentions scientifically based research 110 times – 'rigorous, systematic and objective procedures to obtain valid knowledge ... using experimental or quasi-experimental designs, preferably with random assignments'.

Within the now prevalent managerial discourse (a discourse of 'performance indicators' and 'audits', of 'curriculum delivery' and 'efficiency gains', of 'targets' and 'value addedness', of 'clients' and 'stakeholders'), the means/end model of educational planning and engagement seems almost self-evidently correct. There is a logical separation of the 'ends' of education from the 'means' of achieving those ends. The connection is purely contingent, a matter solely of empirical investigation. And in the educational encounter, the teacher is the expert (hopefully on the basis of the right evidence) in knowing what 'means' will most effectively attain those 'ends'. The teacher's expertise lies not in the deliberations over the 'ends' themselves.

Such a language, which lends itself to a particular understanding of evidence-based policy and practice, is superficially plausible, but is a quite impoverished way of talking about and understanding education, for the 'ends' are more often than not embedded within the 'means'. The way in which one analyses a poem is not assessed in terms of being the most effective way of attaining goals, logically distinct from the reading and the analysis of the poem. The goal, end or purpose shapes the way in which the teacher teaches – it is captured and 'shown' in the very act of teaching. Teaching is a transaction between the teacher and the learner, not the delivery of something to the learner. An *educational* practice embodies the aims and values; it is not something distinct from them. Indeed, to ask for the aims of such a transaction is to ask for the values which the transaction embodies. There may well be 'spin-offs' from teaching Macbeth, but the main educational purpose lies in the engagement with a valuable text. The language of 'engagement' with a text, of 'transaction between teacher and learner', of 'intrinsic value' of an activity, of 'struggle to understand', of 'personal enrichment' seems inimical to the language of targets and of standardized performance indicators or of generalized conclusions drawn from systematic interventions. And it is this view of an educational practice which underpinned the seminal work of Stenhouse (1975), referred to and developed by Elliott in this volume.

Conclusion

There are different levels at which one can examine and appraise evidence-based policy and practice in education. Educational policies aiming to improve the quality of learning and to increase the number of people who successfully participate in education at different phases need evidence to show that one policy rather than another will make things better. Teachers, in the myriad judgements they make every day, would be more professional in those judgements if these were based upon the accumulated evidence from their own practice and from that of the profession as a whole. Of course, that is what they claim to do. Staffroom talk is as much about what has worked, or about advising others in the light of what has been seen to work, as it is about anything else. And so at one level there cannot be much dispute about the idea of evidence-based policy and practice. Teachers, ministers and civil servants give reasons for what they do and those reasons necessarily call upon evidence.

The advocates of evidence-based policy and practice, however, argue that the gathering and the application of evidence has not been rigorous enough. It lacks the systematic investigation, indeed the scientific rigour, which has transformed other areas of public life. Educationists are chastised for their failure to search for evidence systematically enough. Thus Slavin (2002: 16) states:

> At the dawn of the 21st century, education is finally being dragged, kicking and screaming, into the 20th century. The scientific revolution that utterly transformed medicine, agriculture, transportation, technology and other fields early in the 20th century almost completely bypassed the field of education. If Rip Van Winkle had been a physician, a farmer, or an engineer, he would be unemployable if he awoke today. . . . It is not that we have not learnt anything since Rip Van Winkle's time. It is that applications of the findings of educational research remain haphazard, and that evidence is respected. only occasionally, and only if it happens to correspond to current educational or political fashions.

The problems arise, therefore, not over the need for evidence in the adoption of policies or in the improvement of practice, but, first, over what is to count as evidence, second, over the extent to which the scientific rigour in some areas are equally applicable to educational policy and practice, and, third, over whether there is something so distinctive and peculiar about an 'educational practice' that there are strict limits to the relevance of the means/end model of educational improvement and effectiveness.

Thus, as I argued, evidence is of different kinds relative to the form of discourse through which a problem is being addressed. For some (and there are hints of this in the contribution to this volume by Hodkinson and Smith), such an admission leads to the sort of relativism which makes a nonsense of the evidence-based movement. But that does not follow. The different forms of discourse are not arbitrarily developed; they are the best window we have upon the world; and they have built into them the criteria of appropriate evidence without which one would not be able to engage in any intelligible argument – including arguments about evidence-based policy and practice.

Given the range of possible discourses about education, then the danger lies in the imperialism of any one form of discourse, together with its distinctive notion of evidence. Two false consequences are frequently drawn from this, exemplified in the contributions to this book. On the one hand, a narrow and thus too demanding a notion of evidence is adopted, thereby excluding, as irrelevant or as not rigorous or as arbitrary, deliberations about educational policy and practice. On the other hand, in recognizing the distinctively practical, context bound and value-laden nature of educational deliberations, many will reject completely the large-scale experimental search for evidence. Thus is created the false dualism between the quantitative and qualitative approaches to research, which has caused so much damage (see Pring, 2000, where this point is developed much more thoroughly).

There are three conclusions that need to be drawn from this as we look to the future. The first is that evidence-based policy and practice need to look much more carefully at the different kinds of evidence which legitimately enter into educational deliberations at the policy and pro-fessional practice levels. Notions like deliberation, personal and craft knowledge, as well as the different kinds of evidence which enter into educational discourse should be examined critically. It is important to explore what 'systematic' means within these different kinds of appeal to evidence. Second, despite the rather eclectic nature of educational discourse, there are lessons to be learnt from the insistence by the advocates of evidence-based policy and practice for the more rigorous search for evidence. These are the constant attempt to synthesize and reconcile the different research findings, the search for the logical con-nection between conclusions drawn from different kinds of research, the assessment of the degree of reliability of the research for future policy and practice, the evaluation of the conclusions in the light of the explicitly reported data and methodology, the reporting of the research in clear and focused way. Third, the political and often highly charged context of educational research (reflected so powerfully in Gallagher's paper) needs to be recognized. It cannot be wished away. And that political context invades not only the policies and practices themselves, but also the dif-ferent philosophical advocacies of different sorts of research. However pure and systematic the research should ideally be, it never will be like that. Slavin acknowledges the way in which 'educational and political fashions' affect the research, preventing the scientific objectivity which he is so anxious to promote. But his own paper, in persuading us of his position, is not without its own political rhetoric to get the point across.

References

Altrichter, H., Posch, P. and Somekh, B. (1993) *Teachers Investigate Their Work: An Introduction to the Methods of Action Research*. London: Routledge.

Andrews, R. (2002a) A hard road to measure, *The Times Educational Supplement/ TES Online* 26 April: 16.

Andrews, R. (2002b) ICT's impact on literacy learning in English: where's the research?, *Staff and Educational Development International*, 6(1): 87–98.

Andrews, R. (ed.) (forthcoming) *The Impact of ICT on Literacy Education*. London: RoutledgeFalmer.

Andrews, R., Burn, A., Leach, J., Locke, T., Low, G. and Torgerson, C. (2002) *A Systematic Review of the Impact of Networked ICT on 5–16 year olds' Literacy in English*, (EPPI-Centre Review), in *Research Evidence in Education Library*. Issue 1. London: EPPI-Centre, Social Science Research Unit, Institute of Education, 106 pp.

Andrews, R. and Elbourne, D. (eds) (forthcoming) *Evidence-based Education* (series). London: RoutledgeFalmer.

Anon (1995a) Evidence-Based Everything, *Bandolier*, 12: 1.

Anon (1995b) Evidence based medicine; in its place [editorial], *Lancet*, 346: 785.

Armstrong, E. (1999) The well-built clinical question: the key to finding the best evidence efficiently, *Wis Med J*, 98: 25–8.

Askew, M., Brown, M., Rhodes, V., Johnson D. and Wiliam, D. (1997) Effective teachers of numeracy, final report: report of the study carried out for the Teacher Training Agency 1995–96 by the School of Education, King's College London. London: King's College.

Aucoin, P. (1990) Administrative reform in public management: paradigms, principles, paradoxes and pendulums, *Governance*, 3(2): 115–37.

Avis, J., Bloomer, M., Esland, G., Gleeson, D. and Hodkinson, P. (1996) *Knowledge and Nationhood: Education, Politics and Work*. London: Cassell.

Balint, M. (1957) *The Doctor, His Patient and the Illness*. London: Pitman.

Barton, S. (2000) Which clinical studies provide the best evidence?, *British Medical Journal*, 321: 255–6.

Barton, S. (2001) Using Clinical Evidence (letter), *British Medical Journal*, 323: 165.

Bates, R. (2002) The impact of educational research: alternative methodologies and conclusions, *Research Papers in Education*, 17: 403–8.

Batstone, G. and Edwards, M. (1996) Achieving clinical effectiveness: just another initiative or a real change in working practice?, *Journal of Clinical Effectiveness*, 1: 19–21.

Beach, L.R. and Lipshitz, R. (1993) Why classical decision theory is an inappropriate standard for evaluating and aiding most human decision making, in G.A. Klein *et al. Decision Making in Action: Models and Methods*. Norwood, NJ: Ablex.

BERA (2001) Evidence based practice. Symposium at the British Educational Research Association annual conference. Leeds: University of Leeds.

Bernardo, J.M. and Smith, A.F.M. (1994) *Bayesian Theory*. London: John Wiley and Sons.

Bernstein, R. (1983) *Beyond Objectivism and Relativism*. Philadelphia: University of Pennsylvania Press.

Bero, L.A., Grilli, R., Grimshaw, J.M., Harvey, E., Oxman, D., Thomson, M.A. (1998) Getting research findings into practice: Closing the gap between research and practice: an overview of systematic reviews of interventions to promote the implementation of research findings, *British Medical Journal*, 317: 465–8.

Billett, S. (1998) Constructing vocational knowledge: situations and other social sources, *Journal of Education and Work*, 11(3): 255–73.

Black, P. and Wiliam, D. (1998) Inside the black box: raising standards through classroom assessment. London: School of Education, King's College.

Blaser, M.J. (1996) The bacteria behind ulcers, *Scientific American*, 274(2): 92–8.

Bloom, B.S. *et al.* (1956) *Taxonomy of Educational Objectives: I Cognitive Domain*. Longmans: London.

Bloom, B.S. (1971) Mastery Learning, in J.H. Block, *Mastery Learning: Theory and Practice*. Holt, Rinehart and Winston: New York.

Bloomer, M. (1997) *Curriculum Making in Post-16 Education: the Social Conditions of Studentship*. London: Routledge.

Bloomer, M. and Hodkinson, P. (2000) Learning Careers: Continuity and Change in Young People's Dispositions to Learning, *British Journal of Educational Studies*, 26(5): 583–98.

Blunkett, D. (1999) Secretary of State's address to the annual conference of the Confederation of British Industry.

Blunkett, D. (2000) Influence or irrelevance: can social science improve government? (speech to the Economic and Social Research Council, 2 February), *Research Intelligence*, 71: 12–21.

Boston Medical and Surgical Journal (1909) The reporting of unsuccessful cases. Editorial, 19 August 1909. From James Lind Library www.jameslindlibrary.org

Boud, D. (1998) How can university work-based courses contribute to lifelong learning?, in J. Holford, P. Jarvis, P. Griffin and C. Griffin (eds) *International Perspectives on Lifelong Learning*. London: Kogan Page.

Brantlinger, E. (1997) Using ideology: Cases of nonrecognition of the politics of research and practice in special education, *Review of Educational Research*, 67(4): 425–59.

Britten, N., Campbell, R.F., Pope, C., Donovan, J., Morgan, M. and Pill, R. (2002)

Using meta-ethnography to synthesize qualitative research: a worked example, *Journal of Health Services Research and Policy*, 7(4): 209–15.

Brown, A. and Keep, E. (1999) *Review of Vocational Education and Training Research in the United Kingdom.* Luxembourg: Office for Official Publications of the European Communities.

Budge, D. (1998) Welcome to the new age of research, *Times Educational Supplement*, 13 November.

Bunn, F., Lefebvre, C., Li Wan Po, A., Li, L., Roberts, I. and Schierhout, G. (2000) Human albumin solution for resuscitation and volume expansion in critically ill patients. The Albumin Reviewers, *Cochrane Database Systematic Review*, (2) CD001208.

Buntić, C.G. (2000) Can teaching be a research-based profession?, Unpublished M.Litt. thesis. Oxford: University of Oxford.

Burnham, J. (1941) *The Managerial Revolution.* Harmondsworth: Penguin.

Burrows, P., Gravestock, N., McKinley, R.K., Fraser, R.C., Baker, R., Mason, R., Zouita, L., Ayers, B. (2001) Assessing clinical competence and revalidation of clinicians, *British Medical Journal*, 322: 1600–1.

Cabinet Office (1999) *Modernising Government.* London: The Stationery Office.

Cabinet Office (2003a) What Do We Already Know? – Guidance Notes on Systematic Reviews, in *The Magenta Book: A Guide to Policy Evaluation*, Cabinet Office, www.policyhub.gov.uk.

Cabinet Office (2003b) The Quality of Qualitative Evaluation, Report undertaken by the National Centre for Social Research for the UK Cabinet Office.

Campbell, D.T. (1978) Qualitative Knowing in Action Research, in Brenner, P., Marsh, P., and Brenner, M. (eds) *The Social Context of Method*, London: Croom Helm.

Campbell, D.T. (1999a) The Experimenting Society, in D.T. Campbell, and Russo M. Jean (eds) *Social Experimentation.* Thousand Oaks: Sage Publications.

Campbell, D.T. (1999b) An Inventory to Threat to Validity and Alternative Designs to Control Them, in D.T. Campbell and Russo M. Jean (eds) *Social Experimentation.* Thousand Oaks: Sage Publications.

Campbell, D.T. (1999c) Sociology of Applied Scientific Validity, in D.T. Campbell, and Russo M. Jean (eds) *Social Experimentation.* Thousand Oaks: Sage Publications.

Campbell, R., Pound, P., Pope, C., Britten, N., Pill, R., Morgan, M. and Donovan, J. (2002) Evaluating meta-ethnography: a synthesis of qualitative research on lay experiences of diabetes and diabetes care, *Social Science and Medicine*, 56(4): 671–84.

Carnine, D. (1999) Campaigns for moving research into practice, *Remedial and Special Education*, 20(1): 2–6, 35.

Carr, W. and Kemmis, S. (1986) *Becoming Critical: Education, Knowledge and Action Research.* Lewes: Falmer.

Carter, Y.H., Shaw, S. and Macfarlane, F. (2002) Primary Care Research Team Assessment (PCRTA): development and evaluation. London, Royal College of General Practitioners: 1–72.

Chalmers, I. (2001) Invalid health information is potentially lethal, *British Medical Journal*, 322: 998.

Chalmers, I. (2003) Trying to do more good than harm in policy and practice:

the role of rigorous, transparent, up to date, replicable evaluation. Paper commissioned for the Annals of the American Academy of Political and Social Science.

Chalmers, I., Hedges, L.V. and Cooper, H. (2002) A brief history of research synthesis. *Evaluation and the Health professions*, 25(1): 12–37.

Chandler, A. (1977) *The Visible Hand*. Cambridge, MA: Harvard University Press.

Chandler, A., with Takashi Hikino (1990) *Scale and Scope: The Dynamics of Industrial Capitalism*. Cambridge, MA: Harvard University Press.

Chapman, J. (2002) *System Failure: Why Governments Must Learn to Think Differently*. London: DEMOS.

Chisholm, R. (1973) *The Problem of Criteria*. Milwaukee, WI: Marquette University Press.

Cibulka, J., Coursey, S., Nakayama, M., Price, J. and Stewart, S. (2000) The creation of high-performance schools through organizational and individual learning. Part I: Schools as learning organisations: a review of the literature. Washington: Office of Educational Research and Improvement, US Department of Education.

Clarke, J. and Newman, J. (1997) *The Managerial State*, London: Sage.

Coady, C.A.J. (1992) *Testimony: A Philosophical Study*. Oxford: Clarendon Press.

Cochrane Collaboration (2003) http://www.cochrane.org/cochrane/archieco.htm

Cochrane, A. (1972) *Effectiveness and Efficiency. Random Reflections on Health Services*. London: Nuffield Provincial Hospitals Trust.

Cochrane, A. (1989) Foreword, in I. Chalmers, M. Enkin and M. Keirse (eds) *Effective Care in Pregnancy and Childbirth*. Oxford: Oxford University Press.

Cohen, J. (1994) The Earth is round (p<.05), *American Psychologist*, 49(12): 997–1003.

Coles, G. (2002) *Reading the Naked Truth: Literacy, Legislation and Lies*. Boston: Heinemann.

Colley, H. and Hodkinson, P. (2001) The problem with 'Bridging the Gap': the reversal of structure and agency in addressing social exclusion, *Critical Social Policy*, 21(3): 335–359.

Commission on the Social Sciences (2003) *Great Expectations: The Social Sciences in Britain*. London: Academy of Learned Societies for the Social Sciences and at www.the-academy.org.uk/

Connolly, T. and Wagner, W.G. (1988) Decision cycles, in R.L. Cardy, S.M. Puffer and M.M. Newman (eds) *Advances in Information Processing in Organisations*, Vol. 3, pp. 183–205. Greenwich, CT: JAI Press.

Cook, T.D., Cooper, H., Cordray, D.S., Hartmann, H., Light, R.J., Louis, T.A. and Mosteller, F. (1992) *Meta-Analysis for Explanation*. New York: Russell Sage Foundation.

Cooper, H. (1982) Scientific principles for undertaking integrative research reviews, *Journal of Educational Research*, 52: 291–302.

Cooper, H. and Hedges, L.V. (eds) (1994) *The Handbook of Research Synthesis*, New York: Russell Sage Foundation.

Cooper, H., DeNeve, K., and Charlton, K. (1997) Finding the Missing Science: The case for using institutional review boards as prospective registers of psychological research, *Psychological Methods*, 2: 447–52.

Cordingley, P. (2000a) Teacher Perspectives on the Credibility and Usability of Different Kinds of Evidence, Paper presented to the British Educational Research Association Annual Conference, Cardiff.

Cordingley, P. (2000b) Teacher Perspectives on the Accessibility and Usability of Research Outputs, Paper with the National Teacher Research Panel to the BERA 2000 conference. London: TTA.

Cordingley, P. and Bell, M. (2001) *Literature and Evidence Search: Teachers' Use of Research and Evidence as They Learn to Teach and Improve their Teaching*. London: TTA.

Cordingley, P., Bell, M., Curtis, A., Evans, D., Hughes, S. and Shreeve, A. (2002) Bringing research resources to practitioner users via web technology: lessons learned to date. Paper presented at the British Educational Research Association Annual Conference. Coventry: Centre for the Use of Research and Evidence in Education (CUREE).

Crombie, I. (1996) *The Pocket Guide to Critical Appraisal*, London: *British Medical Journal* Publishing Group.

Cronbach, L.J. (1975) Beyond the two disciplines of scientific psychology, *American Psychologist*, 30: 116–27.

David, P.A. (2002) Public dimensions of the knowledge-driven economy. A brief introduction to the OECD/OERI project. Paper presented at the Knowledge Management in Education and Learning Forum, Oxford, March 2002.

Davies, H.T.O., Nutley, S.M., Smith, P.C. (eds) (2000) *What Works? Evidence-based Policy and Practice in the Public Services*. Bristol: Policy Press.

Davies, P. (1999) What is evidence-based education?, *British Journal of Educational Studies*, 47(2): 108–21.

Davies, P. (2000a) The relevance of systematic reviews to educational policy and practice, *Oxford Review of Education*, 26(3/4): 365–78.

Davies, P. (2000b) Contributions from qualitative research, in Davies, H.T.O. *et al.* (eds) *What Works? Evidence-based Policy and Practice in the Public Services*. Bristol: Policy Press.

Davies, P. (2003) Systematic reviews: how are they different from what we already do?, in L. Anderson and N. Bennett (eds) *Developing Educational Leadership for Policy and Practice*. London: Sage.

Davis, D.A., Thomson, M.A., Oxman, A.D. and Haynes, R.B. (1992) Evidence for the effectiveness of CME. A review of 50 randomized controlled trials, *Journal of the American Medical Association*, 268: 1111–17.

Davis, D.A., Thomson, M.A., Oxman, A.D., Haynes, R.B. (1995) Changing physician performance. A systematic review of the effect of continuing medical education strategies, *Journal of the American Medical Association*, 274: 700–5.

De Bruyn Ouboter, R. (1997) Heike Kamerlingh Onnes's discovery of super-conductivity, *Scientific American*, 276(3): 84–9.

Deeks, J.J., Altman, D.G. and Bradburn, M.J., (2001) Statistical methods for examining heterogeneity and combining results from several studies in meta-analysis, in M. Egger, G. Davey Smith, and D.G. Altman (eds) *Systematic Reviews in Health Care: Meta-Analysis in Context*. London: *British Medical Journal* Publishing Group.

Delamont, S. (1976) *Interaction in the Classroom*. London: Methuen.

Department of Education, Training and Youth Affairs (DETYA) (2001) *Educational Research: In Whose Interests*, Higher Education Series, Report no 39, Australia.

Department of Trade and Industry (dti) (2000) *Foresight: Making the Future Work for You: Information, Communications and Media (ICM) Panel*, London: dti Publications or www.foresight.gov.uk

Derrida, J. (1978) *Writing and Difference*. London: Routledge and Kegan Paul.

Desforges, C. (2000a) Knowledge Transformation. Paper presented to the ESRC Teaching and Learning Research Programme Seminar, Leicester University, November.

Desforges, C. (2000b) *Familiar Challenges and New Approaches: Necessary Advances in Theory and Methods in Research on Teaching and Learning*, The Desmond Nuttall/ Carfax Memorial Lecture, BERA, Cardiff. Southwell: BERA.

Desforges, C. (2003) Evidence-informed practice in teaching and learning, in L. Anderson and N. Bennett (eds.) *Developing Educational Leadership: Using Evidence for Policy and Practice*. London: Sage.

Devine, P.J., Lee, N., Jones, R.M. and Tyson, W.J. (1985) *An Introduction to Industrial Economics*. London: Unwin Hyman.

Dickersin, K. and Manheimer, E. (1998) The Cochrane Collaboration: Evaluation of health care and services using systematic reviews of the results of randomized controlled trials, *Clinical Obstetrics and Gynecology*, 41: 315–31.

Dillon, S. (1994) A class apart: Special education soaks up New York's resources, *The New York Times*, 7 April: A16.

Downie, R. and Macnaughton, J. (2000) *Clinical Judgement-evidence in Practice*. Oxford: Oxford University Press.

du Boulay, C. (2000) From CME to CPD: getting better at getting better?, *British Medical Journal*, 320: 393–4.

Dweck, C. (1989) Motivation, in A. Lesgold and R. Glaser (eds) *Foundations for a Psychology of Education*. Hillsdale, New Jersey: Erlbaum.

Dyson, A. and Desforges, C. (2002) Building research capacity: some possible lines of action. Paper commissioned by the National Education Research Forum at www.nerf-uk.org

Dyson, F. (1997) *Imagined Worlds*. Cambridge, MA: Harvard University Press.

Earley, P. (ed.) (1998) *School Improvement After Inspection? School and LEA Responses*. London: Paul Chapman.

Ebbutt, D. and Elliott, J. (eds) (1985) Issues in Teaching for Understanding, Longmans/Schools Curriculum Development Committee (SCDC).

Edwards, A. and Elwyn G. (2001) *Evidence-based Patient Choice – Inevitable or Impossible*. Oxford: Oxford University Press.

Edwards, W. (1954) The theory of decision making, *Psychological Bulletin*, 51: 380–417.

Egger, M., Davey Smith, G. and Altman, D.G. (eds) (2001) *Systematic Reviews in Health Care: Meta-Analysis in Context*. London: British Medical Journal Publishing Group.

Elbourne, D., Torgerson, C., Rees, R. and Andrews, R. (2002) *Quality Assurance in Systematic Reviews in Education: Experience from a New Review Group and From the Review Co-ordinating Centre*, 4th Symposium on Systematic Reviews: Pushing the Boundaries, University of Oxford, July 2002.

Elliott, J. (1978) Classroom Research: Science or Commonsense, in R. McAleese and D. Hamilton (eds) *Understanding Classroom Life*. Slough: NFER Publishing Company.

Elliott, J. (1988) The State v Education: The Challenge for Teachers, in H. Simons, (ed.) *The National Curriculum*, British Educational Research Association, pp. 46–62.

Elliott, J. (1989) *Teacher Evaluation and Teaching as a Moral Science*, in M. Holly and C.S. McLoughlin (eds) *Perspectives on Teacher Professional Development*, Falmer Press: London.

Elliott, J. (1991) *Action Research for Educational Change*. Milton Keynes and Philadelphia: Open University Press.

Elliott, J. (1994) Research on Teachers' Knowledge and Action Research, *Educational Action Research*, 2(1): 133–7.

Elliott, J. (1998) *The Curriculum Experiment: Meeting the Challenge of Social Change*, Milton Keynes: Open University Press.

Elliott, J. (2000) Revising the National Curriculum: a comment on the Secretary of State's proposals, *Journal of Education Policy*, 15: 2.

Elliott, J. (2001) Making evidence based practice educational, *British Education Research Journal*, 27(5): 555–74.

Elliott, J. (2002) What is Applied Research in Education?, *Building Research Capacity*, Issue 3, July, 7–10.

Elliott, J. and Adelman, C. (eds) (1974) Ford Teaching Project Publications, CARE. Norwich: University of East Anglia.

Elliott, J. and MacDonald, B. (eds) (1975) People in Classrooms, CARE Occasional Publications No. 2, Norwich: University of East Anglia.

Elliott, J., MacLure, M. and Sarland, C. (1996) Teachers as Researchers in the context of award bearing courses and research degrees: Final Report to ESRC. Norwich: Centre for Applied Research in Education, University of East Anglia.

Ellis, J., Mulligan, I., Rower, J. and Sackett, D. (1995) Inpatient general medicine is evidence based, *Lancet*, 346: 407–10.

Ely, J.W., Osheroff, J.A., Ebell, M.A., Chambliss, L.A., Vinson, D.C., Stevermer, J.J. and Pifer, E.A. (2002) Obstacles to answering doctors' questions about patient care with evidence: qualitative study, *British Medical Journal*, 324: 710.

Engestrom, Y. (2001) Expansive Learning at Work: towards an activity-theoretical reconceptualisation, *Journal of Education and Work*, 14(1): 133–56.

Eraut, M. (2000) Non-formal learning and tacit knowledge in professional work, *British Journal of Educational Psychology*, 70: 113–36.

Eraut, M. (2003) Transfer of knowledge between education and workplace settings, in H. Rainbird, A. Fuller and A. Munro (eds) *Workplace Learning in Context*. London: Routledge.

Eraut, M. and Du Boulay, B. (2000) Developing the Attributes of Medical Professional Judgement and Competence, Report to the UK Department of Health.

Eraut, M., Alderton, J., Cole, G. and Senker, P. (1998) Learning from other people at work, in F. Coffield (ed.) *Learning at Work*. Bristol: Policy Press.

Eraut, M., Alderton, J., Cole, G. and Senker, P. (2000) Development of knowledge and skills at work, in F. Coffield (ed.) *Differing Visions of a Learning Society*. Bristol: Policy Press, p. 231–62.

Erikson, F. and Gutierrez, K. (2002) Culture, rigor, and science in educational research, *Educational Researcher*, 31(8): 21–4.

Essex County Council (2003) *The Research Engaged School*, FLARE, Forum for Learning and Research Enquiry, Chelmsford: Essex County Council.

Evans, J. and Benefield, P. (2001) Systematic Reviews of Educational research: does the medical model fit?, *British Educational Research Journal*, 27(5): 527–41.

Eve, R. (2000) Learning with PUNs and DENs a method for determining educational needs and the evaluation of its use in primary care, *Education for General Practice*, (11): 73–9.

Fenstermacher, G. (1986) The Philosophy of Research on Teaching: Three Aspects, in M. Wittrock (ed.) *Handbook of Research on Education* (3rd edition). New York: Macmillan.

Ferlie, E., Ashburner, L., Fitzgerald, L. and Pettigrew, A. (1996) *The New Public Management in Action*, Oxford: Oxford University Press.

Feur, M.J., Towne, L. and Shavelson, R.J. (2002) Scientific culture and educational research *Educational Researcher*, 31(8): 4–14.

Feyerabend, P. (1993) *Against Method* (3rd edition). London: Verso/New Left Books.

Figgis, J., Zubrick, A., Butorac, A. and Alderson, A. (2000) Backtracking practice and policies to research, in Department of Education, Training and Youth Affairs, Australia, *The Impact of Educational Research*, pp. 279–373. (Available at: http://www.dest.gov.au/highered/respubs/impact/pdf/impact.pdf)

Flanagin, A., Carey, L.A., Fontanarosa, P.B., Phillips, S.G., Pace, B.P., Lundberg, D. and Rennie, D. (1998) Prevalence of articles with honorary authors and ghost authors in peer-reviewed medical journals, *Journal of the American Medical Association*, 280(3): 222–5.

Foray, D. and Hargreaves, D. (2002) The development of knowledge of different sectors: a model and some hypotheses. Paper presented at the Knowledge Management in Education and Learning Forum, Oxford, March 2002.

Ford Teaching Project (1974) *Implementing the Principles of Inquiry/Discovery Teaching, Ford Teaching Project Publications*. Norwich: University of East Anglia.

Forness, S.R., Kavale, K.A., Blum, I.M. and Lloyd, J.W. (1997) Mega-analysis of meta-analysis: What works in special education and related services, *Teaching Exceptional Children*, 29(6): 4–9.

Fowler, P.B.S. (1995) Letter, *Lancet*, 346: 838.

Freeman, A. and Sweeney K. (2001) Why general practitioners do not implement evidence: qualitative study, *British Medical Journal*, 323: 1100.

Fuchs, D. and Fuchs, L.S. (1995a) What's 'special' about special education?, *Phi Delta Kappan*, 76(7): 522–30.

Fuchs, D. and Fuchs, L.S. (1995b) Special education can work, in J.M. Kauffman, J.W. Lloyd, D.P. Hallahan and T.A. Astuto (eds) *Issues in Educational Placement: Students with Emotional and Behavioral Disorders*. Hillsdale, NJ: Lawrence Erlbaum Associates, pp. 363–77.

Fuchs, D. and Fuchs, L.S. (1995c) Counterpoint: Special education – ineffective?, immoral?, *Exceptional Children*, 61(3): 303–6.

Fuchs, D. and Fuchs, L.S. (2001) Editorial: The benefits and costs of like-mindedness, *The Journal of Special Education*, 35(1): 2–3.

Furlong, J. (1998) Educational Research: Meeting the Challenge. Inaugural lecture, University of Bristol.

Gadamer, H. (1995) *Truth and Method*, trans J. Weinsheimer and D. Marshall. New York: Crossroad.

Gage, N.L. (1972) *Teacher Effectiveness and Teacher Education: The Search for a Scientific Basis*, Palo Alto, CA: Pacific Books.

Galton, M. (2002) *The Role of Steerers in the Teacher Research Grant Scheme*. London: TTA.

Garfunkel, J.M., Ulshen, M.H., Hamrick, H.J. and Lawson, E.E. (1990) Problems identified by secondary review of accepted manuscripts, *Journal of the American Medical Association*, 263: 1369–71.

Gersten, R., Baker, S. and Lloyd, J.W. (2000) Designing high-quality research in special education: Group experimental design, *The Journal of Special Education*, 34(1): 2–18.

Gibbons, M., Limoges, C., Nowotny, H., Schwartzman, S., Scott, P. and Trow, M. (1994) *The New Production of Knowledge*. London: Sage.

Giddens, A. (1976) *New Rules of the Sociological Method*. London: Hutchinson.

Gillborn, D. and Gipps, C. (1996) *Recent Research on the Achievements of Ethnic Minority Children*. London: Office for Standards in Education, HMSO.

Glass, G.V. (1976) Primary, secondary and meta-analysis of research, *Educational Researcher*, 5: 3–8.

Glass, G.V. and Smith, M.L. (1979) Meta-analysis of research on class size and achievement, *Educational Evaluation and Policy Analysis*, 1: 2–16.

Glass, G.V., McGraw, B. and Smith, M.L. (1981) *Meta-Analysis in Social Research*. Beverly Hills: Sage.

Glass, G.V., Cahen, L.S., Smith, M.L. and Filby, N.N. (1982) *School Class Size: Research and Policy*, Beverly Hills: Sage Publications.

Glasziou, P. and Irwig, L. (1995) An evidence based approach to individualising treatment, *British Medical Journal*, 311: 1356–9.

GMC and Department of Health (2002) The guide to appraisal and revalidation – The Toolkit.

Godlee, F., Gale, C. and Martyn, C.N. (1998) Effect on the quality of peer review of blinding reviewers and asking them to sign their reports, *Journal of the American Medical Association*, 280(3): 237–40.

Goldstein, H. (2000) Excellence in research on schools – a commentary at www.ioe.ac.uk/hgoldstein

Goldstein, H. (2002) Designing social research for the 21st Century. Inaugural professorial address, University of Bristol, 14 October.

Goodman, N. (1978) *Ways of Worldmaking*. Indianapolis, IN: Hackett Books.

Gough D. and Elbourne, D. (2002) Systematic research synthesis to inform policy, practice and democratic debate, *Social Policy and Society*, 1(3): 225–36.

Gough, D.A., Kiwan, D., Sutcliffe, S., Simpson, D. and Houghton, N. (2003) A systematic map and synthesis review of the effectiveness of personal development planning for improving student learning. London: EPPI-Centre, Social Science Research Unit.

Grahame-Smith, D. (1995) Evidence based medicine: Socratic dissent, *British Medical Journal*, 310: 1126–7.

Grant, J. (2002) Learning needs assessment: assessing the need, *British Medical Journal*, 324: 156–9.

Gray, J.A.M. (1997) *Evidence-Based Healthcare: How to Make Health Policy and Management Decisions*. London: Churchill Livingstone.

Grayson, L. (2002) *Working Paper 7: Evidence Based Policy and the Quality of Evidence: Rethinking Peer Review*. London: ESRC UK Centre for Evidence Based Policy and Practice.

Greenhalgh, T. (1997) *How to Read a Paper: The Basics of Evidence-based Medicine*, London: *British Medical Journal* Publishing Group.

Greenhalgh, T. (2000) What can we learn from narratives of implementing evidence? (Commentary), *British Medical Journal*, 320: 1114–18.

Guyatt, G.H., Meade, M.O., Jaeschke, R.Z., Cook, D.J., Haynes, R.B. (2000) Practitioners of evidence based care, *British Medical Journal* 320: 954–5.

Haas, C. (1996) *Writing Technology: Studies on the Materiality of Literacy*. Hillsdale, NJ: Lawrence Erlbaum Associates.

Hager, P. (2000) Knowledge that Works: Judgement and the University Curriculum, in C. Symes and J. McIntyre (eds) *Working Knowledge: The New Vocationalism and Higher Education*. Buckingham: SRHE/Open University Press.

Haines, A. and Donald, A. (1998) Making better use of research findings, *British Medical Journal*, 317: 72–5.

Hallahan, D.P. (1998) Sound bytes from special education reform rhetoric, *Remedial and Special Education*, 19(2): 67–9.

Hallahan, D.P., and Kauffman, J.M. (1997) *Exceptional Children: Introduction to Special Education* (7th Edition). Needham Heights, MA: Allyn and Bacon.

Hammersley, M. (1993) On the teacher as researcher, in M. Hammersley (ed.) *Educational Research: Current Issues*. London: Paul Chapman.

Hammersley, M. (1997) Educational research and teaching: a response to David Hargreaves' TTA lecture, *British Educational Research Journal*, 23(2): 141–61.

Hammersley, M. (2000) The sky is never blue for modernisers: the threat posed by David Blunkett's offer of 'partnership' to social science, *Research Intelligence*, 72, June.

Hammersley, M. (2002a) On 'systematic' reviews of research literature: a 'narrative' response to Evans and Benefield, *British Educational Research Journal*, 27(5): 543–54.

Hammersley, M. (2002b) *Educational Research, Policy-making, and Practice*. London: Paul Chapman.

Hammersley, M. (2003) Media representation of social and educational research: the case of a review of ethnic minority education, *British Educational Research Journal*, 29(3): 327–344.

Hampton, J.R. (1997) Evidence-based medicine, practice variations and clinical freedom, *Journal of Evaluation in Clinical Practice*, 3(2): 123–31.

Hanson, N. (1958) *Patterns of Discovery*. Cambridge: Cambridge University Press.

Harden, A. (2002) Choosing appropriate criteria for assessing the quality of 'qualitative' research for inclusion in systematic reviews: a review of the published literature. Poster presented at the 1st Campbell Collaboration Methods Group Conference, Baltimore, 17 to 19 September.

Harden, A., Oliver, S., Rees, R., Shepherd, J., Brunton, G., Garcia, J. and Oakley, A. (2003) A new framework for synthesising the findings of different types of research for public policy. Paper presented at the 3rd Campbell Colloquium, Stockholm, February.

Hargreaves, D. (1996) Teaching as a Research-based Profession: possibilities and prospects, The Teacher Training Agency Annual Lecture, London, TTA.

Hargreaves, D. (1997) In Defence of Research for Evidence-based Teaching: a rejoinder to Martyn Hammersley, *British Educational Research Journal*, 23(4).

Hargreaves, D. (1998) The Knowledge Creating School. Paper presented to the British Educational Research Association Annual Conference, Belfast.

Hargreaves, D. (1999a) The knowledge-creating school, *British Journal of Educational Studies*, 47(2): 122–44.

Hargreaves, D. (1999b) Revitalizing Educational Research: lessons from the past and proposals for the future, *Cambridge Journal of Education*, 29(2).

Hargreaves, D. (2003) From Improvement to Transformation. Keynote lecture, International Congress for School Effectiveness and Improvement, Sydney, Australia, 5 January.

Havelock, R. (1973) *Planning for Innovation Through Dissemination and Utilization of Knowledge Centre for Research on Utilization of Scientific Knowledge*. Ann Arbor: Michigan.

Haynes, R. and Haines, A. (1998) Barriers and bridges to evidence based clinical practice, *British Medical Journal*, 317: 273–6.

Haynes, R.B., Devereaux, P.J. and Guyatt, G.H. (2002) Physicians' and patients' choices in evidence based practice, *British Medical Journal*, 324: 1350.

Hearnshaw, L.S. (1979) *Cyril Burt: Psychologist*. London: Hodder and Stoughton.

Hedges, L.V. (1984) Estimation of effect size under nonrandom sampling: The effects of censoring studies yielding statistically insignificant mean differences, *Journal of Educational Statistics*, 6: 61–85.

Heshusius, L. (1989) The Newtonian mechanistic paradigm, special education, and contours of alternatives: an overview, *Journal of Learning Disabilities*, 22(7): 403–15.

Heshusius, L. (2003) *From Creative Discontent Toward Epistemological Freedom in Special Education: Reflections on a 25 Year Journey*, in D.J. Gallagher (ed.), *Challenging Orthodoxy in Special Education: Dissenting Voices*. Denver, CO: Love Publishing.

Hewison, J., Dowswell, T. and Millar, B. (2000) Changing patterns of training provision in the health service: an overview, in F. Coffield (ed.) *Differing Visions of a Learning Society*, Research Findings, Volume 1. Bristol: Policy Press.

Hibble, A., Kanka, D., Pencheon, D. and Pooles, F. (1998) Guidelines in general practice: the new Tower of Babel?, *British Medical Journal*, 317: 862–3.

Higgins, S. and Moseley, D. (1999) Ways forward with ICT: effective pedagogy using information and communications technology for literacy and numeracy in primary schools, Newcastle: University of Newcastle upon Tyne.

Hillage, J., Pearson, R., Anderson, A., and Tamkin, P. (1998) *Excellence in Research in Schools*. London: Department for Education and Employment/Institute of Employment Studies.

Hockenbury, J.C., Kauffman, J.M. and Hallahan, D.P. (1999–2000) What is right about special education, *Exceptionality*, 8(1): 3–11.

Hodkinson, P. (2001) Response to the National Strategy Consultation Paper, for the National Educational Research Forum, *Research Intelligence*, 74, February.

Holton, G. (1995) The controversy over the end of science, *Scientific American*, 273(4): 168.

Honey, P. and Mumford, A. (1986) *Using Your Learning Styles*, 2nd edition. Maidenhead: Peter Honey.

Howard, G.S., Maxwell, S.E. and Fleming, K.J. (2000) The proof of the pudding:

an illustration of the relative strengths of null hypothesis, meta-analysis, and Bayesian analysis, *Psychological Methods*, 5(3): 315–32.

Iano, R.P. (1986) The study and development of teaching: With implications for the advancement of special education, *Remedial and Special Education*, 7(5): 50–1.

Jackson, G.B. (1980) Methods for integrative reviews, *Review of Educational Research*, 50: 438–60.

Joyce, E. and Showers, B. (1988) *Student Achievement through Staff Development*. London: Longman.

Kamin, L.J. (1977) Burt's IQ data, *Science*, 195: 246–8.

Kauffman, J.M. (1994) Places of change: Special education's power and identity in an era of educational reform, *Journal of Learning Disabilities*, 27: 610–18.

Kauffman, J.M. (1996) Research to practice issues, *Behavioral Disorders*, (22): 55–60.

Kauffman, J.M. (1999) Commentary: Today's special education and its message for tomorrow, *Journal of Special Education*, 32(4): 244–54.

Kauffman, J.M. (1999–2000) The special education story: Obituary, accident report, conversion experience, reincarnation, or none of the above?, *Exceptionality*, 8(1): 61–71.

Kavale, K.A. and Forness, S.R. (1998) The politics of learning disabilities, *Learning Disabilities Quarterly*, (21): 245–73.

Kerridge, I., Lowe, M. and Henry, D. (1998) Ethics and evidence based medicine, *British Medical Journal*, 316: 1151–3.

Klein, G.A. *et al.* (eds) (1993) *Decision-Making in Action, Models, and Methods*. Norwood, NJ: Ablex.

Kogan, M. (1999) The impact of research on policy, in F. Coffield (ed.) *Speaking Truth to Power: Research and Policy on Lifelong Learning*. Bristol: Policy Press.

Kolb, D.A. (1984) *Experiential Learning: Experience as the Source of Learning and Development*. New Jersey: Prentice Hall.

Kuhn, T. (1962) *The Structure of Scientific Revolutions*. Chicago, University of Chicago Press.

Kuhn, T. (1970) The Structure of Scientific Revolutions (2nd edition). Chicago: University of Chicago Press.

Kulik, J.A. and Kulik, C-L.C. (1989) Meta-analysis in education, *International Journal of Educational Research*, (13): 221–340.

Lagemann, E.C. (2000) *An Elusive Science: The Troubling History of Educational Research*. Chicago: Chicago University Press.

Laurance, J. (1998) Experts' 10 steps to health equality, *Independent*: 14.

Lave, J. and Wenger, E. (1991) *Situated Learning*. Cambridge: Cambridge University Press.

Leakey, L.B. and van Lawick, H. (1963) Adventures in the Search for Man, *National Geographic*, January: 132–52.

Levins, R. and Lewontin, R. (1985) *The Dialectical Biologist*. Cambridge, MA: Harvard University Press.

Light, R.J. and Pillemer D. (1984) *Summing Up: The Science of Reviewing Research*. Cambridge, MA: Harvard University Press.

Lilford, R.J., Pauker, S.G., Braunholtz, D.A. and Chard, J. (1998) Decision analysis and the implementation of research findings, *British Medical Journal*, 317: 405–9.

Lindblom, C. (1979) Still muddling, not yet through, *Public Administration Review*, 39: 517–26.

Lipman, T. and Price, D. (2000) Decision making, evidence, audit, and education: case study of antibiotic prescribing in general practice, *British Medical Journal*, 320: 1114–18.

Llewelyn, H. and Hopkins, A. (eds) (1993) Analysing how we reach decisions. London: Royal College of Physicians of London.

Lloyd, J.W., Forness, S.R. and Kavale, K.A. (1998) Some methods are more effective than others, *Intervention in School and Clinic*, 33(4): 195–200.

Louis, P.-C.-A. (1836/1986) Researches on the Effects of Bloodletting in Some Inflammatory Diseases, and on the Influence of Tartarized Antimony and Vesication in Pneumonitis. Boston: Hilliard Gray. Reprinted, Birmingham, AL: Classics of Medicine Library.

Luntley, M. (2000) *Performance, Pay and Professionals*. London: Philosophical Association of Great Britain.

Macdonald, G. (1996) Ice therapy? Why we need randomised controls, in Barnardos *What Works? Effective Social Interventions in Child Welfare*. Ilford: Essex, Barnardos.

MacIntyre, A. (1981) *After Virtue: A Study in Moral Theory*. London: Duckworth.

Marris, R. (1971) The economic theory of 'managerial' capitalism, in G. Archibald (ed.) *The Theory of the Firm*. Harmondsworth: Penguin.

Matthews, R. (1998) 'Silly science', *Prospect*, December: 17–19.

Matthews, R. (2001) Methods for assessing the credibility of clinical trial outcomes, *Drug Info Journal*, 35 (4).

Mayne, J. and Zapico-Goni, E. (eds) (1997) *Monitoring Performance in the Public Sector*. New Brunswick: Transaction Books.

Mays, N. and Pope, C. (2000) Assessing quality in qualitative research, *British Medical Journal*, 320: 50–2.

McCall Smith, A. (2001) Obtaining consent for examination and treatment, *British Medical Journal*, 322: 810–11.

McIntyre, D. (1997) The profession of educational research, *British Educational Research Journal*, Vol. 23(2): 127–40.

McIntyre, D. and McIntyre A. (1999) *Capacity for Research into Teaching and Learning*, Final Report to ESRC Teaching and Learning Programme, Cambridge: School of Education, University of Cambridge.

McMaster University, Evidence-Based Medicine Working Group (1992) Evidence-based medicine, a new approach to teaching the practice of medicine, *Journal of the American Medical Association*, 268 (17): 2420–5.

McNutt, R.A., Evans, A.T., Fletcher, R.H. and Fletcher, S.W. (1990) The effects of blinding on the quality of peer review, *Journal of the American Medical Association*, 263(10): 1371–6.

McSherry, R., Simmons, M. and Abbott, P. (eds) *Evidence-Informed Nursing: A Guide for Clinical Nurses*. London: Routledge.

Medawar, P. (1982) *Pluto's Republic*. Oxford: Oxford University Press.

Medwell, J., Wray, D., Poulson, L. and Fox, R. (1998) Effective teachers of literacy: a report of a research project commissioned by the Teacher Training Agency. Exeter: University of Exeter.

Misakian, A.L. and Bero, L.A. (1998) Publication bias and research on passive smoking, *Journal of the American Medical Association*, 280(3): 250–3.

Morton, S. (1999) Systematic Reviews and Meta-Analysis, Workshop materials on Evidence-Based Health Care, University of California. San Diego, La Jolla: California, Extended Studies and Public Programs.

Mostert, M.P., and Kavale, K. (2001) Evaluation of research for usable knowledge in behavioral disorders: ignoring the irrelevant, considering the germane, *Behavioral Disorders*; 27(1): 53–68.

Moynihan, R., Heath, I. and Henry D. (2002) Selling sickness: the pharmaceutical industry and disease mongering, *British Medical Journal*, 324: 886–91.

Muir Gray, J.A. (1998) Where's the chief knowledge officer?, *British Medical Journal*, 317: 832–40.

Nagel, T. (1986) *The View from Nowhere*. Oxford: Oxford University Press.

Nastasi, B. and Schensul, S. (2001) Criteria for coding the use of qualitative research methods in studies, interventions and programs (Qualitative research coding criteria section of the procedural and coding manual for identification of evidence-based interventions), American Psychological Association and Society for the Study of School Psychology.

National College of School Leadership (2002) *Networked Learning Communities*. Nottingham: NCSL.

National Educational Research Forum (NERF) (2000a) *A National Strategy Consultation Paper*, Nottingham: NERF Publications.

National Educational Research Forum (NERF) (2000b) *The Impact of Educational Research on Policy and Practice*, Sub-group report, London: NERF and at www.nerf-uk.org.

National Institute of Child Health and Human Development (2000) Report of the National Reading Panel. Teaching Children to Read: An Evidence Based Assessment of the Scientific Research Literature of Reading and its Implications for Reading Instruction. Washington DC: US Government Printing Office.

Newman, M., Hayes, N. and Sugden, M. (2001) Evidence-based practice: a framework for the role of lecture-practitioner, *Clinical Effectiveness in Nursing*, 5: 26–9.

Nicoll, A. (ed.) (2000) *Chapman's Homer: The Odyssey* (with preface by Garry Wills). Princeton: Princeton University Press, 208–24.

Noblit, G.W. and Hare, R.D. (1988) *Meta-Ethnography: Synthesizing Qualitative Studies*. Newbury Park: Sage Publications.

Noblit G. and Hare R. (1988) *Meta-Ethnography: Synthesizing Qualitative Studies*. London: Sage.

Norris, C. (1987) *Derrida*. London: Fontana.

Norris, N. (1990) *Understanding Educational Evaluation*. London: Kogan Page.

Nove, A. (1980) *The Soviet Economic System*, 2nd edition. London: Allen and Unwin.

NTRP (2000) Teacher perspectives on the accessibility and usability of research outputs: a paper prepared by Philippa Cordingley and the National Teacher Research Panel to the BERA 2000 Conference. Cardiff University: 7–9 September.

Nutley, S., Davies, H.T. and Walter, I. (2002) What is a Conceptual Synthesis? ESRC Research Unit on Research Utilisation: (www.evidencenetwork.org).

Nutley, S., Percey-Smith, J. and Solesbury, W. (2003) *Models of Research Impact: A Cross-Sector Review of Literature and Practice*. London: Learning and Skills Research Centre.

O'Neill, O. (2002) *A Question of Trust.* London: BBC Publications.

Oakeshott, M. (1962) *Rationalism in Politics, and Other Essays.* London: Methuen.

Oakeshott, M. (1967) Learning and teaching, in R.S. Peters (ed.) *The Concept of Education,* pp. 156–76. London: Routledge and Kegan Paul.

Oakley, A. (1998) Public policy experimentation: lessons from America, *Policy Studies,* 19 (2): 93–114.

Oakley, A. (2000) *Experiments in Knowing: Gender and Method in the Social Sciences.* Cambridge: Polity Press.

Oakley A. (2001) Making evidence-based practice education: a rejoinder to John Elliott, *British Educational Research Journal,* 27, 5: 575–6.

Oakley, A. (2002) Research evidence, knowledge management and educational practice: lessons for all? Paper for High-level Forum on Knowledge Management in Education and Learning. Oxford: 18–19 March.

Oakley, A., Gough, D. and Harden, A. (2002) Quality Standards for Systematic Synthesis of Qualitative Research, Research project, EPPI-Centre, Institute of Education, University of London.

Oakley, A., Harlen, W. and Andrews, R. (2002) Systematic Reviews in Education: myth, rumour and reality, British Educational Research Association annual conference, University of Exeter: September.

OECD (2002) *Educational Research and Development in England: Examiners' Report.* Paris: OECD.

Oliver, S. (1999) Users of health services: following their agenda, in S. Hood, B. Mayall and S. Oliver (eds) *Critical Issues in Social Research: Power and Prejudice.* Buckingham: Open University Press.

Oxman, A.D., Thomson, M.A., Davis, D.A. and Haynes, R.B. (1995) No magic bullets: a systematic review of 102 trials of interventions to improve professional practice, *Can Med Assoc J,* 153: 1423–31.

Parlett, M. and Hamilton, D. (1987) Evaluation as illumination: a new approach to the study of innovatory programmes, in: R. Murphy and H. Torrance (eds) *Evaluating Education: Issues and Methods.* London: PCP, pp. 57–73.

Paterson, B., Thorne, S., Canam, C. and Jillings, C. (2001) *Meta-study of Qualitative Health Research: A Practical Guide to Meta-analysis and Meta-Synthesis.* London: Sage.

Pawson R. (2002a) Evidence and policy and naming and shaming, *Policy Studies,* 23(3/4): 211–30.

Pawson, R. (2002b) Evidence-based policy: the promise of 'realist synthesis', ESRC Evidence Network, Queen Mary College, London (www.evidence network.org)

Pawson, R. and Tilley, N. (1997) *Realistic Evaluation.* London: Sage.

Peile, E. (2000) Is there an evidence base for intuition and empathy? The risks and benefits of inviting an older person to discuss unresolved loss, *Journal of Primary Care Research and Development* 1: 73–9.

Peters, R.S. (1966) *Ethics and Education.* London: Allen and Unwin.

Peters, R.S. (1973) Aims of Education – A Conceptual Inquiry, in R.S. Peters (ed.) *The Philosophy of Education, Oxford Readings in Philosophy* Oxford University Press, Ch. 1, pp. 11–57.

Petrosino, A., Turpin-Petrosino, S. and Buehler, J. (2003) 'Scared straight' and other juvenile awareness programs for preventing juvenile delinquency. Cochrane Review, in the Cochrane Library Issue 1. Oxford: Update Software.

Polanyi, M. (1959) *Personal Knowledge*. Manchester: Manchester University Press.

Polanyi, M. (1966) *The Tacit Dimension*. Garden City, NY: Doubleday.

Polanyi, M. (1969) The logic of tacit inference, in M. Grene (ed.) *Knowing and Being: Essays by Michael Polanyi*. London: Routledge and Kegan Paul.

Pollitt, C. (1990) *Managerialism and the Public Services*. Oxford: Blackwell.

Popay, J., Rogers, A. and Williams, G. (1998) Rationale and standards for the systematic review of qualitative literature in health services research, *Qualitative Health Research*, 8(3): 341–51.

Popay *et al.* (2002) Putting effectiveness into context: Methodological issues in the synthesis of evidence from diverse study designs.

Poplin, M.S. (1987) Self-imposed blindness: The scientific method in education, *Remedial and Special Education*, 8(6): 31–7.

Power, M. (1997) *The Audit Society: Rituals of Verification*, Oxford: Oxford University Press.

Pressley, M. and Harris, K.R. (1994) Increasing the quality of educational intervention research, *Educational Psychology Review*, 6: 191–208.

Pring, R. (2000) *Philosophy of Educational Research*. London: Continuum.

Pring, R. (2002) False dualisms: quantitative and qualitative research, *Journal of Philosophy of Education*, 34(3).

Putnam, H. (1981) *Reason, Truth, and History*. Cambridge: Cambridge University Press.

Relyea, H.C. (1999) Silencing scientists and scholars in other fields: power, paradigm controls, peer review, and scholarly communication, *Government Information Quarterly*, 16(2): 193–5.

Rennie, D. (1998) Editorial: Peer review in Prague, *Journal of the American Medical Association*, 280, 3: 214–15.

Reynolds, D. (1998) Teacher Effectiveness: better teachers, better schools, Teacher Training Agency Annual Lecture, reprinted in *Research Intelligence*, 66: Oct. 26–9.

Ridgeway J., Zaojewski J.S. and Hoover M.N. (2000) Problematising evidence-based policy and practice. Evaluation and Research in Education, 14, (3 and 4): 181–92.

Riding, R.J. (1997) On the Nature of Cognitive Style, *Educational Psychology*, 17: 29–49.

Roberts, K. (2002) Belief and subjectivity in research: an introduction to Bayesian theory, in *Building Research Capacity*, 3: 5–7, Cardiff: Cardiff University School of Social Sciences, Research Capacity Building Network, July.

Rorty, R. (1979) *Philosophy and the Mirror of Nature*. Princeton: Princeton University Press.

Rorty, R. (1985) Solidarity or objectivity, in J. Rajchman and C. West (eds) *Post-analytic Philosophy*. New York: Columbia University Press.

Rosenberg, W. (1995) Evidence based medicine: an approach to problem solving, *British Medical Journal*, 310: 1122–6.

Russell, B. (1956) Galileo and scientific method, in A.F. Scott (ed.) *Topics and Opinions*. London: Macmillan.

Sackett, D. and Haynes, R. (2002) Evidence base of clinical diagnosis: The architecture of diagnostic research, *British Medical Journal*, 324: 539–41.

Sackett, D. and Straus, S. (1998) Finding and applying evidence during clinical rounds: the 'evidence cart', *Journal of the American Medical Association*, 280: 1336–8.

Sackett, D.L. *et al.* (1997) *Evidence-based Medicine*.e London: Churchill Livingstone.

Sackett, D.L., Richardson, W.S., Rosenberg, W. and Haynes, R.B. (1997) *Evidence-Based Medicine: How to Practise and Teach EBM*. New York: Churchill Livingstone.

Sackett, D.L., Rosenberg, W., Gray, J.A.M., Haynes, R.B. and Richardson, W. (1996) Evidence-based medicine: what it is and what it isn't, *British Medical Journal*, 312: 71–2.

Sackett, D.L., Straus, S.E., Richardson, W.S., Rosenberg, W. and Haynes, R.B. (2000) *Evidence-Based Medicine: How to Practise and Teach EBM*. Edinburgh: Churchill Livingstone.

Sargant, N. (1995) Consumer power as a pillar of democracy, in G. Dench, T. Flower and K. Gavron (eds) *Young at Eighty: The Prolific Public Life of Michael Young*, Manchester: Carcanet Press.

Sasso, G.M. (2001) The retreat from inquiry and knowledge in special education, *The Journal of Special Education*, 34(4): 178–193.

Savage, J.D. (1999) *Funding Science in America: Congress, Universities, and the Politics of the Academic Pork Barrel*. Cambridge: Cambridge University Press.

Schatzman, L. (1991) Dimensional analysis: notes on an alternative approach to the grounding of theory in qualitative research, in D.R. Maines (ed.) *Social Organisation and Social Process: Essays in Honor of Anselm Strauss*, pp. 303–14. New York: Aldine.

Schön, D. (1971) *Beyond the Stable State*. Temple Smith: London.

Schön, D. (1991) *The Reflective Practitioner: How Professionals Think in Action*. Aldershot: Avebury.

Schwandt, T.A. (1998) The interpretative review of educational matters: is there any other kind?, *Review of Educational Research*, 68(4): 409–12.

Sebba, J. (2003) A government strategy for research and development in education, in L. Anderson and N. Bennett, (eds) *Evidence-informed Policy and Practice in Educational Leadership and Management: Applications and Controversies*. London: Paul Chapman.

Shahar, E. (1997) A Popperian view of 'evidence-based medicine', *Journal of Evaluation in Clinical Practice*, 3(2): 109–16.

Shapin, S. (1994) *A Social History of Truth*. London: University of Chicago Press.

Shapiro, J.P., Loeb, P., Bowermaster, D., Wright, A., Headden, S. and Toch, T. (1993) Separate and unequal: How special education programs are cheating children and costing taxpayers billions each year, *U.S. News and World Report*, pp. 46–54.

Shavelson, R.J. and Towne, L. (eds) (2002) *Scientific Research in Education*. Washington, DC.: National Academy Press.

Sheldon, T.A., Guyatt, G.H. and Haines, A. (1998) When to act on the evidence, *British Medical Journal*, 317: 139–42.

Skrtic, T.M. (1991) *Behind Special Education: A Critical Analysis of Professional Culture and School Organization*. Denver, CO: Love Publishing.

Slavin, R.E. (1984) Meta-analysis in education: How has it been used?, *Educational Researcher*, 13(8): 6–15.

Slavin, R.E. (1995) Best evidence synthesis: an intelligent alternative to meta-analysis, *Journal of Clinical Epidemiology*, 48(91): 9–18.

Slavin, R.E. (2002) Evidence-based education policies: transforming educational practice and research, *Educational Researcher*, 31(7): 15–21.

Smith, A.F.M. (1996) Mad cows and ecstasy: chance and choice in an evidence-based society, *Journal of the Royal Statistical Society A*, 159(3): 367–83.

Smith, J.K. and Heshusius, L. (1986) Closing down the conversation: The end of the quantitative-qualitative debate, *Educational Researcher*, 15(1): 4–12.

Smith, J.K. (1989) *The Nature of Social and Educational Inquiry: Empiricism versus Interpretation*. Norwood, New Jersey: Ablex.

Smith, M.L. (1980) Publication bias and meta-analysis, *Evaluation Education*, 4: 22–4.

Smith, M.L. and Glass, G.V. (1980) Meta-analysis of research on class size and its relationship to attitudes and instruction, *American Educational Research Journal*, 17: 419–33.

Smith, M.L., Glass, G.V. and Miller, T.I. (1980) *The Benefits of Psychotherapy*. Baltimore: Johns Hopkins University Press.

Social Exclusion Unit (1999) *Bridging the Gap: New Opportunities for 16–18 Year Olds Not in Education, Employment or Training*. London: Stationary Office.

Southgate, L., Cox, J., David, T., Hatch, D., Howes, A., Johnson, N., Jolly, B., Macdonald, E., McAvoy, P., McCrorie, P. and Turner, J. (2001b) The assessment of poorly performing doctors: the development of the assessment programmes for the General Medical Council's Performance Procedures, *Medical Education*, 35 (suppl. 1): 2–8.

Southgate, L. and Dauphinee, D. (1998) Maintaining standards in British and Canadian medicine: the developing role of the regulatory body, *British Medical Journal*, 316: 697–9.

Southgate, L., Hays, R.B., Norcini, J., Mulholland, H., Ayers, B., Woolliscroft, J., Cusimano, M., McAvoy, P., Ainsworth, M., Haist, S. and Campbell, M. (2001a) Setting performance standards for medical practice: a theoretical framework, *Medical Education*, 35: 474–81.

Southgate, L. and Pringle, M. (1999) Revalidation: Revalidation in the United Kingdom: general principles based on experience in general practice, *British Medical Journal*, 319: 1180–3.

Spencer, L., Ritchie, J., Lewis, J. and Dillon, L. (2003) Quality in Qualitative Evaluation: A framework for assessing research evidence. Government Chief Social Researcher's Office, Occasional Papers Series No. 2. London: Cabinet Office.

Spiegelhalter, D.J., Myles, J.P., Jones, D.R. and Abrams, K.R. (1999) An introduction to Bayesian methods in health technology assessment, *British Medical Journal*, 319: 508–12.

Stenhouse, L. (1970) Some limitations of the use of objectives in curriculum research and planning, *Paedagogica Europaea*, 6: 73–83.

Stenhouse, L. (1975) *An Introduction to Curriculum Development and Research*. London: Heinemann.

Stenhouse, L. (1977) Problems and Effects of Teaching about Race Relations, a report to the Social Science Research Council on Project HR 2001/1, (lodged in the British Library).

Stenhouse, L. (1979a) Research as a Basis for Teaching, Inaugural Lecture at the University of East Anglia, Norwich, in L. Stenhouse (1983) *Authority, Education and Emancipation*. London: Heinemann Educational.

Stenhouse, L. (1979b) *Using Research Means Doing Research* (mimeo version), in H. Dahl, A. Lysne and P. Rand, (eds) *Spotlight on Educational Problems*. University of Oslo: Oslo Press: pp. 71–82.

Stenhouse, L., Verma, G. Wild, R. and Nixon, J. (1979) *Problems and Effects of Teaching about Race Relations*. London: Ward Lock.

Stenhouse, L. *et al.* (1970) The Humanities Curriculum Project: an introduction, Heinemann Educational, revised 1983 by Jean Rudduck, University of East Anglia School of Education, Norwich.

Straus, S. and Sackett, D. (1998) Getting research findings into practice: Using research findings in clinical practice, *British Medical Journal*, 317: 339–42.

Sweeney, K. (1996) Evidence and uncertainty, in M. Marinker (ed.) *Sense and sensibility in health care*. London: British Medical Journal Publishing, pp. 59–87.

Sylva, K. and Hurry, J. (1995) *The Effectiveness of Reading Recovery and Phonological Training for Children with Learning Problems*. London: Thomas Coram Research Unit.

Symes, C. and McIntyre, J. (eds) (2000) *Working Knowledge: The New Vocationalism and Higher Education*. Buckingham: SRHE/Open University Press.

Thomas, G. and Loxley, A. (2001) *Deconstructing Special Education and Constructing Inclusion*. Buckingham: Open University Press.

Tiner, R. (2002) The pharmaceutical industry and disease mongering (letter), *British Medical Journal*, 325: 216.

Tooley J. and Darby, D. (1998) *Educational Research – a Critique*. London: Office for Standards in Education.

Torrance, H. (2001) Assessment for Learning: Developing Formative Assessment in the Classroom, *Education*, 3–13, 29(3): 26–32.

Torrance, H. and Pryor, J. (1996) Teacher Assessment at Key Stage 1: Accomplishing Assessment in the Classroom. Final Report of Research Grant R000234668 to ESRC, ESRC, Swindon.

Torrance, H. and Pryor, J. (1998) *Investigating Formative Assessment: Teaching, Learning and Assessment in the Classroom*. Philadelphia: Open University Press.

Torrance, H. and Pryor, J. (1999) Investigating and Developing Formative Teacher Assessment in Primary Schools. Final Report of Research Grant No. R000236860 to ESRC, ESRC Swindon.

Torrance, H. and Pryor, J. (2001) Developing Formative Assessment in the Classroom, *British Educational Research Journal*, 27(5): 615–31

Trinder, L. (ed.) (2000a) *Evidence-Based Practice: A Critical Appraisal*. Oxford: Blackwell Science.

Trinder, L. (2000b) Introduction: the context of evidence-based practice, in L. Trinder (2000a).

TTA (1996) Teaching as a research-based profession: promoting excellence in teaching. London: TTA.

TTA (2002) Leeds primary schools consortium: summary of the final report. London: TTA.

Tuckett, D. *et al.* (1985) *Meetings Between Experts: An Approach to Sharing Ideas in Medical Institutions*. London: Tavistock Publications.

Usher, R. (2000) Imposing structure, enabling play: new knowledge production and the 'real world' university, in C. Symes and J. McIntyre (eds) *Working Knowledge: The New Vocationalism and Higher Education*. Buckingham: SRHE/Open University Press.

Valentine, J.C. and Cooper, H. (2003) What Works Clearinghouse Study Design and Implementation Assessment Device (Version 1.0). Washington, DC: U.S. Department of Education.

Viadero, D. (2002) British researchers first to compile key findings, *Education Week*, 4 September.

Vietor, R.H.K. (1994) *Contrived Competition: Regulation and Deregulation in America*. Cambridge, MS: Harvard University Press.

Von Neumann, J. and Morgenstern, O. (1947) *Theory of Games and Economic Behaviour*. Princeton, NJ: Princeton University Press.

Walker, H.M., Forness, S.R., Kauffman, J.M., Epstein, M.H., Gresham, F. M., Nelson, C.M. and Strain, P.S. (1998) Macro-social validation: Referencing outcomes in behavioral disorders to societal issues and problems, *Behavioral Disorders*, 24(1): 7–18.

Walker, H.M., Sprague, J.R., Close, D.W. and Starlin, C.M. (1999–2000) What is right with behavior disorders: Seminal achievements and contributions of the behavior disorders field, *Exceptionality*, 8(1): 13–28.

Walter, I., Nutley, S. and Davies, H. (2003) Developing a taxonomy of interventions used to increase the impact of research. Unpublished paper, Research Unit for Research Utilisation, University of St Andrews, Scotland.

Watkins, S.J. (2000) Editorial: Conviction by mathematical error?, *British Medical Journal*, 320: 2–3.

Watts, A.J. (2001) Career guidance and social exclusion: a cautionary tale, *British Journal of Guidance and Counselling*, 29(2): 157–76.

Wax, M. (1979) *Desegregated Schools: An Intimate Portrait Based on Five Ethnographic Studies*. Washington DC: National Council of Education.

Weick, K.E. (1983) Managerial thought in the context of action, in S. Srivastva (ed.) *The Executive Mind*. San Francisco: Jossey-Bass.

Weinstein, M.C. and Fineberg, H.V. (1980) *Clinical Decision Analysis*. Philadelphia: W.B. Saunders.

Wennerås, C. and Wold, A. (1997) Nepotism and sexism in peer review, *Nature*, 387: 341–3.

Wiliam, D. and Lee, C. (2001) Teachers developing assessment for learning: Impact on student achievement. Paper presented at the British Educational Research Association Conference, University of Leeds. London: King's College.

Winch, P. (1958) *The Idea of a Social Science and its Relation to Philosophy*. London: Routledge and Kegan Paul.

Winerip, M. (1994) A class apart: A disabilities program that got out of hand, *The New York Times*. 8 April.

Wright Mills, C. (1970) *The Sociological Imagination*. New York: Holt.

Wyatt, J. (2001) Management of explicit and tacit knowledge, *Journal of Research in Social Medicine*, 94: 6–9.

Index

DISCOURSE IN EDUCATIONAL AND SOCIAL RESEARCH

Maggie MacLure

> With wonderful clarity Maggie MacLure shows how deconstructionism opens new avenues of critical inquiry and understanding for educational researchers. In exposing the hidden, ideological side of terms like clarity, certainty, mastery, and relevance she allows us to see schooling and educational policy in new ways. In so doing she allows us to imagine classrooms as liberating, pedagogical places, as places where new forms of desire, knowledge, and learning take place
>
> Norman K. Denzin, University of Illinois at Urbana-Champaign

This book is both practical and provocative. It demonstrates the insights and the challenges of a discourse-based orientation to educational and social research. Drawing on a variety of educational and social science 'texts' – including press articles, life history interviews, parent–teacher consultations, policy debates and ethnographies – the author shows how knowledge, power, identities and realities are constructed and problematized in discourse.

The book also deals with research itself as discursive practice, examining the texts that qualitative researchers produce and consume: reports, monographs, journal articles. Practical examples are included for researchers and graduate students wishing to 'interrogate' their own data from a discourse perspective. The author develops a critical awareness of the researcher's role as writer/reader of texts.

The book makes the case for 'discursive literacy' in research. While its primary allegiances are to poststructuralism and deconstruction, it draws from a wide range of disciplines, including interaction sociology, feminist ethnography, literary theory, critical discourse analysis and art history. What holds the book together is the persistent question: how to do educational research and social research within a 'crisis of representation' that has unsettled the relationship between words and worlds?

Contents

256pp   0 335 2019 0 3 (Paperback)   0 335 20191 1 (Hardback)

UNDERSTANDING, DESIGNING AND CONDUCTING QUALITATIVE RESEARCH IN EDUCATION
FRAMING THE PROJECT

John F. Schostak

- How do I get my research off the ground and ensure that it is 'new', 'novel' and 'important'?
- How do I make sense of data, build theories and write a compelling thesis?
- How can my research bring about change?

This book is more than an introduction to doing research – it aims to help readers identify what is new and important about their project, how their research relates to previous work and how it may be used to bring about change at individual, community, national or even international levels. A total strategy is offered focusing on the notion of the 'project' as an organizing framework that ensures that the methods chosen are appropriate to the subject and aim of the study. The intention throughout is to help readers move from being able to apply methods to being able to interrogate the theoretical underpinnings of particular perspectives so that they can feel confident about the particular kinds of knowledge claim they are making. The book will be important reading for students at masters' and doctoral level and will be particularly helpful for professionals from education, health, social work, criminal justice and business who carry out research in their workplace and who need to reflect upon the consequences and possibilities for action and change.

Contents
Introduction – Finding bearings – Subjects: choices and consequences – The other: its objects and objectivity – Handling complexity and uncertainty – Sense and nonsense: braving the postmodern, broaching the novel – Being shy of the truth – Framing texts and evidence: con/texts, intertextuality and rhetoric – Framing ethics and political issues – Framing ethical actions – Writing it – Conclusion – References – Index.

256pp   0 335 20509 7 (Paperback)   0 335 20510 0 (Hardback)

ACTION RESEARCH AND POSTMODERNISM
CONGRUENCE AND CRITIQUE
Tony Brown and Liz Jones

Make something new, Derrida says, that is how deconstruction happens. This book exemplifies such a move in the way it addresses the stuck places of practitioner oriented research with its rational, intentional agents seeking to empower both teacher self and students. An example of putting postmodernism to work in educational research, the book asks hard questions about necessary complicities ... grounded in nursery teaching and math education, it attempts to develop a better language toward a more complicated understanding of what knowledge means ... without reverting to the quick and narrow scientism of the past.

Patti Lather, Ohio State University

- How can we move forward from or develop traditional approaches to Action Research which have dominated teacher research for many years now?
- How can teachers work at improving their teaching when there are so many different understandings of what education is trying to achieve?
- In which ways can post-structuralism, which has had such a major impact in other disciplines, offer practical support to teachers developing their own professional practices?

A premise of much teacher research is that reflection on practice can lead to a development of that practice. Such reflection, it is purported, enables the practitioner in organizing the complexity of the teaching situation, with a particular emphasis on how 'monitoring of change' can be converted to 'control of change'. This book questions the notion of construing developing practice as 'aiming for an ideal' and suggests that such a pursuit has a questionable track record. The very desire for control, and the difficulties encountered in trying to document it can cloud our vision from the very complexities we seek to capture. The book offers detailed discussion of teacher research enquiries carried out in the context of masters' and doctoral degrees. It focuses in particular on how the reflective writing generated by the teacher might build towards an assertion of professional identity through which professional demands are mediated.

Contents

208pp   0 335 20761 8 (Paperback)   0 335 20762 6 (Hardback)